MODERNIST EMPATHY

This book shows how reading modernist literature gives us a fresh and necessary insight into both the tensions within the empathetic imagination and the idea of empathy itself. Writers such as Thomas Hardy, Ford Madox Ford, Mary Borden, T. S. Eliot, and Virginia Woolf encourage us to enter other perspectives even as they question the boundaries between self and other and, hence, the very possibility of empathy. Eve C. Sorum maintains that we must think through this complex literary heritage, focusing on the geographic and elegiac modes of the empathetic imagination, and revealing empathy as more fraught, threatening, and even uncanny than it first appears. *Modernist Empathy* thereby forges a theory of literary empathy as an act not of orientation, but of disorientation, thereby enriching our contemporary understanding of both modernist literature and the concept of literary empathy.

EVE C. SORUM is Associate Professor of English at the University of Massachusetts, Boston and was a Fulbright Scholar in Burkina Faso in 2013–2014. She has published articles and essays on a range of topics, including the masochistic aesthetics of T. S Eliot and Virginia Woolf, poetic self-elegies, and the democratic nostalgia of W. H. Auden.

MODERNIST EMPATHY

Geography, Elegy, and the Uncanny

EVE C. SORUM

University of Massachusetts Boston

CAMBRIDGE
UNIVERSITY PRESS

CAMBRIDGE
UNIVERSITY PRESS

University Printing House, Cambridge CB2 8BS, United Kingdom

One Liberty Plaza, 20th Floor, New York, NY 10006, USA

477 Williamstown Road, Port Melbourne, VIC 3207, Australia

314–321, 3rd Floor, Plot 3, Splendor Forum, Jasola District Centre,
New Delhi – 110025, India

79 Anson Road, #06–04/06, Singapore 079906

Cambridge University Press is part of the University of Cambridge.

It furthers the University's mission by disseminating knowledge in the pursuit of
education, learning, and research at the highest international levels of excellence.

www.cambridge.org
Information on this title: www.cambridge.org/9781108498722
DOI: 10.1017/9781108595667

© Eve C. Sorum 2019

First published 2019

Printed and bound in Great Britain by Clays Ltd, Elcograf S.p.A.

A catalogue record for this publication is available from the British Library.

Library of Congress Cataloging-in-Publication Data
NAMES: Sorum, Eve, 1976– author.
TITLE: Modernist empathy : geography, elegy, and the uncanny / Eve Sorum, University of
Massachusetts, Boston.
DESCRIPTION: First edition. | Cambridge, United Kingdom ; New York : Cambridge
University Press, 2019. | Includes bibliographical references and index.
IDENTIFIERS: LCCN 2019003140 | ISBN 9781108498722 (hardback)
SUBJECTS: LCSH: English literature – 20th century – History and criticism. | Modernism
(Literature) – Great Britain. | Empathy in literature. | BISAC: LITERARY CRITICISM /
European / English, Irish, Scottish, Welsh.
CLASSIFICATION: LCC PR478.M6 S67 2019 | DDC 820.9/112–dc23
LC record available at https://lccn.loc.gov/2019003140

ISBN 978-1-108-49872-2 Hardback

for John

Contents

Illustration

Acknowledgments

I could not have written this book without the help and support of so many people. Thanks first to my three anonymous readers, whose thoughtful feedback pushed my writing in such useful directions. Thanks also to my editor, Ray Ryan, for his guidance and encouragement, and to Edgar Mendez, for his help with all parts of the process.

I'm fortunate to have worked with many wonderful colleagues at the University of Massachusetts Boston; several, in particular, have provided support for this book at various points. Thanks to Sari Edelstein, Holly Jackson, Betsy Klimasmith, Cheryl Nixon, Nadia Nurhussein, Louise Penner, and Rajini Srikanth for their encouragement and help with the process over the past years; to Liz Roemer and my fellow participants in the Mid-Career Faculty Research Seminar; to Brian Halley for invaluable help getting my prospectus out the door; to Matt Brown for his illuminating readings of early chapters and his continued friendship; to Sam Regan, for making everything better at work. Friends at other universities deserve special thanks: to Patricia Rae, who has guided me in ways tangible and intangible as an editor, supporter, and friend; to Madelyn Detloff, whose golden thread image (and encouragement) kept me going; and to a wonderful group of interlocutors over the years at the MSA and beyond: Jon Hegglund (collaborator extraordinaire), Bill Hogan, Marjorie Levinson, Meredith Martin, Jeff McCarthy, Gabrielle McIntire, and Jenny Sorenson. John Whittier-Ferguson has been a constant mentor and example. Phil Weinstein helped make me the modernist I am. Thanks to my fellow participants, especially Emily Setina and Frances Dickey, at a perfectly timed National Humanities Center seminar on Eliot.

Thanks also go to so many people outside my professional life: in particular, to my inspiring early-morning running friends – Bonnie Duncan, Emily Edwards, Ashley Lanfer, and Michelle LeBlanc – for their empathetic listening and wise words. I also am so grateful for the friendship and support provided over the years, whether as writing, hiking, or dinner companions, by Sabra Brown, Michele Clark, Amanda Cook, Gareth Cook, Sarah Elmendorf, Lianne Fisman, Synne Henriques, Jonas Henriques, Chyld King, John Sarnecki, Robbie Singal, Rebecca Weintraub, and Sam Weschler. Many thanks to my extended family – particularly the Elliott and the Fulton clans – for their love. Most of all, thanks to Mary-Catherine Harrison: best friend and soul mate since we first met in graduate school; catalyst for thinking about modernism and empathy; ideal reader and interlocutor throughout the process. This book would not have come into being without her, and I can only hope it will live up to her level of lucidity, insight, and imaginative range.

I can't express enough gratitude to my father, Paul Sorum, whose intellectual curiosity always inspires me and whose ever-present love and patience (and untiring ability to edit!) have made this book far better than it would otherwise be. The hardest part of writing these acknowledgments is knowing that one deep source of influence and support is not here to read them. Losing my mother, Christina Elliott Sorum, far too early changed the trajectory of my research, pushing me to delve into elegy and mourning practices in ways that I had not anticipated. The memory of her is, on the most basic and primal level, what motivated me to continue with this book. She was my model of a scholar, teacher, leader, and mother; I wish every day that she was still here.

Finally, my love to Zoë and August, who bring wonder and meaning to each day, and who have taught me that parenthood opens up the world in marvelous and unanticipated ways. And my total gratitude goes to John Fulton for being my first and best reader, constant interlocutor, and partner in everything from adventures around the world to the banalities of a Monday morning. I think of Woolf's line in *To the Lighthouse*, which describes so lyrically the radiance with which little James Ramsay's excitement infuses even the most ordinary object: the surrounding world becomes "fringed with joy" (*To the Lighthouse*, 3). How fortunate I am to be with someone who makes the edges of my own world shimmer and glow. Thank you.

Needless to say, what this book achieves was only possible through the efforts of all those mentioned above; any errors you find are purely my own.

Portions of Chapter 2 first appeared in two articles, and acknowledgment is gratefully given to The Johns Hopkins University Press, for their permission to reprint revised versions of "'The Place on the Map': Geography and Meter in Hardy's Elegies," Copyright © 2009 The Johns Hopkins University Press, which first appeared in *Modernism/Modernity*,

Vol. 16, Issue 3, September 2009, 553–574; and "Hardy's Geography of Narrative Empathy," Copyright © 2011 The Johns Hopkins University Press, which first appeared in *Studies in the Novel*, Vol. 43, No. 2 (Summer 2011), 179–199.

Acknowledgment is also gratefully given to Associated University Presses, for permission to reprint in Chapter 3 revised portions from "Mourning and Moving On: Life After War in Ford Madox Ford's *The Last Post*," which first appeared in *Modernism and Mourning*, ed. Patricia Rae (Bucknell University Press, 2007), 154–167.

Other sections from Chapter 3 first appeared in my chapter, "Empathy, Trauma, and the Space of War in *Parade's End*," in *War in the Mind: Ford Madox Ford's* Parade's End, *Modernism, and Psychology*, eds. Ashley Chantler and Rob Hawkes (Edinburgh University Press, 2015), 50–62.

CHAPTER I

Modernizing Empathy, Locating Loss

> But art, if it means awareness of our own life, means also awareness of
> the lives of other people – for style for the writer, no less than colour
> for the painter, is a question not of technique but of vision: it is the
> revelation, which by direct and conscious methods would be impos-
> sible, of the qualitative difference, the uniqueness of the fashion in
> which the world appears to each one of us, a difference which, if there
> were no art, would remain for ever the secret of every individual.
> Through art alone are we able to emerge from ourselves, to know
> what another person sees of a universe which is not the same as our
> own of which, without art, the landscapes would remain as unknown
> to us as those that may exist on the moon. Thanks to art, instead of
> seeing one world only, our own, we see that world multiply itself and
> we have at our disposal as many worlds as there are original artists,
> worlds more different one from the other than those which revolve in
> infinite space.[1]

I find it hard to imagine that anyone who has picked up my book, with its
clear literary focus, can read that statement from Marcel Proust's final
volume of *In Search of Lost Time* and not feel a thrill of recognition and, if
not agreement, at least hope. The vision that Proust accords art (here he
means literature, specifically) illuminates the singularity of every experience; literature reveals the differences, rather than the unity, between our
understandings of the world. Art, in this formulation, occupies a privileged
position as the catalyst to what could only be called an empathetic imagination, where we can "know what another person sees."

If we could just take these lines out of context and be gratified by their
reassuring claim, I might not have felt compelled to write *Modernist
Empathy*. Yet, of course, Proust's statement comes at the end of many
volumes in which the narrator is unable to access not simply others'
experiences, but also his own, except perhaps in brief retrospective
glimpses; indeed, just a page earlier he has noted that it is almost impossible
to know even oneself; art may be the one thing that can "make us fully

aware of that reality, remote from our daily preoccupations . . . that reality which it is very easy for us to die without ever having known and which is, quite simply, our life."[2] The issue is revealed: literature may provide the means (may, for Proust, provide the only means) for understanding the multiplicity of perspectives and experiences, including the understanding that is within oneself, but access to such moments is rare and fleeting, if ever experienced at all. Moreover, such knowledge may come at a price; the narrator goes on to think about love and the benefits of having suffered, for "it is only while we are suffering that we see certain things which at other times are hidden from us."[3] Knowledge and art emerge from such suffering; pain brings us the insight and the vision to render the world in such a way that it reveals what Proust describes as the reality beneath the surface.

Let me jump forward from Proust to a more contemporary literary moment – a speech given by the critic James Wood on a late September day in 2009, introducing the Turkish novelist and Nobel laureate Orhan Pamuk, that year's Norton lecturer at Harvard. I was in the audience that day and was struck by Wood's introduction, which revolved around the issue of literature's project of imagining others and, therefore, of promoting empathy. People, Wood argued, believe that fiction expands our moral imagination through the act of viewing the world through another perspective – a proposition that is, he recognized, open for debate.[4] What Wood was arguing for (and was saying that Pamuk works toward in his own writing) was finding a balance between two extremes: absolute identification with characters versus absolute rejection of that possibility. He described how what we need is to experience some kind of middle ground between, on the one hand, engaging so deeply with a novel that we lose ourselves in the characters and their trials, often to the point of experiencing their frustrations and pain on a visceral level, and, on the other, rejecting the possibility of such engagement as a humanist fantasy. Literary empathy is important, Wood claimed, even if the practice is more fraught than people might believe.

I agree with this assessment, though perhaps not quite for the same reasons, and I argue in this book that modernist literature can show us both why empathy is more challenging than we might today assume, and why it is still essential to pursue. My argument goes a step further; I posit that there is a specifically *modernist* empathy that complicates our understanding of the empathetic act. As the lines from Proust suggest, there is something painful in the act of crossing the boundaries of the self and attempting to enter into another perspective; this acknowledgment and celebration of the inevitable loss and probable failure at the heart of any act of perspective-taking characterizes the "modernist empathy" uncovered in this book. In short, modernist literature encourages us to enter other perspectives even as it also questions the very idea of a self and an other, and, hence, the very possibility of empathy.

Modernist Empathy argues that we must look back to modernist litera-ture, which was written when the term "empathy" first came into circula-tion, in order to rediscover the complexity of empathy as an imaginative act. Attention to modernist literature's exploration of empathy reveals that every act of moving outside the perspective of the individual subject exposes the fragility and the isolation of each person's perspective; to empathize is to realize how alone and singular we actually may be. At the same time, we confront how hard it is to return after this movement outside the self; our sense of an uninhibited autonomy of perspective is gone. Modernist literature asks us to take the radical leap into otherness even as it reveals there is never a coherent self on which to base that leap. Yet it is only through attempts to reach outside of the idea of the "self" that we can come to realize the ephemerality and the contextual nature of our own subject positions. Modernist empathy is therefore paradoxical in its very nature and process.

Defining Empathy

My choice of the term "empathy" is deliberate and deserves some explana-tion; throughout the rest of this chapter I will further explore and con-textualize theories of empathy, ending by explicating the three registers through which I read modernist literature's engagement with empathy: space, form, and psychology. But let me start with some background on the word itself. Even though empathy did not come into common parlance until the second and third decades of the twentieth century, both its emergence as a critical term during the rise of literary modernism and the dominance of its current use make it the most appropriate term for my examination.[5] In contemporary discussions, the idea of empathy has become part of everyday political and literary discourse: think about President Obama's emphasis on the importance of empathy for Supreme Court Justices when he was choosing a replacement for Justice David Souter in 2009,[6] or bestsellers such as Leslie Jamison's 2014 essay collec-tion, *The Empathy Exams*. For an amazing merging of the literary and the political, we could look at President Obama's discussion with Marilynne Robinson, published in the fall of 2015 in the *New York Review of Books*. President Obama notes, "the most important stuff I've learned I think I've learned from novels. It has to do with empathy . . . And the notion that it's possible to connect with some[one] else even though they're very different from you"[7] – words that speak directly to our idea that empathy is both a deep good and that literature, above all, teaches us how to experience it. The importance of being able to understand another's experience seems unquestionable, even though there has been significant debate in literary studies and beyond about whether empathy, and particularly literary empathy, actually leads to altruistic actions – a point I will touch upon further.[8]

As a term, "empathy" is of relatively recent coinage, only entering into English usage in 1909 when the psychologist Edward Bradford Titchener translated the German term *Einfühlung* (in-feeling) into "empathy" in his *Elementary Psychology of Thought Processes*. *Einfühlung* was itself another new word, presented by Robert Vischer in his 1873 essay "On the Optical Sense of Form: A Contribution to Aesthetics," and then taken up by Theodor Lipps in his discussions of how we can experience aesthetic objects.[9] Chronologically, therefore, empathy developed as a concept alongside literary modernism. Two of the most influential writers to introduce the terms to the British literary world were Vernon Lee (Violet Paget), in essays starting in the late 1890s and culminating in the collection *Beauty and Ugliness* in 1912,[10] and T. E. Hulme, whose 1914 lecture brought German art historian Wilhelm Worringer's theories from the 1908 *Abstraction and Empathy* to the attention of the British modernist avant-garde.[11] Lee has received short shrift for her role for reasons explored recently by the scholar Benjamin Morgan,[12] but her discussion of how empathetic imagining both defines our aesthetic experience and is rooted in the body can illuminate the projects of writers ranging from Hardy to Woolf. Hulme, on the other hand, has been far more respectfully treated both by his contemporaries and by future readers, and his argument (which he acknowledges having essentially transcribed from Worringer's lectures) that empathy was antithetical to abstraction has meant that empathy seemed an *undesirable* force when thinking about many kinds of modernist literary experimentation. Hulme says that abstraction reflects an essential distance between the artist and the world, a "feeling of separation in the face of outside nature," while empathy is the result of a realist mode that "can only occur in a people whose relation to outside nature is such that it admits of this feeling of pleasure and its contemplation."[13] Following critic Megan Marie Hammond's belief that "modernist writers reject *sympathetic* fellow feeling and seek a more radical *empathic* fellow feeling," and that "empathy and abstraction can work together in modernist literature,"[14]

I resist Hulme's vision of empathy and abstraction as always dichotomous and instead argue that the urge to separate and the feeling of separation, which were so central to Hulme's understanding of abstraction, can also be found within the modernist empathetic imagination. My own reading of modernist empathy as often operating within a lyric mode of perception – with a focus on how, as Mutlu Blasing describes it, lyric "enables us to share a 'virtual common subjectivity,' which exists only at the symbolic, thoroughly social, level" – provides one way to think about the abstracting and distancing nature of the empathetic imagination; the sharing of perspectives may always be a virtual act, even when there are attempts to root it in immediate, sensory experience.[15] Yet I do not stop with that effort to reconcile Hulme's oppositions: central to *Modernist Empathy* is the argument that the very structure of modernist empathy is defined by an acute awareness of the "separation in the face of outside nature" that Hulme sees as the urge to abstraction.

While writers such as Keen, Greiner, and Hammond have performed much of the necessary foundational work of excavating the connections and the divergences between empathy and sympathy, I should explicate the definitions and valences, particularly in relation to literary modernism. Although our sense of the distinction between empathy and sympathy is well developed now, "sympathy" was the operative term in eighteenth- and nineteenth-century discussions of the relationship between subjects; Adam Smith wrote in *The Theory of Moral Sentiments* (1759) that sympathy involves an imaginative act of perspective-taking – "changing places in fancy with the sufferer" – in such a way that we then can experience some version of the sufferer's experiences.[16] Smith is careful to say that this form of perspective-taking is something that occurs in the realm of the imagination only, and that our experience of sympathy is constituted of "impressions of our own senses only, not those of his, which our imaginations copy."[17] This definition of sympathy resonates more with our current vision of empathy than it does with how we now conceptualize sympathy. Sympathy became too much of a baggy and inclusive concept by the end of the nineteenth century, and Hammond argues that the "strain" on the idea of sympathy was exacerbated by "the rise of modern psychology, which had to deal with the matter of extracting evidence from other minds" (Hammond, 8). *Einfühlung* or empathy evolved as a term to designate the imaginative sharing that Smith first described, while sympathy came to mean feeling *for*, rather than feeling *with*.

With both of these definitions, the emotional side (a sharing of feelings) of empathy is at the forefront. Indeed the earlier term, sympathy, is now often defined as an emotion in and of itself (you feel *for* someone, as critic Robert Solomon has helpfully explained).[18] Yet Greiner argues that we need to see sympathy not as a feeling but as a "complex formal process, a mental exercise, not an emotion" (418) in which, Greiner states, the distance between sympathizer and sympathized is maintained, rather than collapsed.[19] Empathy, she argues – and we could also turn to Vischer's 1873 essay, where he used the word *Einfühlung* to describe the process of viewing objects – involves the elision of the distance between self and other (418); it is different from sympathy not because it is more or less about feeling but because it involves a structurally different way of operating. I argue that this idea (and sometimes ideal) of fusion is in fact not realized in empathy in the way that Greiner suggests; indeed, it is precisely those limits on the possibility of fusing that are explored by the writers discussed in *Modernist Empathy.*

Greiner uses her definition to explore sympathy's connection to metonymy and to the realist novel and to connect empathy with the metaphoric and the lyric. Her focus is on analyzing the realist novel, but her comments on empathy resonate with my approach. I argue that we must see empathy as a lyric act, not because it is mainly on display in poetry, but because the lyric is defined by obscuring or highlighting those boundaries between self and other in ways that frighten and challenge our understanding of the limits of subjectivity. One of the recent points of contention in discussions of the lyric emerges in the claim, made most notably by Jonathan Cullers, that we should not read the lyric as presenting persona, as we might in a novel, but instead as engaging in acts of enunciation that do not posit a fictional imitation of actual speech, but that instead "create effects of voicing."[20] We are in the realm of William James's description of the self in his *Psychology: A Briefer Course* (1892), where he claims, "the thoughts themselves are the thinkers."[21] Lyric makes language itself the subject of the text; as Blasing describes it, "The lyric makes audible a virtual subjectivity in the shape of a given language, a mother tongue, and the historical permutations of the concept and status of an 'individual' are not of help in understanding poetic subjectivity."[22] In other words, our desires to embody the voices of lyric into recognizable individual identities is an understandable but often mistaken response; lyric differs from narrative in its ability to move away from the need for a "someone" speaking, and instead toward the idea of speech itself as the subject.[23] The act becomes the actor. While this idea about the "effects of voicing" may seem extreme, if we take this explanation of the lyric as a starting point for thinking not simply about a genre of writing, but as a *mode of perception,* then we can see how it might begin to open up how to think about empathetic engagement so that we can foreground the possibilities for inhabiting other subjectivities (through voicing them, or attempting to enter into their voice). Concomitantly, such a lyric empathy also suggests the frightening amorphous or polymorphous nature of the very idea of singular subjectivity; if language produces the subject, then the boundaries of subjectivity become linguistically permeable. We may be able both to engage in that critical act of a "momentary suspension of such awareness [of the other's otherness] that sympathy does not allow" (Hammond, 67), and be terrified of the consequences of such a suspension.

This is what I see as the simultaneously radical and frightening aspect of empathy – the experience that modernist writers both embrace and avoid. The moment of suspension of awareness and all the dangers and promises it brings are the focus of my book, as well as why I look at empathy, rather than sympathy, even when the authors themselves do not yet use the term. I argue that it is at pressure points such as this one – the momentary experience when the boundaries of the subject seem permeable – that the modernist empathetic imagination becomes both most fertile and most troubled. And yet I reject Greiner's claim that empathy's elimination of the distance between self and other erases an awareness of alterity. When that instant of fusion occurs, I argue, its unsustainability reinforces, rather than obscures, the sense of the other's difference.

In this way, modernist empathy complicates a critique made in recent years about the ethical *immorality* of empathy. On the one hand, scholars such as Rajini Srikanth have foregrounded the political potential of the imaginative act, writing that "Empathy is a relationally imaginative approach to living that underscores interdependence – whether of individuals, communities, or nations – and has at its foundation the call to imagine our lives always in the context of similar and dissimilar others."[24] Yet Srikanth also acknowledges the complexity of engaging in empathy with those others that are not only different, but reviled – those who may seem more deserving of antipathy than empathy – and this political ambiguity is what scholars ranging from Lauren Berlant to Suzanne Keen have emphasized. Berlant, for example, describes empathy as a "civic-minded but passive ideal" that thwarts the "ethical imperative toward social transformation" because it transforms structural inequity and trauma into private and personal affect, thereby redirecting anger and action into the realm of feeling.[25] Keen, in examining the arguments of various critics of empathy-derived altruism, similarly contends that there is a tenuous link between empathy and action: "empathetic reading experiences that confirm the empathy-altruism theory, I argue, are exceptional, not routine" (65).

Yet this is where, I argue, modernist empathy can offer an alternative way of thinking about the ethics of empathy: in its insistence on the dangerous nature of empathetic identification *and* on the way that it might reveal the fissures in the façade of the singular self, modernist empathy allows us to understand empathy as neither altruistic nor simply self-soothing, but self-altering in sometimes surprising ways. Berlant, in talking about the perils and the potential of sentimental literature, makes a claim that applies to modernist empathy as well: "the possibility that through the identification with alterity you will never be the same remains the radical threat and the great promise of this affective aesthetic."[26] That vibrating space between threat and promise is the site of the modernist empathetic imagination that I will be probing here.

Modernist Empathy

While the quotation from Proust that opened this chapter might suggest that modernist literature and questions of empathy have deep and self-evident links, we do not normally think of empathy when we first encounter a high-modernist text, whether we come to it through the rhythmic cadences of Virginia Woolf's prose or the aural acrobatics of T. S. Eliot's early poetry; dissociation and alienation are terms that are more likely to come up in both criticism and classroom discussion. If you love to read, likely there is a formative moment (or many such moments) in your past when you have fallen so deeply into a book that you cringe when Dorothea Brookes decides to marry Mr. Casaubon, you weep when Beth dies in *Little Women*, and you exult when Esther is finally revealed as an heiress in *Bleak House*. Yet moments like these are harder to come by in books and poetry such as Thomas Hardy's surreal elegies for his dead wife, Woolf's *Jacob's Room* with its inaccessible protagonist, Eliot's polyphonous *The Waste Land*, Ford Madox Ford's fragmented and massive war tetralogy, *Parade's End*, or Mary Borden's lyrical *The Forbidden Zone;* the characters and voices are either too much or too little embodied, are overly flattened, or are entwined in a sea of styles, voices, and references. In fact, perhaps part of what makes literature like that so "hard" is the way that the writing forces us to work in order to understand the characters and, so often, then seems itself to work *against* allowing any understanding to emerge. While the same might be said for poetry more broadly – aside from some narrative poems and the occasional dramatic monologue – it is even more apparent in modernist poetry, which may be why scholars interested in empathy have generally avoided it.

I have chosen extreme examples on both sides in the instances above – those characters and texts that seem to advertise the possibility of empathetic engagement with characters versus those that startle and alienate. I have also deliberately periodized my examples; the group that invites us to empathize with the characters is all taken from the nineteenth-century canon; the group that does not is from the late nineteenth- and early twentieth-century "modernist" period. While these short lists are necessarily reductive, I do want to argue that there is a particular version of nineteenth-century fiction and empathy that colors the literary-historical lens through which we might theorize empathy; as Vincent Sherry argues, from Romanticism through the nineteenth century, "a primary goal for poet and reader is to achieve union with the aesthetic object."[27] This lens is not only focused on the Victorian period, but it is also deeply embedded in a theory of *narrative*, not poetic, empathy. Since Suzanne Keen's 2006 article on "A Theory of Narrative Empathy" (which she expanded upon in her 2007 book on *Empathy and the Novel*), empathy studies have resided in the domain of narrative theory (and often within the realm of Victorian studies).[28] As the titles of Keen's article and book suggest, she is primarily interested in theorizing empathy in relation to fiction and other narrative forms; this interest is both logical and useful because it focuses our attention on the kinds of interpersonal empathy at work. The narrative-theory approach to empathy foregrounds, first, intratextual acts of empathy between characters (we see the characters experiencing the perspective of another character), and, second, the extratextual act involving the reader's ability to empathize with characters.

It is no surprise that we see this interpersonal empathetic imagination, whether originating from within or without the text, aligned with the project of Victorian fiction; as Keen notes, "the reinvention of the novel as a form that might do something positive in the world by swaying readers' minds rather than activating their passions we may also date to the Victorian period" (*Empathy and the Novel*, 38). In other words, Victorian writers were acutely interested in how acts of empathetic engagement might both be represented and be enacted. Relevant to my book and the question that it raises about the effects and purposes of literary empathy is Rebecca Mitchell's argument that Victorian fiction insists upon the essential difference and distance between individuals and promotes empathy despite this inherent distance between subjects. She writes that we see the characters in realist novels making the same mistake that we do in our own lives; they think that they can know one another fully, which is what often leads to some of their most egregious errors in judgment. The readers, on the other hand, make a different sort of error. While Victorian novels "insist on the distinction – in both form and content – between that unknowability of the person and the knowability of art," the reader tends to confound these realms and to think that people, not just books, are knowable.[29] Mitchell argues that realist novels work to underline and emphasize the difference, and thereby allow for the possibility of an ethical engagement with another. Critic Mary-Catherine Harrison goes even further, positing that realism "emerged in an attempt to alter the very reality that it represents, a literary 'intervention' in the actual world."[30] The social action project of realist fiction raised the stakes of both creating characters with whom readers could empathize and showing characters who could model acts of perspective-taking. As Caroline Levine describes it, "realist writers developed techniques of omniscient narration: narrative perspectives not lodged in any single consciousness but able to move in and out of multiple spaces and minds and to present connections among people which they themselves might not be aware of."[31] The formal techniques of realist narrative blend with what Frederic Jameson calls its "epistemological claim (for knowledge or truth)"; indeed, he writes, this claim is what "masquerades as an aesthetic ideal."[32] The apparent transparency of "omniscient" realist narration, which suggests the possibility of understanding multiple perspectives, is both a formal and a philosophical stance; Victorian realism is created by and creates an idea of the world as potentially known or knowable, even as it acknowledges the alterity that is behind any act of thinking through another's perspective.

While empathy (as an act or an experience) may seem to have an easy connection to omniscience (as a literary technique or mode), this is an assumption that a turn to modernist literature allows us to probe. While empathy is often compared to experiences of omniscience, it does very different work if it depends on and highlights alterity. Nicholas Royle has argued for a sociohistorical basis to the waning of the omniscient narrative as we move into the late nineteenth and early twentieth century; he points to the concomitant waning of Christian religious belief. Omniscience from its initial uses in narrative was "a definition based on the presumed analogy between the novelist as creator and the Creator of the cosmos, an omniscient God."[33] With the validity of belief in the all-knowing Christian God foundering, the possibility of omniscience likewise loses its steady foundation; conceptualizing omniscience is more challenging if we reject the idea of an omniscient creator.[34] For his part, Royle argues that we should think of "telepathy" rather than omniscience when looking at shifts in perspective in the literature, since it is a term that allows for movement into other minds without positing an overarching master of the fictional cosmos.[35]

Royle is proposing a shift in terms – from the omniscient narrator to the telepathic narrator – but when looking at modernist literature, telepathy falls short. While this literature does move away from the mastery and the *all*-knowing nature of the omniscient narrator, signaling a turn to narratives that are more firmly embedded in individual consciousnesses who have awareness of their limits and boundaries, telepathy does not connote the intellectual and affective labor so central to the narrative and poetry emerging at the turn of the twentieth century and lauded in numerous literary and artistic manifestos of that period. Telepathy is inadequate, I posit, as a description of the varieties of perspective-taking that emerge in modernist literature. This is where empathy comes in as a more nuanced and useful term.

Let me turn to Woolf's aesthetic manifesto, "Mr. Bennett and Mrs. Brown," as an example here, since it has been so formative in definitions of high modernism and the idea of character. While there is no definitive break between Victorian realism and modernist narrative forms, despite claims like Woolf's that "on or about December 1910 human character changed,"[36] we can begin to chart some ways in which certain terms and strategies shift and take hold. To begin, we can identify the primacy of an idea of work as central to the aesthetic process and product; this is something at the core of "Mr. Bennett and Mrs. Brown," in which Woolf emphasizes the labor involved in writing and, more specifically, in accurately and truly expressing character – what Woolf describes as "the appalling effort of saying what I meant" (18). "Saying what I meant," which seems like a quotidian activity, is shown to be one of the most challenging processes and projects – the labor at the heart of the modernist aesthetic – whether described by Woolf here, or by Hulme in "Romanticism and Classicism," when he describes how each "man sees a little differently, and to get out clearly and exactly what he does see, he must have a terrific struggle with language."[37] Central here is not only the emphasis on struggle and work, but also the way that these formulations put the author in the forefront; before labor can occur, there must be a laborer. Art as inspiration or divine word has no place in these formulations, since that would bypass the work of and the work with language that both Woolf and Hulme experience. Art may serve to create a common bridge to others, but it emerges from the solitary struggle of the writer to find that bridge and make common ground. Thus, Woolf notes, to have got at what I meant I should have had to go back and back and back; to experiment with one thing and another; to try this sentence and that, referring each word to my vision, matching it as exactly as possible, and knowing that somehow I had to find a common ground between us, a convention which would not seem to you too odd, unreal, and far-fetched to believe in. (18)

Woolf's process aligns with Hulme's definition of the artist as "the man who simply can't bear the idea of that 'approximately.' He will get the exact curve of what he sees whether it be an object or an idea in the mind."[38] Whether it is Woolf's "should have had to go back and back and back" or Hulme's "will get," both writers emphasize the time, the work, and the difficulty of finding an adequate form. As Hulme would have us notice, the labor seems a different kind from that described in a text like William Wordsworth's "I wandered lonely as a cloud," where reflection, rather than strenuous (almost physical!) exercise, is the necessary work of the poet. Wordsworth writes:

> For oft, when on my couch I lie
> In vacant or in pensive mood,
> They flash upon that inward eye
> Which is the bliss of solitude[39]

Even though, as Peter Howarth has argued while speaking specifically about Hulme's essay, "modernist classicism is in fact based on the same Coleridgean ideas about autonomy as the Romanticism it despised,"[40] we can see that the focus on effort is different between Wordsworth's and Hulme's (or Woolf's) description of the writer. Vision is there for all three, but the kind of work involved in writing that vision differs; Hulme and Woolf do not, we might note, talk about the pleasure or bliss in the act.[41]

Yet along with this effort and work comes the sense of the cost of the creative act – and this is where we come back to the question of occupying other perspectives. On the one hand, that cost is occasioned by the destruction of the old methods of narration; it is a destruction of the conventions of genre as well as the expectations of the audience. The foundation of the contemporary writing, Woolf notes, is the rubble of the old methods and forms; contemporary writers engage in destructive creation and a creative destruction. She describes the demolition: "And so the smashing and the crashing began. Thus it is that we hear all round us, in poems and novels and biographies, even in newspaper articles and essays, the sound of breaking and falling, crashing and destruction" (20). On the other hand, there is a quieter sort of vital absence at the center of the writerly project – this is the pursuit of Mrs. Brown, which is described almost as a practice in necromancy or spiritualism: "Few catch the phantom; most have to be content with a scrap of her dress or a wisp of her hair" (3). While the "Mr. Bennett" in the title refers to the actual writer, Arnold Bennett, whose narrative techniques Woolf critiques in this essay, Mrs. Brown is the figure who stands for Woolf's concept of character itself. Writing Mrs. Brown stands in for trying to write character in the modern age. Embedded, therefore, in the center of the narrative project and the experience of any writer in dealing with this "phantom" is the *absence* of that presence they are trying to conjure, and thus also the presence of that which has escaped, been lost, or been overlooked. In this description Woolf therefore presents the act of writing fiction as one that is both always already elegiac and always engaged in trying to tether the subject enough so that Mrs. Brown's perspective can be understood.

We can think of Royle's argument about the loss of omniscience – the loss of overarching faith in God and/or God's omniscience – as influencing narrative and even cultural perspectives; there is the need, if we have rejected the idea of the omniscient perspective, to think carefully about how to understand and feel with other perspectives. Indeed, "Mr. Bennett and Mrs. Brown" starts from the assumption that something has shifted radically in terms of perspective: the change manifests itself most strikingly in terms of the physical movement of the servants from downstairs to up: "The Victorian cook lived like a leviathan in the lower depths, formidable, silent, obscure, inscrutable; the Georgian cook is a creature of sunshine and fresh air; in and out of the drawing-room, now to borrow *The Daily Herald*, now to ask advice about a hat" (5). While literalizing this change in perspective with her example about the movement between floors of the servants, Woolf also gestures to shifts in internal perspectives as well; the modern reader, she posits, sympathizes with Clytemnestra and feels sorry for Carlyle's wife, unlike readers of the Victorian period. The authority of a character – of a character in a great book, in particular – is "that it has the power to make you think not merely of it itself, but of all sorts of things through its eyes" (11); character, in other words, is assessed in terms of its ability to provoke empathy – in fact, to make the reader engage in an act of empathy, almost whether or not she wants to. At the heart of Woolf's theory of fiction is an act of empathy, an inevitable engagement in perspective-taking.

Why would this be modernist, we might ask, since hasn't Woolf herself acknowledged that *all* novelists "are lured on to create some character which has thus imposed itself upon them" (1)? Perspective-taking, by both novelist and then reader, is thereby inescapably at the heart of all fiction, regardless of period. Woolf's formulation follows Vernon Lee's revision of Lipps's theory of empathy, for Lee insists that the "contemplated object lives in the mind which contemplates it,"[42] rather than the subject moving into the contemplated object. While we can profitably argue that literary language has always been concerned with acts of imaginative perspective-taking, Woolf, with her images of creative destruction, along with other writers that I will examine here as well, foregrounds the shaky ground on which our ideas of the autonomous subject rest: they present an empathy that requires work and that can be seen as in some way troubling the empathizing subject. Even though the very idea of empathy presents a vision of the world in which there is a distinction between subjects and objects (for how can there be an attempt at fellow feeling without the presence of another "fellow"? How can we stand in someone else's shoes, without there being a someone else?),[43] the act of empathy suggests the ways in which that barrier can be breached; that very breach has to be read as equally invasive of the empathizing subject as it is of the object of empathy.

Indeed, in Lee's formulation, empathy is all about the entry into the empathizing *subject*, rather than into the object of empathy. The alterity that Mitchell emphasizes therefore needs to be read back onto the self; in contemplating the other, we are learning something more about the self, perhaps, than about the other. We might think about theories of aesthetic mimesis here; Walter Benjamin most usefully revealed how the empathetic imagination might be an offspring of the mimetic imagination. He writes in his essay, "On the Mimetic Faculty" (1933) that, "The highest capacity for producing similarities, however, is man's. His gift of seeing resemblances is nothing other than a rudiment of the powerful compulsion in former times to become and behave like something else. Perhaps there is none of his higher functions in which his mimetic faculty does not play a decisive role."[44] Mimesis derives from a desire linked to the empathetic imagination; it is the desire to see and act and know what someone else sees and knows, for the mimetic faculty allows us to model others and the world around ("become and behave like something else," as Benjamin writes). Yet as Benjamin's description makes clear, such a mimetic faculty reveals the self more than the world around; what the mind reflects in its mirror transforms the self into the other. In a world in which the "mirror was broken," as Virginia Woolf writes in *To the Lighthouse* about the post-World War I period, the reflection itself can no longer be seen as whole. Instead, we enter into the realm of a fractured and divided self like Picasso's "Portrait of Henry Kahnweiler." Such a view renders the self radically other; we can recognize the other that is in and perhaps *is* the self.

As the above discussion suggests, my argument in general is focused on the experience of the *subject* of empathy – the one who engages in the act of trying to imagine, feel, and understand a perspective of an other. At this moment, when we are in such a self-focused world, returning to a self-focused moment of literature can open up ways of thinking about what it might mean to reach outside of the self. This is why modernist literature can be particularly important to examine: not because it teaches us how to be selfless, but because it teaches us both how frightening and how vital it is to recognize the boundaries of the self and to try to open those boundaries. Empathy, especially when talking about emotional empathy, may seem like voyeurism (having and reveling in the feelings of an other from the safety of the self), but when dealing with modernist literature we are reminded of our essential alienation not only from others (like in the monadism that we will see in Eliot, for example) but also from the self. Hammond describes how modernist writers moved from a sympathetic "feeling for" to an empathetic "feeling with" – a kind of merging into the otherness – claiming that "Literary modernism trained readers to believe that a more radical joining of subjectivities was possible. Yet the driving ambivalence of modernist empathy signals that fellow feeling, in whatever form, is an act whose dangers we must constantly assess" (5). If we put even more emphasis on examining this "ambivalence," we can begin to see that modernist representations and expressions of empathy are defined, first and foremost, by this ambivalence about not just the premise of sharing feelings and understanding other minds, but also the effects of doing so.

In claiming this, I am making an argument that the actor, that subject behind the empathetic act, rather than being in control and in a state of authority, is challenged and often threatened when engaging in these cognitive and emotional acts. Judith Butler's vision of the relationship between sovereignty and agency within language is a useful constituting framework here: she claims that "agency begins where sovereignty wanes. The one who acts (who is not the same as the sovereign subject) acts precisely to the extent that he or she is constituted as an actor and, hence, operating within a linguistic field of enabling constraints from the outset."[45] Butler here is arguing (*pace* Austin) that the subject is always constituted by language (by speech acts) and is therefore never fully sovereign, since the relationship with language is never simply instrumental; you are transformed into a subject by language at the very moment that you engage in a speech act.[46]

We can take this formulation and apply it, with some variations, to the empathizing subject. Whether focusing on the act of empathizing or on the object of empathy, authority and even sovereignty – instrumental control over the cognitive and imaginative act of imagining – tend to be awarded to the empathizer. Hence, Marjorie Garber writes that empathy "has come to denote the power of projecting one's personality into the object of contemplation and has been a useful technical term in both psychology and aesthetics. . . . But *empathy* also seems to stress the matter of personal agency and individual emotion."[47] The idea of the "power" of the empathizer stands out here; that projection of self into other – something that we see articulated by Vernon Lee in her discussion of aesthetic empathy – presumes a kind of control over the action and an ability to remain intact in the act itself. Yet that assumption seems inadequate when we probe the act of empathizing more deeply; by positing oneself as an empathizing subject, I argue, one is immediately entered into an engagement with an other that challenges the subject's autonomy and authority. Indeed, the texts I examine reveal that the very *idea* of empathy both depends on and damages a free-standing autonomous subject, since it is predicated on the belief that one can shift perspectives and experience the feelings of an other.

Space: Disorientation

This question of shifting perspectives leads quite naturally to the first of the registers on which I examine modernist empathy: that of space. Empathy is perhaps most commonly glossed as the attempt to "stand in someone else's shoes." Rather than being an act of orientation, however, I argue that modernist literature reveals the essential *disorientation* that occurs in this movement. The positional foundations of empathy can be obscured if we designate the empathetic act as a purely inner movement, but they begin to emerge when we think about the way that empathy involves movements between outer and inner states – when the "out there" becomes the "in here," to quote critic Philip Weinstein.[48] In *Unknowing: The Work of Modernist Fiction* (2006), Weinstein offers a particularly thoughtful and insightful use of Freud in his argument about how the movement toward "unknowing" is defining of modernist fiction. Though such an argument may at first appear antithetical to one about empathy – which, after all, suggests a movement toward knowing (even if unsuccessful) – in fact Weinstein's vision of the modernist subject as always unrealized and unknowable, both to itself and to others, resonates directly with the kind of modernist empathy that I uncover, in which movement into other perspectives reveals only the amount that we do and cannot know, rather than constructing a vision of mastery.

In *On the Problem of Empathy* (1917), phenomenologist Edith Stein argued that empathy not only provides an "orientation" into another's world, but also transforms our understanding of our own world: "from the viewpoint of the zero point of orientation gained in empathy, I must no longer consider my own zero point as the zero point, but as a spatial point among many."[49] This sense of relativity and multiplicity is at the heart of the disorientation; modernist writers reveal this self-knowledge and understanding of the variety of perspectives as essential and important, but often frightening and sometimes even destructive. The danger spots at the boundaries of the subject emerge in their representations of the strange sense of loss that permeates every attempt to know both the self and others.

There are many terms used to define empathetic engagement, and the choice of these terms made by different scholars helps to delineate the particular foci of their own arguments and stakes in both the genealogy of the term and the application of it to texts and fields. Hammond, for example, chooses "fellow feeling," a version that emphasizes the important intersubjective relationships, and one that was connected to sympathy.[50] I choose more often to emphasize "perspective-taking," since this alludes to some of the elements that I find most salient. First, the idea of perspective-taking is deeply rooted in literary study, and I will show how we have to think about empathetic engagement first and foremost as a formal issue, not entirely but certainly in part because empathy was an aesthetic term at its inception. Second, however, the term "perspective-taking" foregrounds the spatial, positional nature of trying to stand in someone else's shoes, and this spatialized understanding of empathetic engagement is one that I examine in many of these chapters, turning to the geographers of the period for insight into the more literal implications of the term perspective-taking. In particular, in the chapter on Thomas Hardy, I examine the geographers involved with the "New Geography" movement, including Patrick Geddes, Archibald Geike, H. R. Mill, and Halford Mackinder, in order to think through the concept of perspective-taking on both the literal and figurative levels, and this informs my discussion of trench spaces in my chapter on World War I. In my discussions of Eliot and Woolf, this idea of spatial movements shifts from the more tangible, geographic level explored in the earlier chapters to an internal (and sometimes metaphysical) level, as they probe primarily mental movements.

Another benefit of thinking about empathy spatially is that it allows us to move beyond the role of "feeling," and toward not only the more locative, but also the cognitive elements of empathy. This approach highlights empathy as a process: it is an *act* (a movement, a shift) of imagination that allows you to understand or experience the other's emotions (or, as I argue, allows you to *try* to understand or experience them). The recognition of the dual affective and cognitive nature of the empathetic act is commonplace now, whether in the work of literary critics such as Keen and Hammond, or in the work of psychologists and neurologists who examine the brain through fMRI scans.[51] My work in some ways aligns with the robust body of research that has grown up around the study of affect, which encourages moving away from a subject-oriented discussion of emotion, with all of its dependence on a vision of the self as defined and controlled by layered aspects of (un)consciousness. Instead, affect theorists tend toward an understanding of a precognitive being whose reactions must be examined on the "preconscious" level as affects rather than emotions, or as immediate and, despite their preconscious origins, surface (unconditioned) responses, rather than multivalenced ones influenced by outside forces.

Yet, as I have indicated, the importance of the subject – full of intentions, motivations, and emotions – should not be dismissed. Literary critics such as Jonathan Flatley and theorists such as the philosopher Gilles Deleuze and psychiatrist Felix Guattari have usefully pointed to the crucial role of the preconscious affects that underlie overt expressions of emotion.[52] Despite the provocative insights of this approach, however, I have not followed it because it moves us away from the questions of emotion and intention – in particular, away from the social and subjective experiences of and reactions to loss and trauma – that are central to modernist literature. A focus simply on affect and automatic responses does not do justice to the layered subjectivity that emerges in the face of loss and to the deep emotional responses, with all their cultural and psychological valences, that are given literary expression in this period and seem to demand new aesthetic forms.

Form: Elegy

As we see in all of the texts I will examine, from Hardy's elegies to Ford's war narrative, to Eliot's poems, to Woolf's early and mid-period novels, the focus on the spatial element of empathy – the possibility of "standing in someone else's shoes" – is especially troubled, and troubling, when the object of empathy may be dead, or when the object of empathy might be an inanimate object rather than a conscious subject. This brings us to a set of questions about the loss that is central to modernist empathy and how it emerges formally as well as spatially: we can see this loss manifest from the level of the poetic line to the level of genre as a whole, and it foregrounds what I call the elegiac nature of modernist representations of empathy.

We might first wonder how these poems and novels that self-consciously break with the forms usually connected with character identification are still able to get their readers to cross the cognitive and emotional boundaries that lead to empathy with the characters. Hammond has discussed the ways that modernist narrative techniques such as stream-of-consciousness narration and shifting focalizations are "empathy-driven" – in other words, how they work to give us immediate access to others' thoughts and feelings (4). These techniques are central in narrative studies, and I examine some texts for which they are useful. But by turning to a poetic term – elegy – and using that as the interpretive wedge into thinking through modernist form and empathy, *Modernist Empathy* proposes a way to think about literary empathy in terms of lyric, not simply narrative, form.[53] Empathy studies may have exhibited this generic bias toward narratives because we see within fiction the most typical template for exploring empathetic engagement – the enactment of movements within characters' perspectives or the movements that characters make in their attempts to experience the perspectives of others. Yet the prosody of Hardy's elegies, for example, provides a way for him to write a multilayered experience of loss – one that simultaneously voices the absence and the presence of his dead wife Emma, the problematic assumption of Emma's voice, and the absolute failure of that movement in terms of truly bridging the unbridgeable distance of death. Similarly, in *The Waste Land* we will see how ghost beats and spots of silence allow Eliot to explore a polyphony of perspectives that suggest both the possibility and the problematics of elegizing and empathizing across distance and time.

While the longing for a lost togetherness has been recognized as integral to an urge to empathize – as Hammond puts it, "empathetic desires mourn a togetherness that never was" (17) – the relationship between this sense of loss has not been probed in terms of the literary form most closely connected to this urge, the elegy. In claiming that modernist empathy is defined by loss, both imagined and experienced, I necessarily focus on the elegiac tone and perspective. Indeed, when discussing texts such as Woolf's *Jacob's Room* or Eliot's *Four Quartets*, I even go so far as to argue that acts of imagining other perspectives become elegiac acts in their very moment of inception. My own reading of modernism, in general, sees a deeply elegiac strain running throughout, not just because of events like World War I, but also because of a broader awareness that loss may be central to how we understand and define the human experience, and that this loss cannot be assuaged by tomes such as the "Mausoleum book" that Virginia Woolf describes her father turning to after the death of his wife. Indeed, one useful way to define modernism in general may be through its attempts to represent and grapple with loss without turning to the forms and rituals central to nineteenth-century mourning practices.

My work on elegy has been informed by the richly textured set of discussions emerging in the terrain originally carved out by Jahan Ramazani's now classic *Poetry of Mourning: The Modern Elegy from Hardy to Heaney* (1994). In the wake of Ramazani's insightful readings and theorized revisioning of the traditional elegy form and its transformation in the hands of twentieth-century poets, a series of pointed explorations of modern and modernist mourning and elegies has emerged. Particularly important for the development of my approach to mourning and loss have been Madelyn Detloff's *The Persistence of Modernism: Loss and Mourning in the Twentieth Century* (2009), where she argues that we should read modernism as "a constellation of discourses about widespread loss and violence,"[54] and Patricia Rae's introduction to *Modernism and Mourning* (2007), which presents modernist mourning as defined by resistance to the project of mourning. Rae's insights led to my own understanding of modernist mourning as illuminating a failure in mourning practices – a movement into the melancholia that Freud presented as the dysfunctional cousin to the mourning process. As Ramazani argued, elegies that depart from a vision of mourning as a successful practice of overcoming loss or, to use Freud's terms, as a cathexsis of the lost object, necessarily become unable to present a coherent trajectory from loss to reconciliation, trauma to wholeness. I read these theories of modernist mourning, with their focus on the permanent impression of loss, in relation to the kinds of loss and trauma that stand at the heart of modernist empathetic imagining.

Yet there is more at stake here than the recognition of the loss inherent in acts of modernist empathy. With the recognition of the elegiac nature of both modernism and empathy, there are methodological implications: I argue for a *poetics* of modernist empathy. In his *Theory of the Lyric* (2015), Jonathan Culler usefully sets out the differences between the interpretive, hermeneutic approaches, which are interested in figuring out meaning, and the practice of poetics, which, he writes, "works in the opposite direction, asking what are the conventions that enable this work to have the sorts of meanings and effects it does for the reader."[55] My interest here is in the poetics of empathy – asking how, as much as why, these texts work toward imagining other perspectives, and what effects they have on readers. I will go even further and posit that another way to think about the absences and gaps that define modernist literary empathy is as a manifestation of a particularly lyric presence, even within narrative texts. Modernist empathy, in my formulation, is far from contributing to a narrative project of character development and plot-building; it should instead be thought of as inserting and gesturing to modes that work against narrative development and highlight the disruptive nature of such perspective-shifting.

In so arguing, I take up Daniel Tiffany's compelling claim in *Infidel Poetics* (2009) that obscurity is "native to the ontology of poetry" and, therefore, that obscurity in poetry should not be met simply with a clarifying hermeneutic impulse, but instead with attention to the "phenomenology of unknowing, of unresolvable obscurity" that might lead to insight about the role and the effects of this obscurity.[56] In other words, Tiffany suggests that we should dwell in the experience of obscurity – dwell in what we cannot know – when reading poetry; to translate it into a clarified paraphrase takes away what is essentially lyric. In the same vein, I hope to expose how acts of empathetic engagement in modernist literature are not always (or ever?) about revealing and explaining another mind. Instead, they make us zero in on what remains unknown and unclear. To return to Tiffany's definition, therefore, modernist empathy has more affinities with lyric, not narrative, impulses and modes; one other way to describe modernist empathy, with its focus on loss and unknowing, may therefore be as a "lyric empathy." Modernist poetry offers surprising insights into the structure and function of literary empathy, giving a more comprehensive understanding of the modernist literary and empathetic imagination, precisely because so often it performs that obfuscation that results from shifts in perspectives. And while poetry might offer the first terrain on which to explore this kind of lyric empathy, modernist fiction offers a similarly exciting set of insights into the dangers and rewards of the empathetic imagination. By thinking through the possibilities for perspective-taking via objects, places, and even the voicing of language itself, our sense of the terrain of empathy is enlarged and challenged.

Psychology: The Uncanny

Finally, this book turns to questions of psychology when thinking of empathy, though primarily through what Berlant describes as the "space

of disinterpellation or uncanny self-misrecognition."[57] Freud's short piece
on "The Uncanny" (1919) is beloved by literary critics for a number of
reasons, perhaps beginning with his first sentence, which proclaims "It is
only rarely that a psycho-analyst feels impelled to investigate the subject of
aesthetics even when aesthetics is understood to mean not merely the
theory of beauty, but the theory of feeling."[58] This opening has some
unexpected resonances with Vernon Lee's book on empathy, *Beauty and
Ugliness*, published seven years earlier. Lee describes her own exploration of
empathy as emerging from the intersection between what she terms "the
science mind which, under the name of psychology, has only lately
detached itself from general philosophy; and the various sciences dealing
with the comparison, the origin and the evolution of artistic form."[59]
The similarity between Freud and Lee's explanation of the overlap between
psychology and aesthetics (and their desire to probe that site of overlap)
suggests some methodological similarities, and the connections that we can
begin to see between empathy and the uncanny will help us uncover some
of the more problematic parts of the empathic experience.

What might uncanny empathy mean? Let me approach this from two
angles. First of all, the very psychological and aesthetic movement that we
can see in the act of empathizing – what Vernon Lee describes in *Beauty
and Ugliness* as "putting ourselves inside" or, for the more literal translation
she gives of the German term *Einfühlung*, "feeling ourselves into"[60] –
involves a perforation of the boundaries between inside and outside, self
and other, in the structure of the action. Empathy challenges the concept
of the unified and autonomous subject, for in the act of feeling into
another, one must absent the perspective of the self, even if only briefly.
The return to the original perspective is not necessarily as seamless as it
might be; we might think about Virginia Woolf's caution to herself in her
diaries that, while it is necessary to take away the screens that protect the
self, "If we had not this device for shutting people off from our sympathies,
we might, perhaps, dissolve utterly. Separation would be impossible."[61]
Edith Stein likewise identifies the complicated equation that occurs for the
empathizing subject:

> when the experience of the other arises before me all at once, it faces me as an
> object (such as the sadness I "read in another's face"). But when I inquire
> into its implied tendencies (try to bring another's mood to clear givenness to
> myself), the content, having pulled me into it, is no longer really an object.
> I am now no longer turned to the content but to the object of it, am at the
> subject of the content at the original subject's place. And only after success-
> ful executed clarification, does the content again face me as an object. (10)

This movement between what Stein terms "primordial" experience (which has an "embodied givenness" and a quality of "being there itself right now" in the subject [6]) and "non-primordial" experience (which represents its object, rather than have it "bodily present" [7]) describes the shifts that occur in every act of empathy; the subject must move from perception of the other's experience as something that is nonprimordial (observed but not experienced) to an experience of the other's experience as having an embodied givenness (where it becomes the experience of the subject). Then the subject again detaches and returns to the state of a nonprimordial experience. This last moment, which Stein describes as a "successful executed clarification," is the danger point that Woolf intuited. What allows for the success of the "clarification," and how can one know that the movement back into a clear subject–object differentiation will be successful? We might think about the law of entropy here: entropy is the amount of disorder in a system; as the Second Law of Thermodynamics shows, a system can never decrease in entropy, it can only increase; things can only grow increasingly disordered, and we can never return to an original state of order. The idea of entropy disrupted the orderly world of Newtonian physics; likewise, modernist empathy disrupts the order of the subject–object universe in which there are discrete boundaries imagined between subjects and objects. While the sympathetic mind can feel *for* someone/thing without challenging the autonomy of the feeling self, the empathetic mind, when it feels *with* someone, necessarily challenges that autonomy. In the act of stepping outside one's own perspective and inhabiting another, whether we think of it in Vernon Lee's sense of absorbing into oneself the object's experience, or in the Steinian sense of occupying the perspective of the object of empathy, we introduce an element of disorder into our prior sense of subjectivity. Paradoxically, it can seem like a loss (loss of order, loss of clarity), even as it could be described as a gain (of another perspective).

This slight difference in the subject pre- and post-empathy is where we can locate the beginning of the uncanny nature of the empathetic act. As Freud emphasizes in his lengthy first section where he explores the etymology of the words canny and uncanny (*heimlich* and *unheimlich*), the two terms contain each other; as Freud notes, "we are reminded that the word *heimlich* is not unambiguous, but belongs to two sets of ideas, which without being contradictory are yet very different; on the one hand, it means that which is familiar and congenial, and on the other, that which is concealed and kept out of sight" (375), and thus "*heimlich* is a word the meaning of which develops toward ambivalence, until it finally coincides with its opposite, *unheimlich*" (377). This containment of the familiar in the unfamiliar, and vice versa, both mirrors and troubles the trajectory of empathy. Most useful here is how it highlights the ambiguity of the movement between the known and the unknown; encountering the uncanny can be, in part, an experience of recognizing the unfamiliar in the familiar and the familiar in the unfamiliar – that is what distinguishes it from something that is merely frightening.

The second way that Freud helps clarify the idea of "uncanny empathy" is in his discussion of what he calls a "theme" that is frequently associated with the uncanny: that of the double. He foregrounds its appearance in one of Hoffmann's texts – not in the story "The Sandman," which is the centerpiece of Freud's exploration of methods of producing the uncanny, but in a novel called *The Devil's Elixir*. Freud notes here that Hoffmann not only creates an uncanny experience by presenting a double, but also "accentuates this relation by transferring mental processes from one person to the other – what we should call telepathy – so that one possesses knowledge, feeling and experience in common with the other, identifies himself with another person, so that his self becomes confounded" (386–387). This confounding of the self, which stands in contrast to the clarification of the states of identification described by Edith Stein, is what Woolf feared; indeed, it is a fear that characterizes enough modernist literary explorations of the empathetic experience that it begins to seem definitive. We might think of the doubling of Clarissa Dalloway and Septimus Smith, which sends a shock of recognition and confrontation through Clarissa – brings her closer to death – even as she is ultimately able to step away from that death because Septimus' choice frees her in some way: "She felt somehow very like him – the young man who had killed himself. She felt glad that he had done it; thrown it away."[62] This is one of the most confounding lines in the novel – why does Clarissa feel like Septimus, a person whom she has never met, and who is separated by gender, class, and age? – but it makes more sense when we think of it as a moment in which a recognition of some repressed impulse in the self (toward death, away from the repressive patriarchy represented by the doctors – specifically Bradshaw) is seen and recognized in an other; it is a moment in which the self is revealed in ways that may have been hidden before. More ambiguous is the empathetic experience of Tiresias in *The Waste Land*; his "throbbing between two lives"[63] takes its toll on his body, marked with the genitalia of both sexes, as well as on his ability to feel anything at all; he views the scene of sexual assault impassively, and the poem emphasizes his mechanistic vision of the world: he is like a "taxi" throbbing between his lives. Tiresias seems the epitome of the confounded self, the self who no longer has a clear distinction between self and other; in this case it is a dual self, rather than an exterior other.

This troubled experience of doubling or the movement between self and other can instigate feelings of the uncanny precisely because it emphasizes that the unity of the subject is not inviolable; the uncanniness occurs in that moment of recognition when the subject has an experience, as Adam Bresnick describes it, "that momentarily undoes the factitious monological unity of the ego."[64] While empathy might first be seen as clarifying the distinction between subject and object because it depends on an awareness of the alterity of the other perspective, the act of empathizing can create an uncanny situation in which, after having attempted that shift in perspectives between her own and another, the empathizer confronts the strangeness of the self when seen from outside. Empathy can be seen as an uncanny act in and of itself because it involves a bringing to light of something that was dark (the illumination of another consciousness, another perspective) – and, according to Freud's essay, a recognition of a self that was formerly unrecognized: the return of the repressed.

* * * *

Aspects of these three ways of viewing modernist empathy – the spatial, the formal, and the psychological – appear in the following chapters, though the terms play different roles. In Chapter 2, "Disorientation, Elegy, and the Uncanny: Modernist Empathy Through Hardy," Thomas Hardy functions as the starting point for my literary case studies, since through the range of his work he provides a template for using all three of these perspectives. On the one hand, like scholars including Sara Crangle and Rosemary Sumner,[65] I use Thomas Hardy as a chronological starting point for an examination of modernism; he is a writer who evocatively describes the "ache of modernism"[66] in *Tess of the D'Urbervilles*, one of my objects of analysis, even as his writing style sometimes seems more akin to George Eliot's than to Virginia Woolf's. On the other hand, Hardy also proves an ideal starting point because clear examples emerge in his varied texts of how to think through empathy from the spatial, formal, and psychological viewpoints.

My focus shifts in the subsequent chapters; while each touches on more than one element, the primary focus in Chapter 3 is on disorientation, in Chapter 4 on elegy, and in Chapter 5 on the uncanny. In Chapter 3, "Disorienting Empathy: World War I and the Traumas of Perspective-Taking," I examine the violent spaces of the Western Front, turning to

Henri Lefebvre's theory of experienced, perceived, and imagined spaces in order to explicate the multiple levels on which questions of orientation, and therefore also of *dis*orientation, define the subject's experience of war space. In the first section, in which I look at the four novels in Ford Madox Ford's tetralogy, *Parade's End*, I argue that Ford's mapmaking experience, combined with the general disorientation of trench life, transforms the tetralogy into a formal project of (dis)orientation that both uses and reworks cartographic methods of representing traumatized war space and postwar loss. In the second section, I begin to turn more decisively to formal questions of attempting empathetic engagement in a space of trauma. I examine the extraordinary experimental text by Mary Borden, *The Forbidden Zone* (1929), in which, I argue, Borden uses the second person and direct address to create zones of silence even in texts that deal with the most violent and noise-filled spaces of modernism. This silence, so often theorized as a gap, a moment of obscurity, or a sign of absence, can play a powerful and disturbing connective role, I posit. In bridging the gap between the "I" and the "you," it offers a distinctly lyric form of empathy.

The gap between the "I" and the "you" – or, more precisely, between subject and object – comes to the foreground in Chapter 4, "Elegizing Empathy: Eliot and the Subject–Object Divide." Here I move from a more literal geographic focus on space to one that examines the more minute movements of the mind, and that leads to an exploration of the elegiac nature of the empathetic imagination. In order to probe this decentering of the self, I parse Eliot's vision of how objects, rather than people, might become the focal point in acts of perspective-taking. If Hardy gave us a prosody of loss and a rationale for the aesthetic and social necessity (if danger) of empathetic engagement, Eliot gives us a theory of empathy that makes perspective-taking and loss inextricably linked.

The uncanny emerges most prominently in Chapter 5: "Uncanny Empathy: Woolf's Half-Life of Objects." I continue the focus on empathy with and through objects, but I also bring in the dialogue between Freud and literary modernism, reading Freud's "The Uncanny" alongside both Woolf's haunted object world in *Jacob's Room* (1922) and the art object in *To the Lighthouse* (1927). Beginning with Lee's provocative description in *The Beautiful* (1913) of empathy as "feeling oneself into some*thing*,"[67] I argue that we must think of empathy as a challenging act of the aesthetic imagination connected to an object world as much as an act of emotional transference in a subject world. Yet empathy with objects can be threatening when the boundaries between inanimate and animate blur. Thus, we again see how loss defines these spatialized movements into other perspectives, and how modernist empathy seems to obscure the borders between known and unknown, the *heimlich* and the *unheimlich*, in ways that are both illuminating and dangerous.

I end with a brief conclusion, "Performing Empathy?," about the possibility of thinking through the relationship between literary empathy and politics. While empathy is often deployed in political rhetoric, with politicians promising that they are engaging in such productive perspective-shifting in order to serve their constituents more fully, one can question whether empathetic engagement can be an effective political tool (and whether it becomes something else in that process). Throughout this book I argue that we need to push against the idea that empathy and abstraction are always antithetical processes, and in this chapter I briefly examine a specific form of politicized abstraction: the abstraction of the individual into an idea. My case study is a public, performative type of poetry – the Mass Declamations of the 1930s in general and, more specifically, one declamation that was enacted to support the Republican forces in the Spanish Civil War. I explain how this particular poetic form might provide a template for how to engage audience empathy (if it is empathy) in service of a political cause. While this declamation might be seen as a project in perspective-taking, it ultimately fails to engage the empathetic imagination in ways central to modernist empathy, I argue, because it transforms the "we" of the poem into a group mind rather than a container for multiple perspectives.

CHAPTER 2

Disorientation, Elegy, and the Uncanny
Modernist Empathy Through Hardy

With whom better to start than Thomas Hardy, with his career that spanned more than five decades of prolific publishing, from his first 1871 novel, *Desperate Remedies*, to his 1925 poetry collection, *Human Shows*; with his generic range from the baggy Victorian serialized novel, to a historical (and experimental) epic poem, to his elliptical modernist elegies; and with his ambiguous critical future, claimed (and sometimes rejected) by both Victorianists and modernists, both theorists of the novel and critics of the lyric?[1] Because of these messy boundaries and definitions, I have chosen to begin with him because his range allows me to explicate my three main apertures into modernist empathy – spatial, formal, and psychological – within one oeuvre. Hardy's novels perform a geography of narrative empathy that reveals the limits and the challenges to empathetic engagement; his elegies take these insights about the effects of geo-empathy and root them in a language of loss, raising questions about the efficacy and the ethics of such retrospective perspective-taking; and, finally, the psychic content of such geo- and elegiac empathy, shaped and stunted by mourning, emerges as the uncanny because of the structural manifestations of a present absence and absent presence. Hardy thus provides a touchstone for the arguments that will come up, in varying degrees, in the chapters that follow.

Disorientation: Hardy's Geography of Narrative Empathy

When it came to the reception of his novels, Hardy was an anxious man. He had some reason to be this way, given the censorship that most of his work faced when it was serialized in literary magazines. In the essay "Candour in English Fiction" (1890), written when he was having problems with the serialization of *Tess of the d'Urbervilles* (1891), Hardy bemoans the power that the editors wield over what gets published, lamenting that, "acting under the censorship of prudery," they "rigorously exclude from the pages they regulate subjects that have been made, by general approval of the best judges, the bases of the finest imaginative compositions since literature rose to the dignity of an art."[2] His anxiety continued when his novels were published in their full and unexpurgated form and, at various points, he attributed his decision to stop writing novels to the vitriolic critical response to *Jude the Obscure* (1895).

Hardy's comments reflect, in large part, his crankiness about being misread, yet they also provide important background to the revisions he made when consolidating and reworking his novels for publication in later editions. Although he stopped writing new novels after the public outrage over *Jude*, Hardy continued to obsess over the reception of his prose work. His books were, according to Virginia Woolf in 1916, "already accepted among the classics,"[3] but Hardy's own perception of his standing was less sanguine. In his efforts to consolidate both his reputation and his economic security, Hardy actively sought further publication opportunities for his novels, revising them in ways that have been carefully charted by such scholars as Simon Gatrell and Michael Millgate.[4]

Even before the trauma of *Jude*, however, Hardy's publication projects were shaped by his combined emotional and economic desire for an appreciative reading audience. This goal, and Hardy's surprisingly concrete methods to achieve it, are the focus of this first section; I argue here that Hardy uses geographic descriptions with the desire to promote empathetic engagement with his characters, and that he brings the experience of narrative empathy off the page by orienting his readers in both real and imaginary spaces, creating what I will call a "geo-empathy." A reading of two of Hardy's later novels, *The Woodlanders* (1887) and *Tess of the d'Urbervilles*, allows me to analyze the geographic descriptions within the novels as well as the geographic apparatuses that surrounded, in particular, *Tess* after the publication of the 1912 "Wessex Edition." Yet since both of these novels hauntingly chart the loss of a deep and fulfilling knowledge of the terrain, the kinds of orienting attempts Hardy engages in reveal the disorienting effects of trying to stand in another person's shoes.

Hardy's characters are often deeply compelling in their own right, of course, but by examining the role played by geographic perspective-taking in the creation of empathy for these characters, we can see how he turned to strategies other than the representation of characters' interiority in order to facilitate readers' connections. Exploring this conjunction between geography[5] and empathy in the novels and in surrounding texts suggests that Hardy offers an alternative narrative practice in which subject-making – the imagining of interior life and emotions – is no longer the primary method of engaging empathy.

In so doing, Hardy brings together two genres of perspective-taking that are seemingly at odds: the geographic viewpoint, which is most often associated with an "objective" or scientific gaze, and the empathetic perspective, which involves an inherently subjective point of view.[6] His use of geography suggests, moreover, an ethical implication of geo-empathy: the possibility of empathy across difference. If empathy can be engaged by occupying the same *spatial* perspective, then differences in period, class, gender, or other social and personal divisors might be bridged. This does not imply a transcendence of such differences, but rather the uncovering of a route to engagement with others. Hardy's novels seek out such routes, even if they often despair of maintaining them.

One question must precede any focus on Hardy's geo-empathy: why is such geographic orientation needed to facilitate empathy? Why, in other words, do such memorable figures as Tess and Jude not simply inspire identification on the basis of their rich characterization? Suzanne Keen has described how a reader's empathy can be activated, even when the characters have alien moral codes, by "successfully exercised authorial empathy" (xiii) – something that Hardy clearly felt for his characters.[7] In her recent *Thomas Hardy's Brains* (2014), Keen has done an especially thorough job of exploring the various influences on Hardy's understanding of psychology, and she points us toward a manuscript note Hardy prepared for inclusion in his posthumously published autobiography (ostensibly a biography written by his wife), and now found in the personal notebooks, which illustrates his own intense "altruism": "It was his habit, or *strange* power of putting himself in the place of those who endured sufferings from which he himself had been in the main free, or subject to but at brief times."[8] While we might be inclined to smile at the irony of Hardy's self-praise about his empathetic mind, this strange power is at work in the novels; Elaine Scarry specifically cites the "vividness" of Tess and the novel's ability to "incite in our imagination the vivacity of the perceptual world," even while she otherwise focuses on the difficulty of imagining other people and the need for constitutional guidelines that make a civic empathetic engagement into law.[9]

Yet Scarry does not say why she finds Tess so vivid; her mention of the "perceptual world" indicates that vivacity may rely on more than a rich interiority of the characters. William A. Cohen, Peter Widdowson, Gilles Deleuze, and J. Hillis Miller, among others, do *not* read Hardy's novels as providing such an intuitive basis for empathetic engagement. As Cohen has persuasively argued, Hardy "erodes distinctions between subjects and objects" with his version of "human subjectivity as material,"[10] thereby doing away with the distinction between self and other that is the necessary first premise of empathy. Likewise, Widdowson writes in an essay on *Tess* that Hardy gives us "precisely *not* a novel attempting to offer us a 'knowable' character, but rather one which exposes *characterization* itself as a humanist-realist mystification."[11] Deleuze asserts even more radically that Hardy's characters "are not people or subjects, they are collections of intensive sensations, each is such a collection, a packet, a bloc of variable sensations" that it functions as an "[i]ndividual without a subject."[12] Even the geographic terrain in the novels appears to work against engagement with the characters, according to Miller, who links the lack of individualized subjectivity he finds in the novels to Hardy's topographical focus by arguing that, for example, *The Return of the Native* "is a novel in which the human relationships are symbolized by the features of the heath."[13]

I also read Hardy as presenting us with characters who evade our attempts to psychologize them. Of course, the problem of perspective-taking is layered, and, as Hardy knew from his reading of Walter Pater, the possibility of seeing and therefore knowing what others experience is uncertain, to say the least.[14] This distinction between perceiving and knowing reflects the divide between an empathetic understanding, which is inherently limited, even though it may take the empathizer out of his or her own viewpoint, and the geographic version of perspective-taking, which, we will see, assumes (even if erroneously) an ultimate final and objective knowledge of the scene. If perspective *is* embodied, then it would also seem to be unalterably closed to others. Yet rather than a transcendent knowledge that would imply an effortless link to another subject, the form of empathy that Hardy forges involves constantly reiterating the perspectival nature of knowing. With regard to both the successes and the failures of empathy presented in his novels, Hardy points to the incessant reorienting that must take place when trying to understand others. The "difficulty of imagining other people" that Scarry argues for is also a difficulty that Hardy's geographically inflected characterizations both implicitly and explicitly acknowledge. Embedded in each act of perspective-taking, therefore, is the recognition of the limits of the act. By rooting perspective-taking in geographic positioning and by exploring both the potential impossibility of successfully standing in someone else's shoes and the waning ability to "know" a space, Hardy locates that sense of limit and loss in the very terrain of the text, even as he strives to enable empathy in his readers. We can see in this project an early manifestation of Hardy's geographically inflected elegizing which, I will argue in my discussion of Hardy's poetry, is an essential element of modernist negotiations of loss.

Empathy and Geography

My choice of the term "empathy" points to Hardy's position as a bridge between Victorian and modernist social and aesthetic norms, for the possibility of imagining others was increasingly up for debate during the period when Hardy was writing and revising his novels, as I have detailed in Chapter 1. Important to reiterate here is how empathy involves a shift in perspective – a movement from one subjective position into another. While Hardy forces us to recognize the embodied nature of our under-standing of the world, he also explores the possibility of working within this embodied form of perspective-taking in order to create a more expan-sive vision. To do this, he borrowed from and reworked contemporary geographic theories about regional studies, in which the act of standing in someone else's shoes was increasingly viewed as a vital practice. The catalogue of Hardy's library reveals his continuing interest in the field: he owned and annotated geographic manuals, guidebooks, and maps, which range from the mid-century textbook, *A Manuel of Geography Physical, Industrial, and Political* (1864), to later books that grew out of the new geography's focus on regions (*A Handbook for Residents and Travellers in Wilts and Dorset* [1899] and *The English Lake District* [1902], for example).[15]

Hardy's lifelong interest in geography – the science of the description of the physical features of a place or region – originated, however, in primary school where, he reports, he "excelled" at the subject (*Early Life*, 20). Until late in the nineteenth century, in fact, primary school was the only place where geography was taught. Though the Ordnance Survey had been officially underway since 1791, geography had a negligible role in education during much of the nineteenth century.[16] Their field not yet recognized as a university subject, early nineteenth-century geographers became increas-ingly defensive about the encroachment of biological and geological sciences on their terrain.[17] In the 1880s the status of geography began to change, due in large part to the efforts of the Royal Geographical Society and to the growing desire among geographers and social scientists for a "new geography" – a label coined by Halford Mackinder during the annual congresses of the British Association of Science and Art in the 1880s.[18] In 1887, when the prominent geographer Archibald Geike claimed in his pedagogical handbook, *The Teaching of Geography*, that the "study of geography ought to begin at home, and from a basis of actual personal experience should advance to the consideration of other countries and of the earth as a whole," the field of geography had just been established as a legitimate university-level discipline and its teaching at lower levels was being transformed.[19] By 1901, H. R. Mill was able to claim that "geography will be found to afford an important clue to the solution of every problem affecting the mutual relations of land and people."[20]

The focus on occupying different perspectives became an integral element of the new geography primarily with the use of regional surveys that were supposed to provide a global intelligence through accrued local knowledge. Practically speaking, regional surveys involved mapping localities on a number of levels – topography, land use, population density, climate, history, and archeology – with the goal of eventually synthesizing these charts so that a complete picture of an area could be composed. A text such as *Great Britain: Essays in Regional Geography* (1928), which collected essays by twenty-six geographers on various regions and with varying levels of examination, epitomized the ideal of bringing together a layered understanding of particular regions. The ultimate goals of regional surveys, however, were much more sweeping. Prominent geographers and social scientists, including Mill, Mackinder, Patrick Geddes, A. J. Herbertson, and H. J. Fleure, saw the potential for this geography both to reveal the unity of human life through a focus on the diversity of local and individual experience (a seeming paradox), and to solidify a sense of regional and national belonging. As Lord Curzon, the president of the Geographical Society, said in a 1912 meeting, "geography is one of the first and foremost of the sciences; it is part of the equipment that is necessary for a proper conception of citizenship, and is an indispensable adjunct to the production of a public man."[21]

In 1892 Patrick Geddes, a Scottish evolutionary biologist, botanist, and geographer (whose influential *The Evolution of Sex* was in Hardy's library), literalized the act of geographic perspective-taking by instituting the world's first geographical "museum": the Outlook Tower, a five-storey structure on a hill outside of Edinburgh. The Tower was supposed to function as an "Index-Museum to the World," topped by a *camera obscura* that looked out on the surrounding countryside. In this museum Geddes put into practice the idea of regional survey, in which the study of a local area provides the basis for and precedes any broader understanding of society. For Geddes, the *camera obscura* was important because it gave the viewer a particular perspective on the surrounding area, emphasizing the aesthetic elements and allowing one "[to] see everything in its true colours with fresh eyes."[22] This new view of the immediate surroundings provided the basis for the levels of the Tower, devoted (in descending order) to Edinburgh, Scotland, Language, Europe, and the World. Both the primacy of local knowledge and the assumption of different individual perspectives as a starting point for a global and globalized understanding were configured in the very layout of the Tower – a manifestation of the central premises of the larger geographic movement.

At the heart of this focus on the local as a microcosm of the international macrocosm was an understanding of "geography as a social practice operating beyond the academy" (Matless, 468). In other words, proponents of the new geography believed that individual citizens could learn how to orient themselves in relation to the surrounding world through their own observations, and that this ability would transform both their comprehension of and their actions toward others. In essence, as Geike argues in his 1887 handbook, attention to one's surroundings is simply a continuation of a child's natural curiosity: if, "even among the youngest children and in every rank of life," people are "encouraged to look at things with their own eyes, and draw from them their own conclusions," then "in this way their conceptions of their immediate surroundings, of their country, and of the whole globe may, from the very outset, be made vivid, accurate, and enduring" (vii). The teaching and learning of geography via regional surveys thereby functions as an equalizing force that transcends difference and allows all individuals to comprehend the larger world, even if they are bound to their own small locality for social and economic reasons. In this way, geographic perspective-taking suggested a method of creating a foundation for empathetic engagement across difference, even as it also made claims to create knowledge about the broader world.[23]

Feeling Locations

This science of space, which aligns with Hardy's own sense of the historically and personally saturated nature of his surrounding world, provided an external structure – the surveys and maps – through which to mediate individual, social, and environmental change. Yet Hardy's use of geography in his writing refines and challenges, as well as represents, the discipline's assumptions.

While Geddes and other geographers were elaborating the role of perspective-taking in geography, Hardy was exploring the possibility of mobilizing a productive version of a geographically based empathy in his novels, even as he also countered the overweaning hopes evinced by

Geddes and others. The opening paragraphs of *The Woodlanders* – Hardy's story of the ill-fated love triangle of the residents, both new and old, in a hidden little forest community – exemplify such attempts, as well as revealing how Hardy's revisions in later editions lent themselves to this pedagogical process. In the revised 1912 Wessex Edition, the novel begins:

> The rambler who for old association's sake should trace the forsaken coach-road running almost in a meridional line from Bristol to the south shore of England, would find himself during the latter half of his journey, in the vicinity of some extensive woodlands, interspersed with apple-orchards. Here the trees, timber or fruit-bearing as the case may be, make the wayside hedges ragged by their drip and shade; their lower limbs stretching over the road with easeful horizontality, as though reclining on the insubstantial air. At one place, on the skirts of Blackmore Vale, where the bold brow of High-Stoy Hill is seen two or three miles ahead, the leaves lie so thick in autumn as to completely bury the track. The spot is lonely, and when the days are darkening the many gay charioteers now perished who have rolled along the way, the blistered soles that have trodden it, and the tears that have wetted it, return upon the mind of the loiterer.[24]

We begin the novel with a subject, "the rambler," who is open-ended in his allegiances to the scene and the forthcoming action, a rural counterpart to Baudelaire's reader-*flâneur*. This flexible, unnamed subject, though somehow connected in the past to the place, provides a perspective that, we begin to learn, educates us in how to view and read the scene; the nostalgia that seems to propel the rambler leads to an awareness of the tone and the connotations of the spot. Yet this is not simply a description of the affective qualities of the place; instead, the opening paragraph also locates the spot both cartographically (halfway along "a meridional line from Bristol to the south shore of England" and "two or three miles" away from High-Stoy Hill) and naturalistically (with the descriptions of the woodlands). Both the place and the natural features lead to the emotional impact of the spot that, with an agency of its own, "return[s] upon the mind of the loiterer."

This crescendo, moving from the open-minded rambler, receptive to the surroundings, to this subject's resulting awareness of the road's affective history, is clearer when compared with the text of early versions (a text that appears in the manuscript, the serials, and the first Harper Brothers edition). At first glance it seems that in this early version Hardy makes the rambler *more* accessible to identification by giving him a broader motive for travelling: he is described as traveling there "for old association *or* other reasons" (my emphasis).[25] Hardy's excision of the vague "other reasons" in later editions points to his increasing control (or desire for control) over the reader's reaction. Such specification continues with the switch from the more general description in the early editions – "At one place, where a hill is crossed" (Harper edn., 3) – to the revised novel's use of actual place names (Blackmoor Vale and High-Stoy Hill) that connect the setting more firmly to a realistic geography. Likewise, the excision in the revised version of an extended metaphor about the road ("the largest of the woods shows itself bisected by the highway as a head of thick hair is bisected by the white line of the parting" [Harper edn., 3]) again involves a move to specification. The most striking difference between the early and later versions occurs, however, in the ending of the paragraph. The first versions end with the abrupt statement, "The spot is lonely," forgoing the description of the effect this loneliness has on the mind of the rambler. In the early version, therefore, Hardy does not immediately tell his reader how to understand this loneliness; in the later one, we are keyed into the type of resonances that the juxtaposition of road and woodland *should* bring.

The attention paid to knowing how to read this lonely spot foregrounds one aspect of Hardy's larger project to revise his descriptions and names in his Wessex novels. As Dale Kramer writes in a discussion of the revisions, Hardy's adjustments of distances (to be more true to real-life distances) and changes from imagined to real places indicate "that while Hardy seemed to have an obsession about distances and angles of perspective, accuracy for its own sake was not his goal so much as, perhaps, a felt need to re-create the sense of actuality, the state of mind in which he had originally written the invented narration."[26] This is more than an interest in cartographic accuracy; it moves into a desire for accurate placement as a way to combat the belief that his perspective (in all senses of the term) might not be understood. As such, Hardy's revisions acknowledge the difficulty of empathetic engagement and foreground his almost obsessive project to work around that difficulty. Here is the labor that centrally defines both modernist aesthetic production (we might recall Hulme's metaphor of the modern poet working to find the words that fit, just as he might bend a metal band into a perfect curve) and empathetic stretching.

We can see this intense interest in how a place is interpreted just a few paragraphs further in *The Woodlanders*, with the introduction of the first human figure on that deserted road. While at first the character (whom we learn a few pages later is Barber Percomb) does appear to experience the loneliness and haunted nature of the road that the opening paragraphs emphasized, this attunement to the tone of the place is brief because, the narrator tells us, he "was mainly puzzled about the way" (*Woodlanders*, 6).

Barber Percomb's indifference to the melancholy of the road is a product of his purpose-oriented trip (which, we later are told, is undertaken to persuade Marty South to sell her hair). Percomb is not the rambler and, with his lack of ability to experience more than the superficial aspects of the space, not the model of how to understand and read the road and landscape. No wonder he has lost his way.

Yet Percomb's lack of intuition about the resonances of the place is not unusual in this book; indeed, it could be seen as a foreshadowing of the novel's overarching concern with both willful and unconscious misreadings and missed chances for empathy. Two of the relative newcomers to the area – the doctor Edred Fitzpiers and the wealthy landowner through widowhood, Felice Charmond – are characterized both by their lack of interest in and understanding of the terrain and by their deep narcissism, which leads them to view the inhabitants in terms of their utility. Even Fitzpiers's method of deciding where to live – he confidently asserts, "'I'll tell you why I came here. I took a map, and I marked on it where Dr. Jones's practice ends to the north of this district, and where Mr. Taylor's ends on the south, and little Jimmy Green's on the east, and somebody else's to the west. Then I took a pair of compasses, and found the exact middle of the country that was left between these bounds, and that middle was Little Hintock; so here I am'" (50) – reveals his inability to understand the terrain (other than cartographically); his sense of isolation from the villagers confirms this.

Problems with understanding the geography and empathizing with others are not confined to the newcomers. Time away from home leads one of the main characters, Grace Melbury, not simply to forget how to understand the landscape and identify the trees, but even to be unable to *see* the terrain at all. As she rides home with Giles Winterbourne, a dealer in apples and apple trees and her childhood sweetheart, he is astounded by her mistaken identification of one species of tree. Yet, we learn, this is not a case of simple forgetting: "the fact at present was merely this, that where he was seeing John-apples and farm-buildings she was beholding a much contrasting scene: a broad lawn in the fashionable suburb of a fast city" (43). Such geographic blindness, while different in scope, is a precursor of Grace's inability to see at the end of the novel (albeit in large part because Giles conceals it from her) that Giles is ill and near death – a death hastened by his sleeping outside his hut in order to give Grace a place of refuge from her unfaithful husband. Grace is not vilified in this later scene; the narrator assures us that her inability to see Giles's illness results more from the lack of light ("the firelight did not enable her to perceive that [his features] were positively haggard" [278]) than her lack of empathetic vision. Yet it is the combination of Grace's lack of understanding along with Giles's overly empathetic nature – he "forgot his own agony in the satisfaction of having at least found her a shelter" (281) – that precipitates Giles's death. More than by a lack of feeling, Grace realizes she was inhibited by a desire to be "selfishly correct" (290), and she understands her role in his demise when she finally finds him, sick and raving, in the lean-to outside his cottage. The true blindness on her part, we and she realize, stems not from being unaware of his physical discomfort, but from not understanding his personality well enough – the "purity of his nature, his freedom from the grosser passions, his scrupulous delicacy" (291) – to see that he would sacrifice himself for her.

Yet Grace, though chastened by this experience, ultimately goes back to her husband, abandoning her devotional visits to Giles's grave, while Marty South, the only other figure who "had approximated to Winterbourne's level of intelligent intercourse with Nature" (306), main-tains the visits. Noting that Grace found the woods "uninteresting" (318) during her time living back in her father's house, the novel suggests, as it did in that early discussion of Grace's and Giles's different perspectives on the landscape, that empathic action springs from an ability to understand not only other people, but also the surrounding natural world and geo-graphy. It is the loss of this type of spatial perspective-taking – the ability to truly see the natural world and navigate the terrain – that has led to the tragedy in the book. John Barrell's reading of Hardy's earlier novel, *The Return of the Native* (1878), is illuminating here, for he argues that, through

> representing the geography of the heathfolk in terms of what we may suspect to be a myth, of primal unity, the novel constructs us, its readers, as alienated observers of their sense of place, who are thus *obliged* to under-stand the process of our alienation in terms of the correlative myth, of history as the progressive differentiation of a lost, an original unity.[27]

While we see in *The Woodlanders* the same kind of special knowledge of terrain available only to a few, there is a difference here, for we learn the consequences of lacking that kind of knowledge. The imperative, there-fore, is to *try* to understand these other perspectives, even if the book suggests the ultimate difficulty of doing so.

Such a connection between geographic and social knowledge is not unique to *The Woodlanders*; it in fact emerged in Hardy's speeches and essays throughout this later period of his writing, often combined with an appeal to the need to read literature that deepens one's sense of connection. In a 1902 speech to the Wessex Society of Manchester, for example, he claimed, "Whatever strengthens local attachments strengthens both individual and national Character [*sic*]," suggesting the real-world effect of reading regional literature (qtd. in Millgate, 422). He posits in his 1888 essay, "The Profitable Reading of Fiction," that these attachments emerge from an affective connection to the characters, arguing that readers respond via "intuitive conviction, and not upon logical reasoning ... for by their emotion men are acted upon, and act upon others" (*Personal Writings*, 115). This last phrase is especially suggestive, for it again presents a vision of reading that imagines *action* as the end product of engagement with fictional texts. Yet it also raises the question of whether writing about a fictional, not real, region could promote this form of attachment, especially for an audience of readers that was primarily middle class, unlike the farmers and peasants that populate the Wessex novels. In the mid and late 1800s, Hardy's readers generally received his books through magazines and then circulating libraries, and access to these libraries cost approximately a guinea a year – not a price that most working-class families could afford.[28] Even the free libraries tended to serve those who occupied a growing class composed of artisans and clerks, who were situated between the middle and the laboring classes.[29] It was not until the 1890s that the hold circulating libraries maintained over the publishing business weakened, and publishers began to print cheap editions right away. Even then, with the exodus to the cities that took place throughout the nineteenth century, reading was still a primarily urban activity, while Hardy's characters were overwhelmingly rural.[30]

In order to bridge the gap between the urban readers and the rural settings, Hardy's narratives worked to locate the reader on the fictional map, familiarizing her with the imagined geography and the characters' local perspectives by connecting them to identifiable spaces in England. Such a connection between imagined and real could counter the response of what Hardy called the "too genteel reader" in his preface to the first edition of *Tess*, and encourage what Hardy praised as "imaginative intuition" in the preface written seven months later for the fifth edition (*Personal Writings*, 26). This phrase, "imaginative intuition," signals a refinement of Hardy's earlier privileging of emotion over cognition, for it brings together terms that engage with those two processes: imagination, which in this case involves the cognitive act of adopting another's perspective; and intuition, which is a prereflective and often emotionally informed process of apprehension. With a combination of the textual regional geography in his novels and, later, the ancillary guidebooks, Hardy asks his readers to occupy the perspectives taken by his characters, thereby provoking them to embrace a form of local knowledge.

Upon the publication of *Tess*, which followed *The Woodlanders*, an anonymous review in *The Bookman* (1891) took quite literally this imperative to locate oneself, arguing in an article on "Thomas Hardy's Wessex" that "[w]anderers through our south and south-western counties, especially that portion of them which would be enclosed by a triangle with the south coast from Exeter to Portsmouth for its base, and Bristol for the apex, will find few better guides than Mr. Hardy."[31] Yet the tone of this piece firmly sets the *Bookman* reader at a distance from the inhabitants of Wessex, describing them as "his rustics, fellows of infinite humour and quaint homeliness" (28) and suggesting that mere placement in the locale will not make these tourists understand the local perspective. The challenge for Hardy, therefore, was to model the process by which spatial positioning can lead to emotional orientation. At the same time, *Tess* was the text in which Hardy's ambivalence about the experience of empathy emerged most strikingly.

Tess was unique in the passion it inspired in readers and critics (it was Hardy's bestselling novel), even after its rocky start as a serial and the numerous changes Hardy had to make to get it published in that form. Contemporaneous reactions tended to emphasize the ways in which the book *both* enabled *and* blocked empathy for the readers, as well as how readerly empathy might emerge from the author's own empathetic engagement with his characters. One of the very first – and overwhelmingly enthusiastic – reviews illustrates this reaction. The anonymous reviewer in *The Speaker* (December 26, 1891) writes: "There are whole chapters of the book so steeped in the sunny atmosphere of Wessex that the reader feels himself to be one of the personages of whom Mr. Hardy writes, falls to their level and sympathises with them in their wants and woes as though he were himself to the manner born."[32] This reviewer presents himself as an ideal reader in his ability to transcend the myriad experiential barriers (spatial, temporal, and economic) separating him from the characters, and to experience the novel from the perspective of those involved – though he does still characterize such identification as a "fall." A few lines later he writes that, "long after the book has been laid aside we find ourselves still living among its characters" (61). In fact, the reviewer suggests that the reader actually experiences more empathy with the characters than the author experienced, for the author does not "falter as he leads his heroine from sorrow to sorrow, making her drink to the last drop the cup of suffering. He is remorseless as Fate itself in unfolding the drama of her life" (61). A century later, critic James Gibbon agrees with the effect on the readers, but thinks that Hardy's own feeling for Tess is the cause: "Compassion manifests itself in feelings of sympathy and the ability to empathize. In creating Tess, Hardy became her and suffered with her, and we feel pity for her" (5).

Such responses grew not only out of Hardy's emotional connection with Tess, but also, as in *The Woodlanders*, out of his careful spatial orientation of both readers and characters. As early as the beginning of the second chapter in *Tess*, the narrator invites the readers to transform their experience of the story from a sedentary to an active one with the observation that "Marlott lay amid the north-eastern undulations of the beautiful Vale of Blakemore or Blackmoor aforesaid – an engirdled and secluded region, for the most part untrodden as yet by tourist or landscape-painter, though within a four hours' journey from London."[33] The narrator extends this description with a passage that orients the reader *qua* tourist on the map of England:

> This fertile and sheltered tract of country, in which the fields are never brown and the springs never dry, is bounded on the south by the bold chalk ridge that embraces the prominences of Hambledon Hill, Bulbarrow, Nettlecombe-Tout, Dogbury, High Stoy, and Bubb Down. The traveler from the coast, who, after plodding northward for a score of miles over calcareous downs and corn-lands, suddenly reaches the verge of one of these escarpments, is surprised and delighted to behold, extended like a map beneath him, a country differing absolutely from that which he has passed through. (18)

Combining the names of real places (Bulbarrow, High Stoy) with those of fictional ones (Dogbury, Bubb Down), the passage locates the reader in an imagined-realistic geography. Positioned in this way, the reader can engage in that empowering, though initially abstract, act of knowing a geographical space. On the one hand, this narrative position may seem problematic when considering empathetic identification; indeed, Barrell claims that this passage distances the reader from a "real" understanding of the local space because the narrator addresses his description to a reader who is familiar with viewing the world as a map – the cosmopolitan who stands in such marked contrast to the naïve Tess's intimate connection to the vale, for whom, Hardy notes, "every contour of the surrounding hills was as personal to her as that of her relatives' faces" (Barrell, 113; *Tess*, 42). On the other hand, I would argue that the distancing involved in taking the reader-tourist perspective actually enables a sense of connection with the heroine.[34] First, it employs a language (aesthetic, pictorial) and a perspective (cartographic) that would be familiar to middle-class readers. Second, by locating the reader as an outsider viewing the scene, Hardy actually situates them in a *more* parallel relationship to Tess, who becomes increasingly able to read the landscape from a dual perspective of both intimate and map-reader. Indeed, as Tess navigates her way across the countryside later in the novel, after having been rejected by her husband and forced to work in a harsh and newly mechanized agricultural world, we see her moving with a combined local and cartographic knowledge: she sees the land below as a chart of her past and her emotions ("in that vale . . . her sorrow had taken shape"), while still "steer[ing] steadily westward" (*Tess*, 316), an act that points to a spatial mastery that is both biographical and directional.

As the story develops, the personal and physical geographies become increasingly aligned. From the fertile dairy land of the Froom Valley, where Tess falls in love, to the barren fields of Flintcomb-Ash, where she works in a state of emotional despair after her separation from her husband Angel Clare, a symbiotic relationship between character and environment emerges. Hardy gives us this geo-empathy in which the land mirrors human experience *and* humans manifest their geography. Tess's journey to Flintcomb-Ash illustrates this dynamic, as she moves from what she describes as the "friendly" (300) topography of Bulbarrow and Nettlecomb-Tout, the spots where she bloomed as a young woman, to the "starve-acre place" where she now works "hacking" (305) on the rough fields. Tess's desire for anonymity and her sense of desolation are manifest not simply in her own drab appearance (she has hacked off her eyebrows, just as she hacks at the swede-turnip roots), but also in the featureless nature of the landscape. Hardy describes how "the whole field was in colour a desolate drab; it was a complexion without features, as if a face, from chin to brow, should be only an expanse of skin. The sky wore, in another colour, the same likeness . . . So these two upper and nether visages confronted each other all day long" (304). Drawn to this area because it offers the only hope of work, however hard and demeaning, Tess and the landscape become linked in their degradation and exploitation.

As the center of this environmental and human give-and-take, Tess becomes an example of empathy incarnate, as well as a cautionary tale of the perils of empathetic imagining for those without power within the patriarchal power structure of Tess's world. She molds herself so acquiescingly to Angel's opinion of her that she contemplates killing herself "to set [him] free without the scandal of the divorce that I thought you would have to get," since, she tells him, "I have no wish opposed to yours" (259). This adoption of others' perspectives even extends to creatures. In the height of her distress on her trek to Flintcomb-Ash, for example, she comes across pheasants who have been wounded in a hunt and, "with the impulse of a soul who could feel for kindred sufferers as much as for herself," reproaches herself for self-pity: "to suppose myself the most miserable being on the earth in the sight o' such misery as yours!" (298). A shared experience of misery is the core of Tess's empathetic engagement, and it suggests both her profound ability to step outside her own perspective and the more distressing idea that, as the prime empathizer, Tess will absorb and reflect more suffering than one person can endure, just as the barren terrain of Flintcomb-Ash points to a land pushed past its endurance and now further pillaged by mechanized change.[35]

In stark contrast, Angel becomes the model of how *not* to respond to others. Tess believes that he will have empathy for her rape and illegitimate child after she learns about his own pre-marriage sexual misadventures, exclaiming, "I am almost glad – because now *you* can forgive *me*!" (*Tess*, 243). Tess assumes that since one of the major barriers to understanding – an inability to imagine oneself in a similar situation – no longer exists, Angel will be able to forgive her as readily as she forgave him. Angel, however, cannot travel this cognitive and emotional distance; within him was "a hard logical deposit" that had "blocked his acceptance of the Church; it blocked his acceptance of Tess" (261). In essence, Hardy suggests, a certain intuitive leap of faith is necessary in order to give oneself over to other perspectives – the same sort of "willing suspension of disbelief" that Coleridge asked of his readers and that continues to garner support from critics today.[36] As Ralph Pite has written, "Angel's inability to sympathize makes him into an epitome of the bad, censorious reader" (319). While Pite attributes this to his refusal "to fill the gaps in the picture" (319), the novel suggests more strongly that he has failed in the crucial test of empathy. Angel cannot identify with Tess's experience; he can neither put himself in Tess's shoes nor see how their perspectives are more closely aligned than ever. His reaction not only leads to his rejection of Tess, but also to the narrative's eviction of him from the Wessex terrain: Angel severs his connection to his homeland and his wife, and heads to South America.

Even Angel's rigid nature is softened upon his return and his experience with Tess's distress and depth of feeling; when she flees to him after murdering Alec d'Urberville, who was the original cause of her traumas, "[t]enderness was absolutely dominant in Clare at last" (*Tess*, 408). Yet with this new balance of emotion in Angel – an increase in compassion that redeems him somewhat from his past harshness – does not come a corresponding tempering of Tess's affective states. Concomitantly, Angel's increased empathy foregrounds the safety of such affective and cognitive acts of imagining others for those who are already in positions of power, versus the perils for those without power. As Angel reflects, "the strength of her affection for himself ... had apparently extinguished her moral sense altogether" (407–408): Tess's identification – or over-identification – with the wrongs suffered by Angel leads to her murder of Alec d'Urberville. Similarly, it leads to her own self-sacrifice at Stonehenge: "It is as it should be!" (418), she exclaims, when she hears that the authorities have come for her. We end the novel at an ambiguous place that echoes the one we experienced with Giles Winterbourne: while Tess's empathy is exactly what makes her a viable heroine despite her seemingly immoral and even violent actions, it is also what has led to her downfall.

This sense of the traumas and danger of empathy revealed in novels such as *Tess* were obscured by some of Hardy's later attempts to secure his reading audience; Hardy's dark vision of the coexisting benefits and threats of empathy seems to lose much of its ambivalence in his efforts to maintain his standing and his novels' sales after the vicious reviews of *Jude the Obscure*. This jarring public reaction pushed Hardy to solidify readers' empathic engagement with his characters by consolidating his Wessex world, both by revising his novels to make them more cohesive in terms of place description (thereby creating a continuous space in which readers could immerse themselves) and by encouraging the creation of a Wessex tourist industry. In 1902 we see an early mention of this when he writes to Frederick Macmillan (whom he was approaching to be his new publisher) to note that "The curious accident of a topographical interest having arisen in 'Wessex' also helps the vitality of the volumes."[37] In that same year one of the earlier guidebooks to Wessex first appeared: Bertram Windle's *The Wessex of Thomas Hardy*. Hardy had written to Windle six years earlier, responding to his request to indicate some of the "real" names of the fictional areas and providing a detailed list of place correspondences. Yet, once the guidebooks to Wessex began to appear, Hardy realized that some of the revenue he could claim was going to others. In March of 1902, his tone in a letter to Macmillan was verging on petulant:

> So many books seem to be coming out concerning "the Wessex of the novels & poems" (the fourth, I see is just announced) that I fancy I shall be compelled, in self defence as it were, to publish an annotated edn giving a really trustworthy account of real places, scenery, &c (somewhat as Scott

did): since it does not seem to be quite fair that capital shd be made out of my materials to such an extent as it promises to be done. (Letters 3, 16)

Accordingly, in the next few years Hardy began to correspond with Hermann Lea, the young photographer and neighbor who would become a close friend, about Lea's desire to create a photographic guidebook to Wessex. In these letters some of his anxiety about the project began to come out, primarily because Hardy did not want to appear to be using Wessex for profit. He wrote to Lea in 1904:

> I do not see how I could reasonably object to such a little handbook *in itself*, as a thing entirely the idea & work of someone else. Only I should not wish to authorize it, or to have any personal connection with it whatever, for the obvious reasons that I do not really *desire* it to be done, but am quite indifferent whether it be done or not; & also that it would seem to be a self-advertizing sort of thing if I were to authorize it. (Letters 3, 140, his emphasis)

Lea was quite willing for Hardy to have both editorial control of and distance from his project. In 1905 his first short publication came out, *A Handbook to the Wessex Country of Thomas Hardy's Novels*, and in 1913 a longer version named *Thomas Hardy's Wessex* appeared, commissioned by Macmillan as an accompaniment to the "Wessex Edition" of Hardy's work.

Despite Hardy's mixed feelings, the economic urge to create a Wessex industry prevailed. In *Thomas Hardy's Wessex*, Lea provides driving and walking routes, along with photographs of buildings and the countryside, which encourage the reader to travel alongside the characters both visually and physically. In doing so, the guidebook proposes another means of having the reader occupy the perspective of the characters: actual travel into a fictional/factual geography. In his introduction, Lea directly raises the question of the relationship between seeing the landscape and empathizing with the characters by employing the pathetic fallacy in his instructions. Although Lea warns that the reader should not fall into the trap of "confusing the ideal with the actual," he encourages us to take the "ideal" fictional narrative as a guide for *how* to experience the actual.[38] He notes "the strange manner in which the scenery adapts itself to, and identifies itself with, the characters themselves" (xxii–xxiii), suggesting that nature responds to and mirrors human experience. He follows this claim with a brief outline of how this works for Tess, giving such examples as the "phase of her hopelessness finds her at *Flintcomb-Ash*, a spot cursed by sterility" (xxiii). With these comments, Lea suggests that the space of

Wessex itself (and, by extension, of the "Wessex" the tourists are visiting) reflects the emotional world of the characters. In this formulation, geographic perspective-taking also necessarily involves emotional perspective-taking.

This turn to the paratextual material has taken us away from Hardy's geographic perspective-taking *within* the novels. The guidebooks do not reflect the ambivalence in Hardy's own writing about the possibility of either mobilizing or maintaining empathy, or, as with his depictions in *Tess*, the dangers of overempathizing. In this way, there is a curious disconnect between the claims of the guidebooks and the experience of empathy in the novels. Hardy's revisions, like the guidebooks, often worked against this ambivalence; for example, Hardy's documented changes in *Jude* to make Sue's character more appealing illustrate his general tendency toward promoting readerly connection to characters in his novels.[39] Yet, even while Hardy was making the revisions to his novels and participating in the guidebook, the darker side of Hardy's geo-empathy – the side that involves questioning the ethics of empathy and underscoring the always-retrospective nature of an act of imagining others – remained and even continued in the poetry he was writing.

Concluding this discussion of his novels, as well as a transitioning to his poetry, I want to turn to an image drawn by Hardy and included in his first volume of poetry, *Wessex Poems* (most of which were written during his years as a novel writer), because it unsettles any remaining belief in an uncomplicated shared perspective (see Figure 1).

Hardy gives us here a picture of a bucolic landscape, complete with sheep in the background, with a pair of strangely positioned spectacles

Figure 1: Hardy's sketch facing "In a Eweleaze near Weatherbury" (*Wessex Poems and Other Verses*, 181).

floating over the scene. These floating spectacles – disembodied and appearing to serve no magnifying or clarifying purpose – seem to act as a metaphor for not only a particular vantage point, but also a particular way of seeing: you are not simply standing in someone's shoes, you are also looking through their lenses. In turn, the landscape (which is identified by the accompanying poem's title, "In a Eweleaze near Weatherbury") seems to be looking back at the viewer, making the picture-viewing a double-sided experience of seeing and being seen. Marjorie Levinson has identified a third perspective: the glasses, empty of eyes, have been set down upon the book, so we are seeing two objects – glasses and book – on their own.[40] According to her interpretation, seeing is divorced from identity – the lenses on the book seem to stand in for the idea of perspective itself, and the ambiguity of this image raises the question of whether the page constructs the perspective or the perspective shapes the page. Landscape and page, place and text – the boundaries blur in this pictorialization of the textual geographies that structure much of Hardy's writing.

Looking at this image allows me, therefore, to extend my earlier argument about Hardy's perspective-based empathy: not only does Hardy want us to glance through the glasses, but he wants us to be aware of how such a viewpoint involves being read by and back into the landscape and the page – a gesture toward the symbiotic relationship between geography and character that we saw in *Tess*. The spectacles locate us both as viewers of the scene, and as viewed by the scene; the bucolic scene looks back, transforming the interpreter into the interpreted. The boundaries of these distinctions (viewer/viewed, reader/read) are ambiguous, however, and trouble any easy identification with either position. The surreal nature of this image forces us to ask where the agency lies in the act of perspective-taking.[41] Hardy's writing might thereby suggest a breakdown of boundaries between subject, object, and empathetic environment, and this may point not to an extension of feeling and an expansion of the self, but to the loss of certainty about the stability of the subject itself.

Elegiac Empathy: Limits of Empathy in Hardy's Elegies

The stability of the subject becomes more fraught when we are dealing with an absent object of empathy. What does it mean to stand in someone else's shoes, we could ask, when there is no spot on which to stand? Indeed, the potential end to feeling *in* and *for* another reaches its peak when we turn to Hardy's poetry, even though much of it was written when he was making those geographic revisions to his novels. While in his novels Hardy saw readerly empathy in terms of creating both a receptive audience and an inclusive feeling of belonging, however problematic that belonging might be, in his lyric poetry Hardy illuminates how this empathy will always be belated and how those places that are supposed to lead us to it reveal most of all the indifference of the world to individual human experience. This is the darker side of Hardy's geo-empathy: the side that involves questioning the ethics of an empathetic act that is necessarily retrospective, and that involves a movement into a past moment, divorcing it from the creation of connection with the living.

Why, we might ask, does this dark poetics of empathy emerge? On the one hand, Hardy's practical and financial desire to make his novels engage readers' empathy did not have to extend in the same way to his poetry. On the other, the change in genre itself may have led to this ambivalence about empathy. The mysterious relationship between poet and reader/ listener may be in part why lyric-based empathy is less transparent; Jonathan Culler's definition of lyric describes the poet "not as a character in a novel, whose motivations must be elucidated, but as a performer picking up traditional elements and presenting them to an audience."[42] Thus, if novels are defined by characters (figures who can both receive and give empathy) and their development, whether through an hour, a day, or a century, then lyric poetry is defined by a rhetorical development. A lyric form of empathetic engagement thereby would proceed from "dwelling in a particular language" – a form of identification that could take place "before the consolidation of subject positions."[43] In other words, the reader is not being asked to identify with or understand a person, but instead to be drawn into the language, the sound, the voices, the images. Lyric empathy approaches the abstract; such experience of the language recalls the kind of engagement that we often imagine occurring while listening to music, and therefore brings out the musical origins of lyric, as well as the way that empathy could move toward the abstraction that Worringer and Hulme saw as its antithesis.

In the elegy, however, which is a lyric form that often depends on prosopopoeia – the trope that involves giving face and voice both to an absent figure and to the mourner's own grief – the possibilities for empathetic engagement seem promising. All along Hardy has been deeply interested in faces; Keen notes, for example, that he "fore- grounds the facial expressions and physiognomy that humans and animals share" (*Hardy's Brains*, 200) in his quest to highlight the commonalities, rather than differences, among humans, animals, and landscapes. The prosopopoeia of elegy asks us to give face to something that is not simply other, but is also absent. Thus, in many ways, the elegy is a literary form ideally suited to performing empathy, for it asks the reader to experience the suffering of the bereaved and, often through the use of the pathetic fallacy, presents a natural world that exhibits this empathetic act of mourning.[44] Yet, we will see, in his revision of the pathetic fallacy and with his exploration of different perspectives, Hardy reveals a version of empathetic engagement that does not lead to the creation of community, but instead to isolation and disappearing perspectives.

Two of the most astute readers of Hardy's elegies, Peter Sacks and Jahan Ramazani, give numerous examples of how Hardy abandons or revises some of the most prominent conventions of the elegy form: the pastoral context and myth of a vegetation deity, the use of repetition, the movement from grief to consolation, the images of resurrection, to name a few of the most prominent.[45] While Sacks argues that Hardy's poems should ultimately be read within the generic framework of the elegy because the poems work to "prov[e] the reality of loss" and "confron[t] guilt and anger" (235), Ramazani counters that Hardy's elegies provide the link between two poles of interpretation: "his vulnerability to loss gives rise to his invulnerable detachment, his 'democratic' empathy spurs into being his 'absolutist' emphasis on pattern, or to switch to literary historical terms, his late Romantic pathos stimulates his modern irony" (34). Yet Keen also is right to note that even as puzzling an example of elegy as Hardy's "The Convergence of the Twain," which was written in response to the sinking of the Titanic, but which "spares neither a word of grief for the dead, nor an expression of consolation for the bereaved," is still a poem "saturated with *Einfülung*";[46] it asks us to imagine the perspective of the iceberg, rather than that of the lost travelers. This makes Hardy seem a monster of callousness, though the perspective-taking that occurs in the poem likewise transforms the event into a monument to the callousness both of fate, and, more dangerously, of the "Spinner of Years" who allows the collision with a striking "Now!" (*Complete Poems*, 307).

If we refine Ramazani's larger antinomies, we can narrow in on Hardy's geography of poetic empathy. Hardy's version of the pathetic fallacy illuminates a world defined by absence and by confusing overlaps between subject and object, viewer and viewed, empathizer and recipient. While the pathetic fallacy does appear in Hardy's elegies, here it suggests a revision – even a thwarting – of the seeming promise of the guidebooks to construct a shared community of reader-tourists primed for empathetic engagement. As mentioned earlier, Donald Davie talks about how the "Poems of 1912–13" give us landscapes that are "stations in a personal purgatory," and his suggestive comment prompts us to wonder whether or not it is possible for the mourner, who tries to occupy the perspective of the dead beloved in so many of the poems, to stand in what are in fact empty shoes: the shoes of the dead. The questions are: Does death inhibit empathy? And, if so, does all empathetic engagement with the dead ultimately mutate into an anticommunal, lonely identification with absence?

Empathy for the Dead

Hardy's interest in the dysfunctional empathy that emerges in the face of loss can be seen in the very beginning pieces of "Poems of 1912–13." In the first poem of the sequence, "The Going," Hardy's accusing tone – "Why did you give no hint that night" and "Why do you make me leave the house" – identifies the dead Emma as the perpetrator of suffering and himself, the poet left behind, as the one in need of sympathy (*Complete Poems*, 338). By the end of this first poem, Hardy has in fact become like Emma, "but a dead man held on end / To sink down soon" (339); as Ramazani has described it, "what had begun as an elegy for Hardy's wife ends as an elegy for Hardy" (Ramazani, 52). While, on the one hand, such poetic replacement is merely an extreme version of standing in another's shoes, the rhetorical effect in this envoi of the cycle is to displace rather than form a connection with Emma.

If the poet seems in danger of overstepping his boundaries and transforming a poetry of object-loss into a poetry of subject-loss – that act that I have identified as central to modernist explorations of empathy – then a turn to the natural world, which so often stands as a mirror to and a compass for human emotion in lyrics, should provide a redemptive structure that will allow Hardy to bring the experience of mourning into contact with a broader community – the shared experience of nature that would allow readers to join him in understanding the loss. Hardy's revision of the pathetic fallacy, however, forces us to ask whether our shared perspective of the world can draw us together when the environment subsumes or ignores human experience – a question that will haunt my discussion of Virginia Woolf's novels as well.[47] While Hardy always searches for traces of the past in the landscape, such traces break down rather than reaffirm subjectivity, ultimately creating isolation, not community. In "Rain on a Grave," for example, Hardy emphasizes the fallacy of attributing human emotion and loyalty to the natural world: the "arrows of rain" wound Emma's grave with "ruthless disdain" for her sensitivity and her love of nature (*Complete Poems*, 341). While "After a Journey" seems to bring some brief respite with his visions of Emma at Pentargan Bay, the poem that follows, "A Death-Day Recalled," refutes the redemptive elements of the trope, for it denies that places mirror human experience in any way. Hardy writes, "Beeny did not quiver, / Juliot grew not gray" (350), the beginning of a list of all of the ways in which the geography did *not* register Emma's death. Instead of Shelley's "Pale Ocean" that "in unquiet slumber lay" and "wild Winds" that were "sobbing in dismay"[48] at the death of Adonais, Hardy's nature is "unheeding" of Emma's death (350). The third and final stanza brings this lack of connection to the fore, ending with the query:

> Why did Bos not thunder,
> Targan apprehend
> Body and Breath were sunder
> Of their former friend?   (350)

By ending on a note of interrogation, Hardy leaves the answer up to the reader. But the only answer, it appears, is because these places do not care about the death of Emma – our attempts to humanize them are poetic devices. This is Hardy ruthless and unyielding in his assertion that the death of an individual has little meaning in the larger scheme of things. As Ramazani notes, Hardy's "dispassionate stare of the Immanent Will would seem to be anathema to elegy: the genre had always depended on involvement, its pathos being born of resistance to death. To look on loss from a great height and see it as part of a fated pattern is to reduce mournful feelings to ironic twinges" (33). Not exactly ironic twinges in this poem, but there is a recognition of the irony of thinking that nature mirrors human experience. In this way, the poem seems a denial of the relationship that appeared to exist between the land and the characters in *Tess* – the relationship that Lea specifies in his guidebook.

Yet the next poem in the cycle, "Beeny Cliff," seems at first to promise a more satisfying communion between subject and space. Rather than the foreshortened trochaic trimeter of "A Death-Day Recalled," "Beeny Cliff" is written in a lush and suggestive dipodic tetrameter – a form that I will explore at further length later in this chapter – and the breaths at the end of the lines suggest continuance, even when unseen. Yet this continuance is not ultimately sustaining. The final stanzas affirm not only nature's permanence in the face of loss ("Still in all its chasmal beauty bulks old Beeny to the sky"), but also how death puts one beyond both the empathy of others and feeling for others:

> What if still in chasmal beauty looms that wild weird western shore,
> The woman now is – elsewhere – whom the ambling pony bore,
> And nor knows nor cares for Beeny, and will laugh there nevermore.   (351)

From the geographic specificity of Beeny and the other spots that Hardy has identified as places where mourning occurs, to the "elsewhere" of death – this is the trajectory we see from the sites where empathy can occur to the unmoored realm where it cannot. "Elsewhere" negates the possibility of such empathy, for when place is ephemeral, both knowing and caring – those fundamental elements of empathetic engagement – are absent. With this articulation of the absence at the heart of these attempts at lyric empathy, Hardy constructs his version of a modernist empathy – an experience of perspective-taking as always rooted in loss – that we will see manifested fully in Eliot's *The Waste Land*.

This triple loss of subject (in "The Going"), of object, and of empathetic environment points to how, for Hardy, empathy for either the poetic subject or object involves a limit to, rather than an extension of, feeling; feeling with the other becomes feeling nothingness. If we think about this in the visual, spatially based terms that have been at the center of Hardy's method of writing about empathetic engagement, it involves a kind of un-seeing – something that Hardy talks about in a poem of that title, "The Self-Unseeing" (from the 1901 volume *Poems of Past and Present*). In this poem, the speaker tries to place himself in a remembered scene, populating an empty space via memory. However, the final line – "Yet we were looking away!" (*Complete Poems*, 167) – points to the central tragedy: it portrays a double failure to see, for the past self did not think to look, and therefore the present self can only see that lack, rather than the fullness of the past moment. At the center of Hardy's ruminations about the effect of perspective and place on one's understanding of others, therefore, is an inability to be present even for oneself. Our attempts to occupy different perspectives – whether our own or those of others – are thwarted by the fact that these visions are always going to be retrospective *and* imagined. If perspective-taking is purely an act of fantasy, then any sense of community or connection based upon it will be similarly "hollowed and thin" (*Complete Poems*, 166). These are the words Hardy uses to describe the floor of the imagined house in "The Self-Unseeing," but the description is, Levinson points out, "too abstract, interpretive, metaphorical for its sequence."[49] The words therefore indicate the nature of recollection in the poem as much, if not more, as they illustrate the condition of the house.

The poem "Places" provides an even more direct rumination on what a lyric place both can and cannot do in relation to creating community and empathetic engagement. The first three stanzas all begin with negations: "Nobody says," "Nobody thinks," "Nobody calls to mind" (*Complete Poems*, 352–353). These introductory negations reveal an inward motion: from speaking, to thinking, to remembering. But each claim is then immediately juxtaposed with the unsaid comment, the unthought idea, or the unremembered place, thereby contradicting the initial negation by describing, for example, the place that nobody talks about. Yet absence and nonbeing are central to the place's existence – it is the place of nobody. While Davie's reading of the poem emphasizes the triumph of the place of love and happy memories (Cornwall) because it is the "here" in the poem, while the "there" is Plymouth, the problematic midpoint between the past and the present places, the final stanza complicates this reading.[50]

> Nay: one there is to whom these things,
> That nobody else's mind calls back,
> Have a savour that scenes in being lack,
> And a presence more than the actual brings;
> To whom to-day is beneaped and stale,
> And its urgent clack
> But a vapid tale.   (*Complete Poems*, 353)

The stanza begins with an overarching negation – "Nay" – which colors the subsequent claims. Though we get the affirmation that "one there is," it is muted by the following line, which makes the "one" structurally parallel to "nobody else's mind," even as it is a contrast in meaning. The third line begins with "Have," but resolves on "lack." We learn in these final lines that Hardy, once again, is proclaiming the primacy of the past over the present: "to-day is beneaped and stale, / And its urgent clack / But a vapid tale." It is a solitary position – he is the only one who will remember or feel this. The experience of place, therefore, is exclusive and singular, and offers no possibility for empathetic engagement on the reader's part. This poem is pivotal, then, in a sense other than that identified by Davie: it shows how immersion into the past and into memory does not allow connection-making aside from within the poet's own mind. The tour of places in Hardy's elegies allows no overview, no promontory, from which to stand in his shoes.

Uncanny Empathy: Slippages in Time and Place in Hardy's Elegies

This strong challenge to perspective-taking as a subject-building act emerges most strikingly in the boundary slippages between the "in-there" and the "out-here" of Hardy's elegiac verse, creating a prosody of the uncanny that allows Hardy to articulate loss as spatially bound and temporally shifting.[51] As Levinson has claimed, "something funereal, melancholy, and haunted defines Hardy's entire corpus" (557). Hardy's elegies, as Ramazani has noted, are characteristic of modern elegies in their performance of a "melancholic mourning," a label that points to the unresolved nature of his poetics of loss.[52] One way that Hardy both expresses and contains this unsettled mourning is through geographic elements (maps, topographic features, toponymic references) as mediators of loss and presence. His poems thereby set up a relationship between the space of the verse and the charted places of Hardy's England, effectively challenging the parameters of both elegiac poetry and geography.[53] His prosodic and geographic experiments also point, I will suggest, to Hardy's development of a particularly modernist form of mourning, and to the loss that is at the heart of this often uncanny empathy.[54]

Spots of Silence

Hardy's alternative vision of the relationship between place and memory emerges throughout the "The Place on the Map," which richly illustrates the complex geographic and metrical patterns that Hardy employed in lieu of fashioning an empathetic natural world. First published in the *English Review* (1913), this poem was written at the height of Hardy's exploration of the elegiac mode and reveals the extent to which spatial orders can serve to both manifest and perpetuate experiences of loss and mourning. The first stanza of this six stanza poem begins:

I

I look upon the map that hangs by me –
Its shires and towns and rivers lined in varnished artistry –
And I mark a jutting height
Coloured purple, with a margin of blue sea.

(*Complete Poems*, 321)

At first glance, the map mentioned in the title seems to function as a touchstone for the speaker's nostalgic reveries on a past event. The speaker (whom Hardy identifies through the original subtitle, "A Poor Schoolmaster's Story") describes an act that takes place in his present moment, but that leads him into the past. This past, we soon realize, embodies multiple losses – a long-ago love affair that has led to what we assume is a pregnancy ("the thing we found we had to face before the next year's prime"), which would never be sanctioned by society and, presumably, resulted in the end of the affair. The speaker, however, begins with his view of the map, an experience that seems to be purely aesthetic in those first lines, as he notices the "varnished artistry" and the vibrant colors of the outlined land and water. Looking leads him to "mark," a term that, in its ability to mean both geographical measurement and the musical "marking" of time, suggests the spatial and temporal overlap this poem will chart.[55] Such marking brings us back into the remembered scene, as the representation spurs the speaker to reconstruct the event. And yet we do not leave entirely the present-day scene of map-reading: the action in the second stanza is "unfolded" like the unfolding of the map and the place is remembered as a "spot" – a poetically resonant term for Hardy – as if the cartographic symbols have *become* the memory. Such a conflation therefore compels a return to the map in the third stanza, setting up the imbrication of memory and map that structures the poem. The speaker illuminates the relationship between abstract representation and remembered event in the first lines of the stanza: "This hanging map depicts the coast and place, / And re-creates therewith our unforeboded troublous case." Hardy's use of the verb "re-creates" points to the double act of creation that this poem grapples with: the spatial (re)presentation that results in a temporal (re)generation. The original event becomes doubly veiled behind these two different orders of re-creation.

The stakes of this movement between map and memory are manifest in the meter of the very first lines. The meter and form of the poem seem fixed in our first impression: the quatrains follow the same rhyme scheme (*aaba*) and the shape of the stanzas stays the same, suggesting a pattern into which the language has been fit.[56] Yet scansion of the lines reveals a more complex relationship between metrical space and marking time. Take the first line: "I look upon the map that hangs by me – ." The line could be scanned as iambic pentameter with the stresses appearing regularly every two beats in the ten-syllable phrase. Yet placing equal stresses on all five of these syllables is awkward and does not account for the marked caesura at the end of the line; we could instead read the line as having three main stresses – on "look," "map," and "me" (words that suggest the central conflict of the poem). To do so means understanding the other two stresses (the "-on" in "up*on*" and "hangs") as secondary or even unstressed. We are left with a line that could easily be in trimeter with two of the feet having four syllables: unstressed, stressed, unstressed, unstressed (or light stress). The metrical reading of the line would appear as follows, with light stresses marked with the forward slash (\):

    ˘ / ˘\ ˘ / ˘\ ˘ / (˘ \) (dipodic trimeter)
    I look upon the map that hangs by me –

Such a scansion would permit us to take into account the dash, allowing it to stand in for the final beats and giving a metrical place to the silences in this poem. The meter aligns with the images, we will see, in this poem that ends on the image of a "pantomime," effectively emphasizing the role of silence in this traumatic memory.

This is more than a mere exercise in the esoteric art of "marking time"; close attention to Hardy's metrics in general is important because of his own interest in a major late nineteenth and early twentieth-century debate concerning whether or not English verse was in essence dipodic. As Denis Taylor has shown, Coventry Patmore's influential and inflammatory 1857 essay on "English Metrical Critics" (later titled "Essay on English Metrical Law") had brought this issue to Hardy's attention.[57] Though discussions of dipody remained on the fringe of prosodic debates, dipodic meter and Patmore's essay still surfaced in texts including Omond's *A Study of Metre* (1903) and the American George Stewart's *Modern Metrical Technique* (1922) and "A Method Toward the Study of Dipodic Verse" (1924).[58] Dipody refers to the idea that a foot can have as many as four beats, which means that a rhythm that we might first identify as, say, iambic tetrameter, might also be considered a dimeter with two feet of four syllables each. This theory entails more than the recounting and relabeling of feet. Rather, it suggests that a larger rhythmic pattern may contain a smaller one. A meter would be dipodic in particular if there seemed to be stresses with alternating levels of emphasis. Instead of having to count them all equally, one could see how they are part of a larger pattern of such alternating stresses. This means that one foot could contain both a primary and a secondary stress, as can be seen in the first line from "The Place on the Map." Moreover, dipodic theory suggests that the silences in the lines may be integral (and countable) parts of the metrical pattern. Hardy's interest in the measurement of silence is clear from passages he copied from

Patmore's essay: "Unless we are ... to regard every verse affected with catalexis (or a deficiency in the number of syllables requisite to make it a full dimeter, trimeter, tetrameter, &c) as constituting an entire metrical system in itself, which is obviously absurd, we must reckon the missing syllables as substituted by an equivalent pause."[59] Spatial absences must be accounted for in temporal measurements.

In this way, Hardy establishes an intertwined relationship between his metrical experiments and his thematic concerns, for a dipodic meter emphasizes the multiple times that can exist in the same verse space, none of which can be completely forgotten or abandoned – a metrical return of the repressed. Indeed, Taylor has identified a number of Hardy poems where he experiments with a dipodic theory of meter, and he argues that it is used most extensively in Hardy's elegies (Taylor, 95). Most significantly, a dipodic meter enforces a back-and-forth movement that emphasizes what is missing each time we settle on one rhythm. The sense of loss in both the present and the past becomes structurally irresolvable. This codification of loss gestures to what critics including Matthew Campbell and Tim Armstrong have described as the "ghostly" nature of Hardy's elegiac metrical experiments. Referring to the same essay on "English Metrical Critics," Campbell notes that Patmore's theory of the immateriality of a metrical beat connects to Tennyson, Yeats, and, ultimately, Hardy's sense that "sounding the verse provides the material experience not only of the verse in its own time, but also the ghosts of other rhythms from the past."[60] Armstrong continues this discussion of Hardy's allusions to other poets and their rhythmic experiments, describing the simultaneous "textual replacement and textual recovery" involved in Hardy's version of mourning.[61] Yet a focus on dipody points us past the question of literary ghosting and toward the particularly temporal *and* spatial issues that the versification of loss presents. Dipodic theory works hand-in-hand with elegy by making material the mourning process.

We can see the blurred boundaries between different times manifested thematically as "The Place on the Map" continues. While the past moment is aestheticized and made cartographic, the present is equally, if not more, obscure. The map – not its context – is what we know of the present moment. And, as the poem turns in stanza four to the past scene, the line between map and scene begins to blur, despite the numbering of the stanzas that suggests a legible divide between these two time periods. Now the scene is distinguished mainly by its colors and lines, just as the map was in the first stanza, while the sky is described as having "lost the *art of raining*" (*Complete Poems*, 322, emphasis mine). Instead of returning to a contemplation of the map in stanza five, representation and remembrance become indistinguishable as the speaker reaches the climactic moment and the event he cannot quite bring himself to describe. We are left with the ambiguous lines in the fifth stanza: "what in realms of reason would have joyed our double soul / Wore a torrid tragic light / Under order-keeping's rigorous control" (*Complete Poems*, 322). The speaker will not specify who or what is keeping order (presumably those social norms that condemn pregnancy outside of marriage); in the context of the poem, such order connects to the varnished lines of the map and to little outside of it, especially without the original subtitle and its suggestion that the scene takes place in a schoolroom.

We appear to return to the original divide between map and memory in the final stanza as the speaker describes how "the map revives her words, the spot, the time," and yet this gesture to Wordsworth's "spots of time" indicates the underlying loss that the poem charts. In Wordsworth's terms, the spots of time have a "renovating virtue" that enables poetic creation and proves the authority of the mind over the senses.[62] Hardy's spot of time, however, is the abstract representation on the map that confronts the speaker, in the end, with his own silence and the impossibility of returning to that moment – a thwarted interpretive episode for both speaker and reader. The "charted coast stares bright, / And its episode comes back in pantomime" (*Complete Poems*, 322) ends the poem. The speaker is distanced even more now than in the beginning from the past scene, which is no longer relived in rich detail, but instead experienced as pantomime – no more than a poor, even absurd, imitation.[63] The scenes of both map-reading and memory lose their temporal rootedness and distinction as the past enters into the present moment and the present transforms the past. In this way, the poem explores the simultaneity of seemingly distant moments through a geographically and metrically bound negotiation of loss and presence. Geography mediates memory and facilitates the mourning process, but it also thwarts the speaker's desire to inhabit fully either past or present. The meter demands this ambiguity by means of verse lines that contain and suggest more than one "time," thereby presenting a record of always-present loss.

Dipody also produces a uniquely formal version of presence where there should be an absence in a way that is characteristic of the uncanny. It is therefore structurally, rather than simply thematically, that we can see Hardy's elegies as verging on the uncanny in their gestures to locate the absent Emma in "Poems of 1912–13," which is positioned shortly after "The Place on the Map" in his *Satires of Circumstance* volume. This poem cycle stands as a deeply interesting and ambiguous exercise of an uncanny lyric empathy, with Hardy assuming the perspective and sometimes the voice of his dead first wife, Emma. Let me clarify: I do not think that we see the encounters with the ghostly Emma in these poems as necessarily uncanny. Instead, these poems *themselves* are uncanny: that "class of the terrifying which leads back to something long known to us, once very familiar,"[64] and that brings into the present something that should, we believe, in fact be absent. These poems travel back to the places of the long ago past of Hardy and Emma, metrically and geographically charting how what was *heimlich* becomes, or is revealed as, *unheimlich*. At work in particular is Hardy's use of silence – that focus on the dipodic rhythm – which allows for the "strange repetitiveness"[65] that characterizes the uncanny – a repetitiveness that leads to, as Nicholas Royle notes, Freud's formulation of the death drive in *Beyond the Pleasure Principle*. The "repetition compulsion" centers on the return of the repressed: the "unconscious repressed content" that struggles to emerge and that cannot be fully remembered by the patient, but only compulsively (and traumatically) repeated.[66] The repetition compulsion bears both structural and thematic connections to Hardy's elegy sequence, which itself circles obsessively around the place of Emma, unnoticed before her death, and her voice, unheard until after she had gone, with the speaker gaining more misery than comfort from this revisiting. The repetition becomes a repetition of silences that are filled with a ghostly voice; Emma becomes most present, located, and even materialized at the moment when she is the least material and the least there.

The structure of the whole "Poems of 1912–13" sequence is based upon a movement between Hardy's home in Dorset and the Cornwall coast where he and Emma met – what Donald Davie calls his "stations in a personal purgatory" (11). But the movement between past and present through a haunted topography and temporally shifting meter likewise occupies the individual poems.[67] I focus on two of the poems that stand at the center of the sequence: "A Dream or No" and "After a Journey," both of which display Hardy's development of a geographically inflected meter and a metrical geography; this development allows the physical and the formal spaces to register the slippage in boundaries and the uncanny presence of what should be absent. In "A Dream or No," Hardy follows a rigid metrical form that allows him to question the assumption that the natural world remains stable, and thereby to point to the resulting crisis of memory. With his shift to dipody in "After a Journey," Hardy begins to synthesize the poetic and the geographic experience of negotiating a space that exists in two times, and the uncanny form of empathy that then results from this kind of metrical space–time travel.

The always-present loss that defines the meter of "The Place on the Map" emerges even more clearly in the title of the twelfth poem in the "Poems of 1912–13" sequence, "A Dream or No." Set up as if presenting a choice of presence and absence, the title actually offers only a movement between fantasy and negation, the ephemeral and the empty. "A Dream or No" begins with two questions that get to the heart of Hardy's concern with memory and place: "Why go to Saint-Juliot? What's Juliot to me?" (*Complete Poems*, 348).[68] Specific locations in this poem both become the (questioned) impetus for movement and the clearest manifestations of the unstable nature of our experience of places. Ending the first line with "me" sets the questions of motive and movement in relation to a spatially based identity. While locations may define the self, self-definition is complicated by the instability of place over the course of the poem. Even in the first stanza, the stability and validity of the speaker's perspective is challenged when he claims, "Some strange necromancy / But charmed me to fancy / That much of my life claims the spot as its key" (348). In these lines, Hardy sets up a chain of connection between communication with the dead, imagination, and geographical places. The links here are being questioned, however, rather than affirmed. The stable identity of the geographical "spot" is based on an act of imagination that grew out of what could be termed a memory or, more accurately, a haunting.

Hardy made a small but telling revision – probably in service of metrical regularity – in lines two and three after their original appearance in the first edition of *Satires of Circumstance* (1914), where they read "I've been made but fancy / By some necromancy."[69] These lines, while less rhythmically regular than his later revision, propose a curious and evocative role for the poet; instead of being charmed into believing that Saint-Juliot is important, he has been made *into* the imagined figure himself through this act of communication with the dead Emma.[70] Thus, we begin the poem not only with a possible link between memory, imagination, and place, but also (in the original version) with a gesture to the destabilization of identity in the face of such space and time travel – a radical form of perspective-taking. Much as in Hoffman's "The Sandman" story that Freud cites in his essay on "The Uncanny," the return of the repressed and absent figure destabilizes the perceiving subject, throwing his grip on reality into question. The speaker is made imaginary; he has imagined himself so thoroughly into this past and now ephemeral moment that his own solidity and subjectivity is now unclear. The meaning of a place is open to debate, and the person constructing that meaning is open to reconfiguration and (fanciful) invention.

Even though the role of place as key to identity and meaning is challenged in the first stanza, Saint-Juliot and its geography still structure the movement in the poem as the "spot" that the poetic imagination takes "as its key." Thus, Hardy's description in the third stanza of how he traveled "coastward bound" to Saint-Juliot both indicates the physical movements that the poem charts and suggests how geography binds and shapes the dream as surely as do the measured stanzas. And yet the bounds of this geography are strangely ephemeral, as ghostly as the dead Emma. The place is not described in any tangible terms: he identifies it first as "that place in the West" (348), which harkens to the abstract geography of the spirit world as much as to an actual location in England. Aside from the lost beloved, the only other inhabitants that we see are the "sea-birds around her" (348), figures that are more of the wind and the water than of the land. Indeed, in the last stanza Hardy questions the very existence of Saint-Juliot and its surrounding geographical features:

> Does there even a place like Saint-Juliot exist?
> Or a Vallency Valley
> With stream and leafed alley,
> Or Beeny, or Bos with its flounce flinging mist?
> *February 1913*   (*Complete Poems*, 348)

The poem ends on the "flounce flinging mist" of Beeny and Bos cliffs, a description that transforms the geographical place into the very ghostly shape of the woman he imagines there. Through the conflation of place and figure, geography and memory, as well as the questioning of the existence of these places outside his memory, Hardy suggests that this quest to locate his loss will result neither in resolution nor in any materialization of the lost Emma, but instead in a dematerialization of the landscape. "Such have I dreamed" (348), Hardy concludes in the fourth stanza after remembering their meeting, even as he strives to empathize with her through his imagined orientation with the shared space.

The meter thereby mirrors the insubstantiality of both the scene and the past. The first and fourth lines of the four-line stanzas are in tetrameters, made up of an opening iamb and three succeeding anapests, which create a lilting, dancing effect.[71] With their rising meters and regular stresses, the stanzas seem to "fling flounces" much in the same way as the misty cliffs. Yet there is a quiet tedium to the inevitability of this rhythm, which has very little of the "cunning irregularity" (*Life II*, 78) that Hardy described as being at the center of his art. As Donald Davie observed, what can offend us in Hardy's poetry is how "its form mirrors a cruel self-driving, a shape *imposed* on the material, as it were with gritted teeth" (33, his emphasis). "Self-driving" seems an appropriate term to use here; the poem takes place just before Hardy's March 1913 trip to Cornwall to visit the sites of his early romance with Emma, and the insistent nature of the metrical movements suggests the rhythm of a moving car or train. Yet movement here has no obvious end: along with the meter, the rhyme scheme – *abba*, etc. – reflects the circular nature of the poet's reflections and limits the movements to the confines of the prosodically mapped space. And, accordingly, Hardy is trying to describe a tortured movement between belief and disbelief, past and present, dream and reality, though the movement between absence and presence is rendered visible and disturbing when the supposedly inviolable boundaries between these states are crossed. With the meter providing, and perhaps even requiring, a structure of psychological and physical movement, we see the futility of the idea of being able to know and hear Emma's responses; the only thing that remains are the questions, and the questions only turn back into the questioning self. An inverse relationship develops between the meter and the geography, as if they are maintaining an internal equilibrium; while the meter becomes increasingly set in its rhythm, the geography loses its structure. The metrical map insistently replaces the physical and emotional topography, and it charts a world in which attempts to empathize with the dead only lead back to the self.

This strange dance between a geographical/temporal location and dis-location brings us to one of the puzzles of Hardy's poetry that Levinson has provocatively articulated: "how can a discourse be at once so *thingified* . . . and at the same time, so blurred, foggy, and amorphous," with explicitly "named suburbs, train stations, holiday spots, etc." existing on the same plane as "landscapes that seem more like interior spaces" (561)? Levinson argues here that, "in a world without spatial or temporal boundaries, loss itself disappears" (568). In "A Dream or No," however, with its ephemeral, spatially based identity juxtaposed against a "self-driving" meter, loss does not disappear altogether. Instead the loss, which was temporally and spatially located in the dead Emma, becomes the pattern of the speaker's experience itself. The landscape of dreams and memory encounters the present moment of the poem's voicing, and the resulting collision involves a loss to both of those times and spaces; neither can bear the interpretive weight that the other wishes to assign. Loss becomes systemic – the meter does not allow for a working through of the absence, but instead only magnifies the original question. Thus the poem ends by asking, "Does there even a place like Saint-Juliot exist?" This question signals not only the loss of the dead Emma and her ghost, but also of Hardy's memory of his past relationship. Yet, with this reworking of the opening question, the poem also brings us back to toponymy[72] as the key to understanding what this loss might mean. The map must not only be reworked, but perhaps even entirely erased, for once the reality and meaning of one place has been questioned, all of the surrounding ones – Vallency Valley, Beeny, Bos – may be similarly lost.

A return to his experiments with dipodic structure in "After a Journey," the most metrically ambitious poem in "Poems of 1912–13," allows Hardy to resolve and (re)present the complications manifested by a landscape and meter that must negotiate past and present spaces. Again topography and toponymy structure the poem, which begins, it claims, "*After* a Journey" (emphasis mine), but only allows the reader to reach that place – Pentargan Bay, which is named as the site at the end of the poem – after traversing the space of the verse. The poem begins:

> Hereto I come to view a voiceless ghost;
>   Whither, O whither will its whim now draw me?
> Up the cliff, down, till I'm lonely, lost,
>   And the unseen waters' ejaculations awe me.
> Where you will next be there's no knowing,
>   Facing round about me everywhere,
>   With your nut-coloured hair,
> And gray eyes, and rose-flush coming and going.
>
> (*Complete Poems*, 349)

The poem's first words, "Hereto I come," suggest that Hardy too must locate himself, but this task is more complicated than the final place-name notation suggests. The poem explores the tensions between the assumed fixity of a topographic space – the bay and surrounding cliffs – and the mourner's multiple and shifting experiences of the place. The setting forms a relationship of mutual dependence with poetic memory: the memories rely on the shaping presence of both geographic and verse space in order to come into being, while the geographic place gains its meaning from the personal and poetic mapping that brings us to the place name. With Pentargan Bay as a catalyst and a structure for memory, a memory that involves an actual revisioning and revisiting of past spaces, Hardy uses both stanzaic and physical mapping to manifest the multiple times at work in the physical space.

The direct experience of the landscape in the poem produces a haunting moment of timelessness within a temporally bounded episode. Even though the narrator gestures to the outside temporal events such as the coming of dawn – "Soon you will have, Dear, to vanish from me, / For the stars close their shutters and the dawn whitens hazily" (349) – he transcends this constraint within the space of the verse as he moves between past and present. We have flux within a closed realm, the traversing of time inside the physical boundaries produced by the bay and the lines of verse. Yet the "voiceless ghost" that draws the narrator to Pentargan Bay is a fleeting subject who appears and disappears, always eluding poetic fetters. Though the first line begins with a demonstrative locator – the deictic term "Hereto" – which suggests a place-bound memory, the verses cannot pin down the remembered woman, despite the final attempt made at the end with the naming of the bay. "Whither, O whither will its whim now draw me?" the speaker despairingly queries. The alliteration of "wh" emphasizes the airy unfixedness of his situation: both the breathlessness of a man running up and down the cliff paths, and the breathiness of the ephemeral shade. This fluctuating tone is embodied by the appearance of the verses on the page; the lines move in and out, as if mimicking the search for a ghost who keeps "coming and going."

In the second stanza, the language of metrical measurement as well as vision appears:

> Yes: I have re-entered your olden haunts at last;
>   Through the years, through the dead scenes I have tracked you;
> What have you now found to say of our past –
>   *Scanned* across the dark space wherein I have lacked you?
>   (*Complete Poems*, 349, emphasis mine)

We realize that the physical travel by the bay is made possible by metrical movements. Memory, the journey "across the dark space," is represented as scansion (the counting of metrical feet); this measurement of the past, Hardy hopes, will provide his "voiceless ghost" with some knowledge emerging from that distance. Yet she is silent, and he must speak for her. In this versification of memory, we gain insight into the project of the poem: an attempt to figure what is lost and to scan past moments by putting them into meter and charting them in space. Just as geographic place spurs memory, so does verse space shape its articulation, for the very forms of his poems provide the necessary shape and structure for his attempt to revisit the past. The opening alternating rhymes (*abab*) produce a forward momentum and a feeling of anticipation as we wait for the next line to connect back. The rhyme aids the rhythm in propelling the verse forward, even as it enforces a moment of return. The second quatrain, however, produces a quite different effect, breaking up the established pattern and installing one (*cddc*) that emphasizes containment rather than movement. In this juxtaposition, the driving forces of the verse connect to the poet's movements through space: he must engage in an almost harried trip around the Bay that provokes and is provoked by the circular motion of memory.

If we delve further into the meter, we can see how it performs a collapse of time within the verse space on both figurative and literal levels. The meter manifests absence and loss in the unspoken beats that occupy each line, which agrees with Dennis Taylor's reading of the poem as essentially dipodic in structure. Taylor argues that the first line's apparent pentameter and the second line's tetrameter (followed by an overwhelmingly tetrameter movement throughout) set up a "metrical conflict" that makes us aware of the submerged extra stress latent in the following lines and "takes us up and down the scale of [English verse] history" (100) in its play with multiple rhythms ("the tetrameter of popular song stanzas and the pentameter of the Keatsian ode" [98]).[73] Geographic and metrical time travel thereby transform both Pentargan Bay and the poem into sites that register loss (the lost love, the past meters) even as they also master and rework that emptiness into a new shape and form. We can read this metrical conflict as a more sinister and problematic venture as well when we think about the kind of empathetic imagination that Hardy posits here: he asserts a kind of mastery and understanding of the object of empathy in the first line of stanza two with the emphatic "Yes." That affirmation is definitively set off by the colon, which suggests that what follows will explain and reinforce the "yes." And, indeed, this is the moment where Hardy attempts to give voice to the voiceless ghost, though the "yes" is then belied by the question marks that end three of the lines. Emma's ghost resists empathetic identification here – perhaps because the speaker cannot fully accept what her perspective would be. The question marks are protective, as well as indicative of Hardy's anxiety.

Thus, it becomes problematic to read "After a Journey," as Peter Sacks does, as suggesting a primarily positive "assertion of continuous identity" and "Hardy's recommitment to his early love" (Sacks, 254). When we take into account the way in which this poem moves between metrical times and spaces (pentameter and tetrameter), the penultimate line – "I am just the same as when" (*Complete Poems*, 349) – carries less authority. If we have learned anything in this poem, it is that there is no such easy adherence to *one* time or identity nor maintenance of one static space: the poem and poet will always be shifting between two times and spaces, if not more. The modern elegy as Hardy presents it does not simply involve repetition – one of the conventions of elegy that establishes continuity and control of grief (Sacks, 23) – but a repositioning that makes the return to the lost moment and place always new, jarring, and a fantasy. The elegy balances between two times within a space that is defined by what it is not: "Scanned across the dark space wherein I have lacked you." Ramazani writes that "Hardy begets his poetry in the dark space of his lack" (58), but we could also think of it as a poetic shaping of absence – the materialization of that dark space into meter and the mapping of loss. "The Place on the Map," "A Dream or No," and "After a Journey" portray a geography and prosody defined by what is absent as much as by what is present. These poems thereby highlight the conceptual and material distance that cartographers themselves try to elide: the gap between immediate spatiotemporal experiences and a patterned understanding of them (and attempt to access them) provided by a map. Hardy here maps the gap between a real place and a past moment, creating a chart in which the loss – the hope and the bitterness of perpetual movement and unresolved mourning – provides the contour lines of the landscape.

With poems that enact this unresolved mourning through their presentation of a geographically and prosodically overlapping space–time, we see Hardy formulating a theory of spatial experience that has decidedly modernist overtones. As geographer Timothy Oakes has argued, place itself may be the site of "modernity's paradoxes and contradictions" where the "tension between progress and loss" is geographically expressed.[74] While Oakes focuses on Hardy's novels as presenting us with an "unstable landscape of process" in which readers negotiate "a tense *relationship* between dwelling and detachment" (517, his emphasis), I think that his terms usefully illuminate how Hardy's elegies formally and thematically explore a version of this spatial paradox. The experience of the subject in place will result in the subject displaced, and this displacement will be provoked and manifested by the multiple (and mutually exclusive) times at work within each place. As such, place no longer functions as "a site of both *meaningful identity* and *immediate agency*" (510, his emphasis), but as a site where identity is unstable and agency is shifting. It is a space in which boundaries are transgressed in ways that create both uncanny moments of identification and frightening shadow selves. Even further, the poetry transforms each place into a new cartographic space in which the key is always changing and the most important map-reading occurs in the negative space.

This unstable version of map-reading leads me back to "Wessex Heights (1896)" which was the poem Hardy used to open *Satires of Circumstance, Lyrics and Reveries* in the first edition, as well as back to questions of the empathetic, perspectival imagination. This original placement underscores the importance of parsing the poem's figurative and literal perspectives, for the verses thereby functioned as a primer to the lyrics that followed.[75] "Wessex Heights (1896)," which moves toward a progressively more abstracted and identity-erasing lyric space, is an awkward piece to read because the tension between rhythm and words at times seems overwhelming. Hardy starts us with a seemingly static location:

> There are some heights in Wessex, shaped as if by a kindly hand
> For thinking, dreaming, dying on, and at crises when I stand,
> Say, on Ingpen Beacon eastward, or on Wylls-Neck westwardly,
> I seem where I was before my birth, and after death may be.
>
> (*Complete Poems*, 319)

Although we begin the poem rooted in time and space – the title presents an identifiable place and a particular year[76] – this sense of fixity is upended by the end of the first stanza. From the specificity of two geographic prominences – Ingpen Beacon and Wylls-Neck – and of the present tense ("when I stand"), the speaker suddenly shifts to a place that evades such charting: the space of the distant past and distant future ("I seem where I was before my birth, and after death may be"). The long heptameter lines crowd the page and, by the end of the stanza, create a tongue-twisting reading experience because of the midline caesuras, which suggest to the reader that, for example, the phrase "I seem where I was before my birth" should fit (though it does not) into the same metrical time as the second half of the line: "and after death may be." Such awkwardness in this instance is deliberate; Hardy decided to use "before" instead of the "ere" that was in the original manuscript, thereby adding another stressed syllable and speeding up the first half of the line as we struggle to make it fit the meter.[77] As Taylor notes, the long lines "invite division into a larger multiple," hinting at the possibility of an alternative dipodic reading (heptameter becoming tetrameter, for example) that might emerge at moments and suggest the possibility of more than one time (or of two coexisting times) at work in the lyric space.[78] This often unwieldy conflict between metrical time and space and the vision of a temporally blurry "I" functions as an aural and visual reminder of one of the central problems grappled with in this piece: on the one hand, negotiating the relationship between specific geographic spots and fixed past events, as well as the "I" that both was and could be; and, on the other hand, acknowledging the ephemeral negative space and time shaped by the Wessex Heights and voiced by the dipodic background.

The movement that Hardy sets up, therefore, in this first stanza is one in which precise physical locations are counterbalanced by a negative space. The temporal and spatial indeterminateness of the first stanza's final line foreshadows the poem's syntactical tendencies. Hardy avoids enjambment and the resulting sense of surfeit meaning and instead breaks the lines in the middle with strong caesuras, pauses that hint at an empty space at the center of this poetic experience. The shape of these lines and the occasional excess of syllables point to the juxtaposing forces at work in the poem: on the one hand, the constraints of the physical and emotional cartography that the poem presents; on the other, a desire to draw a new map of the Wessex Heights that charts spots that are emotionally arid rather than emotionally resonant. In so doing, Hardy brings us back to one of the tenets of the "new geography" and its thematic maps. His stanzas about the lowlands and towns – where he is "tracked by phantoms having weird detective ways" and is "barred by the forms now passed / For everybody but me, in whose long vision they stand there fast" – present us with geographic areas that manifest personal history, a temporally deep set of relationships that form the isolines in this lyric cartography. Yet he charts these layers only to avoid them, proposing instead to escape to the curiously empty toponymy of the heights.

This escape to the heights from which he can view his distant, pre-birth past (irretrievable) and his future death (unforeseeable) points to a different sort of empathetic positioning from the one that we encountered in *The Woodlanders* and *Tess*; it is a far more hopeless vision of perspective-taking that suggests both the multiplicity of subject positions within the self, and the challenge of achieving a viewpoint that will, in any way, allow one to move beyond the vagueness of "seem" and "may." Poems such as "The Place on the Map," "After a Journey," and even "Wessex Heights" turn to dipody to metrically express loss, the return of the repressed, and the layered nature of space–time relationships. At the same time, Hardy takes the layering that contemporary geography proposes and reveals the slippages and fissures in such a project, and the gaps that emerge, therefore, in any attempt at standing in someone else's shoes. Spatiotemporal relationships, these poems suggest, are no longer governed by natural and geographic laws; they suggest an uncanny modernist space, as Philip

Weinstein describes it, not "open to orientation and ownership."[79] Hardy combines contemporary geography's concern with charting space *through* time and prosody's interest in the times *within* lyrical space in order to suggest that the "place on the map" may be in fact the spot that evades, rather than enables, meaning-making. Thus, the melancholic mourning that critics have characterized as central to modernist expressions of grief involves, in Hardy's formulation, a Janus-faced prosody that maps a haunted terrain of loss, and marks uncanny encounters with past selves and failed attempts to see from other perspectives. These attempts are themselves haunted by the ghostly presences of some of the very figures who are the intended objects of the empathetic imagination. But once having left the boundaries of the self in acts of empathetic imagining, any return can only reveal the self as newly strange. What we learn from Hardy's poetry, therefore, is that, as he writes in "Moments of Vision," the first poem to follow *Satires of Circumstance*, the mirror that we turn on others inevitably "throws our mind back on us, and our heart" (*Complete Poems*, 401). We will see this freshly unveiled mind and heart illuminated in the next chapter with the attempts to represent the equally shattered physical and formal spaces of World War I.

CHAPTER 3

Disorienting Empathy
World War I and the Traumas of Perspective-Taking

Wandering through the Newfoundland Memorial in the Beaumont-Hamel area of the Somme – a site where 733 members of a Canadian regiment were killed on July 1, 1916 – produces a distanced but evocative understanding of the experience of trench warfare. Closely shorn grass covers the battlefield now, but it follows the contours of a landscape that is still alien in its shape. The tended ground eerily recalls Carl Sandburg's war poem, "Grass": "Pile the bodies high at Austerlitz and Waterloo. / Shovel them under and let me work – / I am the grass; I cover all."[1] Under this superficial cover of green, the pockmarked land bears witness to the massive destruction that took place a century ago. Hills that would have seemed innocuous or even picturesque have become ominous monuments to the strategic disadvantages of the Canadian position. A lone petrified tree, the only one to remain after the offensive, is the infamous "danger tree" that signaled the midpoint between the trenches, beyond which almost certain death awaited the advancing soldiers.

These traces of the Great War hint at the profound spatial changes that occurred as the shells fell and the trenches were dug and suggest that, in order to read this war's literature, we must unravel the complex relations among the spaces inhabited, perceived, and imagined – to use terms given by French spatial theorist Henri Lefebvre[2] – by both the real and fictional participants. At the center of this negotiation of the war's spaces were also questions that arose, whether for the participants or for those reading their descriptions of the war, about the possibility and the effects of stepping outside one's own perspective while so fully limited by both the physical and the mental constraints of life in the trenches. Meanwhile, cartographic practices and technologies proliferated and changed, leading to a surge in mapping and surveying projects during World War I.[3] The striking juxtaposition between the most important shift in mapping technology – the use of aerial photography – and the chthonian perspectives of the soldier in the trenches points to one of the central dilemmas of writing war space: the gap between the modes of perception on the ground and from afar. The ramifications of this gap appear in the formal aspects of war literature and in the barriers to perspective-shifting that the literature explores.

In this chapter I look at texts by Ford Madox Ford and Mary Borden, both of whom experienced the space of the Western Front first hand: Ford as a soldier and Borden as a nurse. While Hardy gave us an elegiac empathy that grappled with the challenge of empathizing with a lost other, Ford and Borden both confront absence – often physical gaps in and transformations of the body of land and the bodies of the soldiers – as definitive of the spatial, corporal, mental, and linguistic experiences in war. Their texts – Ford's war tetralogy, *Parade's End* (1924–1928),[4] and Borden's slim collection of short stories, *The Forbidden Zone* (1929) – foreground the structural presence of loss in these acts of war writing, and explore how to represent attempts at perspective-taking and empathetic imagining. If Hardy's elegies present a modernist space in which the perspective-taking strategies emerging from the "new geography" reveal the layers of loss embedded in the landscape, both Ford's and Borden's works struggle with the problem of how to represent both the mental and physical absences created by the war. Such erasures and lack of control are made all the more ironic when juxtaposed against the apparent geographic mastery on display in the proliferating maps, charts, and guidebooks of the war years.

War proves especially problematic for acts of empathy, both because of threats of impending loss (of self and other), and because war's guiding imperative – to kill – self-evidently hinders empathy with the "other," since it is that very same other that one must try to kill. There exists in a war space not only the problem of how to imagine others in this space, but also the problem of how to imagine the self; one is simultaneously a would-be killer and a likely victim of injury or death. Attempts to write the war experience, therefore, force writers to reexamine not only the stakes of representation, but also the very idea of entering into another's perspective or the possibility of narrating one's own perspective. Ford's novels, in particular, work to render the isolating and anatomizing nature of the war experience more visible to readers through explorations of the empathetic imagination. *Parade's End* is not just long; the novels are large in scale, serving as social and political critique even as they also portray a domestic drama that mirrors the dysfunctional breakdowns in communication and empathy afflicting Britain. The stakes of Ford's project extend to a diagnosis of a society that is unable to understand action outside of self-interest, and Ford's anachronistic main character, Christopher

Tietjens, charts both the limits and the necessity of an empathetic imagination in such a world.

Borden's book is on another end of the prose spectrum, not only in
length, but also in its scope and focus. *The Forbidden Zone*, which is
a collection of vignettes and stories drawn from (and some written during)
Borden's experiences as a nurse on the Western Front, encircles the reader
with its intensely inward voices and sense of being trapped in the isolating
space of the Front. Rather than diagnosing a national and social inability to
see and comprehend other perspectives, as Ford does through his brilliant
protagonist, Tietjens, Borden's text works to foster awareness of the *otherness* of the various subject positions that can be occupied (reader, writer,
observer, soldier), some of which overlap. Her text is concerned with
silences and with the estrangement or alienation of the *reader* from the
subject; we are in the realm of Hegel's argument that "poetic language
brings an estrangement from the prosaic perception of the world."[5]
Exploring this estrangement in *The Forbidden Zone* shows us how her
abstracting grammatical choices, the isolation of voices, and her use of
textual silence to bridge the space between the "I" and the "you" illuminate
the necessity and the improbability of empathy in this war zone. While it is
not written in verse, I argue that Borden's text, with its complex triangula-
tion of speaker–addressee–reader, can best be understood using a theory of
lyric address that recognizes how it is the act of address itself – the
articulation of the moment of address, often a moment of apostrophe –
that places us in "the special 'now' of lyric articulation."[6]

The uncanny nature of these war texts emerges less in the empathetic act
itself, and more as a constant function of the losses occasioned by war. This
is not only because war texts are so often haunted by the presence of death,
but also because the survivors are so often marked by missing limbs,
missing parts – both physical and mental. Freud notes that
"Dismembered limbs, a severed head, a hand cut off at the wrist, feet
which dance by themselves – all of these have something peculiarly
uncanny about them."[7] Borden's book enacts the sense of corporal absent
presence particularly strikingly; the sensation of the missing limb, the
awareness of a body part that is no longer there – this becomes an occasion
of uncanny presence in and of itself, and signals how the uncanny may
become a normal part of war experience, rather than the exception. Ford,
too, explores this connection between war injuries and the uncanny in the
final postwar volume, *The Last Post* (1928), with the mute body of the
protagonist, Mark Tietjens, which brings back the repressed experience of
war through its silent presence. While this final volume is set in a bucolic

southern English landscape, and with the war-marked Christopher Tietjens notably absent until the very end, Mark's body accuses and disconcerts those around him who would rather forget. By occupying Mark's perspective for almost its entirety, Ford's text performs an act of uncanny perspective-taking, putting a presence into an absence and bringing back the repressed wounds of war in the literally silenced figure of Mark.

This sense of dislocation portrayed by Ford and Borden fits with critic Ruth Ley's definition of trauma as inherently defined by disassociation. It is, she writes, "an experience that immersed the victim in the traumatic scene so profoundly that it precluded the kind of specular distance necessary for cognitive knowledge of what had happened."[8] Trauma can be seen as a "dislocation of the 'subject' prior to any identity and any perceptual object."[9] It might, therefore, seem to prepare the terrain of the subject for the kind of perspective-shifting essential to an act of empathetic imagination – it has already exposed the permeability of the boundaries between self and the world. However, this momentary suspension of the distance between two experiences has threatening consequences in trauma theory; the subject loses control over her own sense of subjectivity. This is one of the potentially haunting experiences that lurk behind the boundary-crossing movement between self and other, subject and object. Transferring an awareness of these threats to the realm of empathy studies helps reveal the potential dangers of empathetic engagement. First, however, Ford's war text will bring us back to a question of geo-empathy that emerged in a different form in Hardy's poetry and novels: what happens when you try to occupy a perspective that is in not simply another space, but in the hostile space of war?

Forms of Trauma: Ford's *Parade's End*: Writing the "territory of Armageddon"

When turning to the literary spaces of representation in war literature – which range from Frederick Manning's autobiographically inflected novel about life on the front, *Her Privates We*, to T. S. Eliot's London poem, *The Waste Land* – we can find a similarity in method. Despite the range in treatment, these works are engaged in what Margot Norris describes as the seizure of "*what is left over* for [art's] own terrain, a leftover in the form of the *human remainder*, the affective residue, the suffering that military histories imply but don't voice, the inner experience that can't be mapped, charted, counted, or otherwise quantified."[10] This definition explicitly sets forth a contrast between perceived space – the maps, charts, and other quantified forms of measurement – and imagined space, which deals with the subjective and "affective residue" of an experience. Yet this division does not work so neatly when the art and literature must deal with a large-scale trauma such as the experience of front-line fighting and the toll it took on European society. The boundaries between objective and subjective begin to collapse when experience is particularly violent and perception is unconditionally violated, and the imagined spaces of these war texts take on the burden of negotiating these boundaries.[11]

If art's strength is in its representation of the affective and subjective realm of the individual, it struggles with its "epistemological inability to totalize"[12] when faced with the mass horror of war. As an examination of *Parade's End* will illustrate, the attempt to resolve this problem of representation leads to a crisis of genre and a breakdown of the barriers between literary forms. Understanding this crisis requires rethinking the distinctions between Henri Lefebvre's three spaces – formal divides that may no longer make sense in a war-torn world.[13] As Hammond notes, Ford's work reveals how the Worringerian thesis that empathy and abstraction are at odds must be revised, for empathy and abstraction can be deeply linked (125). Indeed, in *Parade's End* we see that abstraction is, in fact, mobilized in order to produce empathy, especially when the experienced spaces of war are abstracted into spaces of representation. I scrutinize the imagined map that Ford's protagonist, Christopher Tietjens, visualizes, and which becomes not only a figure on which the problems and possibilities of representing a battlefield are explored, but also, I argue, a synecdoche for the larger questions of how to structure a war novel and how to imagine an abstract literary form that enables an understanding of the war experience, even as the map also suggests that realist, mimetic models are no longer functional. Discussions of the empathetic and the cartographic imagination become interconnected here because both grapple with the profound restrictions on the various senses – sight, in particular – that enable them.

Ford Madox Ford's notorious inaccuracy makes him a most unlikely map-maker, yet both drawing maps and lecturing on war geography were part of his duties as a commissioned officer during World War I.[14] Though not a soldier in the front-line trenches, Ford experienced the muddy, gory mess of Western Front war as a transport officer. In 1915, despite his age (forty-one) and his bad lungs, Ford took a commission in the Welsh Regiment (Special Reserve).[15] When he was finally sent to France in 1916, Ford landed in the notorious Somme valley near the scene of some of the worst fighting – the area around Albert and the Mametz Woods – and was stationed well within range of the larger shells. One such shell exploded near him at the end of July 1916, knocking him unconscious and causing his long-lasting case of shell shock.[16] After returning to duty in August, Ford and his battalion moved to the equally infamous Ypres Salient.[17] Eight months later he was invalided out of his front-line duties and sent back to England, where he stayed in the army until 1919. Ford's active role in the war was finished, but his involvement through his writing had only just begun.

The seeds of Ford's interest in the spatial dynamics of war can be found in his notes for lectures that he gave to soldiers in 1918. The "Lecture on France" hints at his geographically inflected understanding of history and culture. Ford writes that this lecture is "not about War but about Civilisations,"[18] and the two sketch maps that accompany this lecture reveal that he defines civilization in geographic terms. Indeed, he comments that the "Main factor of <u>Frankish</u> Civ[ilisatio]n is the fact that the Rhine at every part of its course is exactly equidistant from Paris" (*War Prose*, 254, his emphasis).[19] Similarly, while the notes are exceedingly rough and unelaborated, some phrases that Ford uses for his lecture on "Geography and Strategy," which was accompanied by three sketch maps, point to his understanding of the emotional resonance of geographic features. Ford describes the relationship between geography and strategy thus:

{Rivers
Main Features of Strategy = {Roads
{Sentiment   (*War Prose*, 252–253)

In this formulation, sentiment, which is placed in an appositive relationship with the rivers and roads, is an integral element of Ford's wartime geography. The three accompanying sketch maps illustrate (1) a skeletal view of the rivers of England (with the Thames prominently marked); (2) some rivers and roads of France (with Paris at the center and the rivers and roads looking like spokes – the term that Ford used to describe them in the note below – radiating outwards); and (3) the Rhine River with marks for battles to the east. The question that arises when the notes are read in relation to the maps is *where* and *how* we locate sentiment on the mapped space. He has connected it in his notes to the cities of London and Königsberg (but not Paris), but these notes do not help us understand the implied multifaceted space of war. An answer will emerge, however, in Ford's fictionalized war map in *Parade's End*. Indeed, I argue that Ford's

geography of war is a geography of war trauma and, therefore, is inextric-
able from a charting of the sentiment that is both frighteningly absent and
present.

  Most of Ford's writing during the years during and immediately following the war, however, was nonfiction or thinly disguised autobiographical
fiction. Two of his most interesting essays, never published during his
lifetime, form a thematic pair even though the first was written in Ypres
in September 1917 and the second almost a year later. In both essays, Ford
struggles with the issue of how to represent or even remember the war.
In "A Day of Battle," Ford claims that he "can write nothing – why
I cannot even think anything that to myself seems worth thinking" (*War
Prose*, 36). Of course, anyone who is familiar with Ford's numerous
publications or who reads through the collected volume of *War Prose*
will smile at this claim, but Ford's point is about the difficulty not just of
putting words on the page, but of translating any kind of coherent and
overarching image of the war into a narrative. This problem with finding
an appropriate literary form – "we have no method of approach to any of
these problems" (59), Ford sighs in an posthumously published essay that
was found in Ezra Pound's papers – becomes an issue of perspective or,
rather, of the lack of a proper perspective. "One is always too close or too
remote" (59), and the challenge of the writer is to find a form that reveals
both the details and the broader picture of the war. Being too close is the
habitual state of the soldier in the trenches, whose perspective is circum-
scribed by the limits of a rifle sight. Ford recalls in "A Day of Battle":

> Dimly, but very tyrannically, there lurk in your mind the precepts of the
> musketry instructors at Splott or at Veryd ranges. The precepts that the
> sights must be upright, the tip of the foresight in line with the shoulders of
> the –v– of the backsight are always there, even when the –v– of the backsight
> has assumed its air of being a loophole between yourself and the sun and
> wind and when the blade of the foresight is like a bar across that loophole.
> And the dark, smallish, potlike object upon whose 'six o'clock' you must
> align both bar and loophole has none of the aspects of a man's head. It is just
> a pot. (*War Prose*, 38–39)

These limits on vision are what allow the soldier to function in the midst of
battle. Focusing on the rules of the instructor forces him to attend to the
technical and mechanical side of his actions, while separating him from the
moral and emotional implications. Killing becomes part of a manageable
process of alignment, while the target loses its humanity and the head
becomes simply a pot, divorced from the rest of the body. The closeness of
the vision leads to remoteness from the actual events. The act of engaging

in battle becomes linked with the inverse of empathetic engagement; rather than imagining oneself in the shoes of another, you have to imagine the other as decidedly nonhuman – simply a pot, a machine, an automaton.[20]

This tension in perspective-taking is at the heart of the kind of narrative empathy that characterizes both the shifting points of view in Ford's tetralogy and those in modernist literature in general. *Parade's End* frustrates attempts at connection and empathy in order then to allow for them, collapsing the easy distinctions between categories of orientation and disorientation. Over the course of the tetralogy, Ford explores the possibility of empathy in a war world in which the failure and even threat of empathy are at the forefront, where mediation between individuals and their environment is through the convoluted paper trails of a distant bureaucracy, and where the characters may be able to experience emotion only at the moment when they think all such emotion has been lost. Yet, despite the structural and affective barriers to perspective-taking, Ford's novels persist in probing these barriers and attempting to traverse the gap.

Arguing this, I hope to provoke thought about the complex labor and formal maneuverings involved in empathetic imagining, as well as to highlight the threat to the idea of the autonomous individual that is implicit in an act of perspective-taking. As Max Saunders has written in his comprehensive biography, Ford's choice to narrate the war through the perspective of a character who was based on his late friend, Arthur Marwood, "has too often been discussed as if it were an easy thing to do" because it is "a self-effacing device, which can be confused with a mere appropriation of the *déja vu* and the *déja dit*," as opposed to the "extraordinary act of imagination" that it actually manifests.[21] While I am less concerned with the authorial empathy at work in this novel, and more with readerly empathy and the representations of empathy between characters, Saunders's comment points to one of the dangers of empathy – the potential loss of the self in the act of imagining other perspectives – as well as to the effort involved in crossing the boundaries of one's individual experience. Perhaps counterintuitively, the stylistic difficulty of Ford's narrative turns out to be central to the project of perspective-taking. As Keen describes it, research by David S. Miall suggests that potential formal barriers to perspective-taking like those found in "difficult and discontinuous texts" may in fact enable readerly empathy *because* of the interpretive work that they ask readers to do.[22] Stylistically disorienting narratives do not necessarily engage in a "refusal of empathy" such as the one Sianne Ngai locates in a text like Herman Melville's *The Confidence Man*, which results from a proliferation of characters and the foreclosure of "sympathetic identification at all levels by foregrounding 'objectified emotion.'"[23] Even though this idea of objectified emotion is pertinent to a discussion of *Parade's End*, as we will see most vividly with the map image in the second volume, *No More Parades*, such moments of objectification fascinate and horrify Ford's characters. Indeed, unlike Melville's Bartleby or the figures in *The Confidence Man*, who present surfaces that resist identification, the characters in *Parade's End* – as a result of their own alienation from their experiences and sense of disorientation within the emotional and experiential terrain – actually invite the reader into a world that might otherwise be inaccessible.

The solution to seeing things clearly is more complicated than it would at first seem, since the act of stepping back and looking down on the scene of battle does not solve this problem of perspective. Indeed, as Jeffrey McCarthy argues, we can see an "anxiety about instrumentalizing relations" and a critique of "the industrial, bureaucratic society behind the war" at the center of the tetralogy.[24] This political focus aligns with the perspectival one that Ford similarly confronts in the impulse to map the battlefield. In the third novel of *Parade's End*, *A Man Could Stand Up –*, the characters voice their desire for a commanding perspective and their inability to find one in the war ("Imagine standing up on a hill! It was the unthinkable thing there!"[25]), while at the same time Ford's own experience reveals the flaws in this commanding outlook. His memory of a view of the battlefields of the Somme focuses on the "immense cloud of smoke [that] hung: black and as if earthy" (*War Prose*, 38) and which, in essence, effectively obscured the ground below. Ford sees "a million men, moving one against the other and impelled by an invisible moral force into a Hell of fear" (38). Not only is the view obscured, but also the knowledge of the enormity of events taking place overwhelms the mind of the viewer. Ford cannot progress beyond this image, for he has no structure that will do justice to the event. Here the remote view from above both hides the war and brings its immensity so close that it becomes an incomprehensible part of a terrifyingly abstract pattern.

This rejection of the abstract is why Ford originally dismisses maps as useful tools in this search for a new form. His experience as a wartime map-maker reinforces this belief. He writes in "War and the Mind":

> When I used to ride in from the line to Divisional HQ in Albert, for the purpose of copying onto the maps for Battalion use, the alteration of trenches that had been made in the night, I know that the lines that I made with blue, yellow, or red pencils, on the map that showed Pozières, Welch Alley, Bazentin le Petit or Mametz and High Wood. . . .

those lines which represented Brigade and Divisional boundaries, new
trenches, the enemy's new lines, MG emplacements and so on, represented
nothing visual at all to my intelligence. (*War Prose*, 43)

Especially to a soldier with intimate knowledge of the actual conditions of
the war and of the human experience of space, these maps cannot portray
the actual events of war, only certain static moments of success or failure.
The colored lines – the trenches and battles made both abstract and
concrete – sterilize the war for both the viewer and the creator, just as
they did in the newspaper and military maps. In fact, Ford claims that these
maps shut down the mind's ability to visualize the represented place,
effectively inhibiting any imaginative creation of war space.

As tools for memory, however, the maps *do* produce images of the space
they represent for those who can connect the representation with the
referent, much in the way that Hardy's speaker in "The Place on the
Map" uses the map to launch his reverie. In the "A Day of Battle" Ford
claims that:

> Today, when I look at a mere coarse map of the Line, simply to read
> "Ploegsteert" or "Armentières" seems to bring up extraordinarily coloured
> and exact pictures behind my eyeballs – little pictures having all the brilliant
> minuteness that medieval illuminations had – of towers, and roofs, and belts
> of trees and sunlight; or, for the matter of that, of men, burst into mere
> showers of blood and dissolving into muddy ooze; or of airplanes and shells
> against the translucent blue. – But as for putting them – into words! No: the
> mind stops dead, and something in the brain stops and shuts down. (*War
> Prose*, 37)

Though it may show a "mere" set of lines, this map of the Western Front
has the power to evoke the images and actions that occurred on that line in
the form of detailed miniatures of the actual events and scenes for the
traumatized soldier. These images are, for the most part, more generalized
than personal, for they describe what we can imagine as the background of
war – that ungraspable combination of views of tranquil towns and sky and
of bloody death and instruments of destruction. He describes the scenes
from the war without naming specific men or battles, as if the map can
allow or produce only an abstracted version of the war experience. And
although Ford says that he is unable to describe the place of war, this
paragraph belies his claim, for the map leads to a description, however
general it may be. In fact, this tension inherent in representation becomes
one of the primary aesthetic and narrative concerns in *Parade's End*.
The challenge of the war writer is somehow to find a form that both reveals
suffering and enables narrative progress.

One of the most elegant and risky solutions Ford discovers in the tetralogy is the use of ellipses as both psychological and narrative erasures and defacements. This mimetic coping with trauma through the efface-ment of the text, memory, and actual events involves the aestheticization of loss, inscribing the absences in both the sentences and the larger structure. Such a mimetic mechanism works when the trauma is immediate and violent, but it becomes problematic when dealing with the aftermath of war, when such narrative silence signifies the failure of a national mourning practice. Yet in all of the books the ellipses not only work to register loss, but also to note the gaps – the distances between meaning and representa-tion, between thought and word, between self and other. We might see the ellipses as moments in which, as well, meaning can emerge: the haunted absences in the text and in the minds of the characters suggest that some-thing horrifying can arise from the repressed war experience.

The traumas of such erasures are most evident in the figure of the protagonist himself. *Parade's End* is the story of Christopher Tietjens, a brilliant man who possesses both an astounding memory and a head for figures that surpasses all others in England, but who has little insight into human relationships. During the war, battlefield trauma and relation-ship angst combine to test his ability to maintain his calm as an officer. Tragically and ironically, Tietjens's primary injury in the war involves shell shock, and he loses the memory that had made him look with disdain at the Encyclopedia as a superficial overview. By the end of the first novel, *Some Do Not* (1924), Tietjens must literally recreate his memory and resort to reading the formerly scorned reference text. His loss of memory means that his thoughts and conversations are punctuated by stutters – "Met ... Met ... It's Met ... "[26] – and by spaces that signal both the obliteration of the prewar world in which optimism, confidence, and unchallenged knowledge could be taken for granted, and the unspeakable nature of the deaths and destruction that he had witnessed.

Contemporaneous debates about the nature of shell shock focused on this relationship between emotional trauma and its physical effects. Several prominent doctors posited that the shell-shocked soldier "unconsciously 'materialized' [his emotions] by converting them into physical or bodily symptoms. Most striking of all, the patient would not remember anything about the horrifying events that lay at the origin of his pitiable state. *Dissociation* or *amnesia* was therefore the hallmark of the war neuroses."[27] Thus, though Christopher Tietjens functions as a notably idiosyncratic hero,[28] he also stands as a representative soldier whose loss of memory encapsulates what Ford saw as a central problem for postwar

Britain: the nation's difficulty with moving past a trauma that it could not quite – in fact, refused to – remember. Only with the help of his wife, Sylvia, who responds with fury to his stutter – "For God's sake say *Metternich* ... you're driving me mad!" (*Some Do Not,* 205) – does Tietjens overcome this mental blankness in the first volume, allowing the narrative to continue. Sylvia's prompting, though profoundly unsympathetic, allows the "reintegration or resynthesis of the forgotten memory" so that the soldier and, in this case, the narrative can "overcome [a] dissociated, fractured state and accede to a coherent narrative" (Leys, 106). By presenting the gaps and allowing them to be resolved, Ford can represent the injuries caused by war while maintaining narrative movement and, at the same time, can highlight an oddly counterintuitive element: that these epistemological gaps enable a kind of empathetic mind reading even between estranged characters.

The close relationship between the action and the narrative structure suggests that Ford approaches the individual experience of loss and silence through experimentation with literary form. The overabundance of ellipses in the sentences of *Parade's End* produces a narrative characterized by the spaces between the words as much as by the words themselves. The ellipses mirror and display the jumps and retreats of the characters' minds, as Tietjens, Sylvia, and Valentine (the woman whom Tietjens loves) attempt to make sense of their world and create a coherent structure of understanding in the face of increasingly confusing social, political, and personal situations. Not surprisingly, the ellipses appear most frequently at moments of stress, when the order of the world is suddenly so disrupted that thought cannot keep up with the necessary reordering. Thus, ellipses overwhelm Tietjens's narrative in *No More Parades* when the dead body of one of his soldiers, O Nine Morgan, pins him to the ground during an attack. In this traumatic moment Tietjens becomes unusually aware of his process of thinking, realizing that his "thoughts seemed to have to shout to him between earthquake shocks."[29] Tietjens's musings are soon punctuated by ellipses that bring the reader's attention to the mechanics of his mind: "It worried him not to know what expression [Valentine's] face would have if she heard of his occupation, now. Disgust?... Perhaps disgust! ... It was impossible to think in this row ... " (30). The phrases are bounded by ellipses that represent Tietjens's mental slips and shifts. The spaces that surround his thoughts act as buffers against a too complete understanding of his situation – a hazard in this infinitely horrific space of war. Even more pointedly, they represent the literally unspeakable acts of violence.

At this moment, when Tietjens seems to suffer from a combination of shell shock and grief over the death of his soldier, he attempts two methods of regaining self-control that involve the aestheticization of trauma. Saying "to himself that by God he must take himself in hand" (*No More Parades*, 37), his first response is to write the rhyme structure of a Petrarchan sonnet – *abba abba* with a sestet – "which ought to make a little plainer what it all meant" (43). The sonnet's rhymes (supplied by a crazed fellow officer) – death, moil, coil, breath – produce a clichéd poem that illustrates very little about the horror of the situation: "Now we affront the grinning chops of *Death* / And in between our carcass and the *moil* / Of marts and cities, toil and moil and *coil* / Old Spectre blows a cold protecting *breath*" (42, his emphasis). Writing it occupies Tietjens's mind so that he can push aside the recent traumas – as Meredith Martin evocatively describes it, joining "military feet and metrical feet . . . in the automatic composition of a *line* meant to discipline and protect" – but it does not do justice to his experience.[30] Of course, that is not the point of the exercise – indeed, it is part of a project to manage, rather than express the war experience.

More than two hundred pages later, though less than twenty-four hours later in narrative time, Tietjens again tries to deal with overwhelming stress. His response is to imagine a map of the Belgian front, a sign that the problem of representation is inseparable from the issue of finding a comprehensible *spatial* perspective (exactly what trench warfare and the shape-shifting shell-pocked land deny the soldier). This passage illuminates the tensions involved in the process of mapping, in the potential creation of a new structure through the abstraction of the old, and in the connections between this geographic mapping and literary form. Ford writes:

> The whole map of the embattled world ran out in front of him – as large as a field. An embossed map in greenish *papier mâché* – a ten-acre field of embossed *papier mâché*, with the blood of O Nine Morgan blurring luminously over it. Years before . . . How many months? . . . Nineteen, to be exact, he had sat on some tobacco plants on the Mont de Kats . . . . No, the Montagne Noire. In Belgium . . . What had he been doing? . . trying to get the lie of the land . . . . No . . . . Waiting to point out positions to some fat home general who had never come. The Belgian proprietor of the tobacco plants had arrived, and had screamed his head off over the damaged plants . . . . (*No More Parades*, 239)

Tietjens's war duties force him to map the landscape for the general – even as he suggests the delusional nature of this duty in his phrasing ("the *lie* of the land") – but his mind also performs the same abstracting gesture in the present narrative moment as he transforms the remembered view into a map. This map image appears at a moment of extreme emotional trauma, for he has recently had a soldier die on top of him, staining his clothes with blood, and he is being questioned by his commanding general, who is also his godfather, about the behavior of the chronically unfaithful Sylvia. Tietjens's memory abstracts and obscures the traumas of his own experience, and he thinks, with resignation, "Now, having lost so much emotion, he saw the embattled world as a map" (241). The map begins with a close representational connection to the land it depicts. Its size ("as large as a field," "a ten-acre field") and its topographic fidelity (it is made of three dimensional papier mâché and, in addition, is "embossed") make it seem less like a map of the world, and more as if the world itself is a map. For the shell-shocked Tietjens, the only view that he can face is this simplified version in which the particulars of the landscape are smoothed over, allowing it to become an abstracted representational system of a uniform color and material. However, though he notes the potentially dehumanizing and abstracting nature of the map, Tietjens does not realize that his map, by making the distortion and destruction visible in the blood that covers its surface, actually reveals the violence and emotion he presumes are lost. The defacement of his map, paralleling the defacement of the land, allows the space of war to be read and recognized. The blood of O Nine Morgan, the soldier whose dead body pins down Tietjens in the first pages of *No More Parades*, signals the destruction enacted on and in the land, even while it also obscures Tietjens's map and empties it of any traditional function or practical military purpose. This frightening swath of red both challenges his reliance on a symbolic representation of a landscape scarred by war and creates a new image – a new kind of map – that acts as a revised sign, and suggests the particular geography produced by war. The image maps both the war-marked countryside of Belgium and the scarred mind of a soldier.

The description of *how* O Nine Morgan's blood distorts the map – "blurring luminously over it" – further points to the presence of war. Like the "misty halos" of meaning that surround the stories of Marlow in Joseph Conrad's *Heart of Darkness*,[31] the blood's movement reveals more about the map than it destroys. It stains the map, highlighting the presence of the war on the bloodied earth. The sign of trauma – the blood – provides a new perspective on the war-torn land. Yet Ford's use of the word "blur" reminds us that this perspective is imperfect; the bloodshed of war obscures as much as it reveals, and a war-inflected aesthetic order and social vision produce mud-spattered and bloody insights. Tietjens's perspective is, therefore, both insecure and powerful, already implicated in a constructive and destructive relationship with the land. Not even a lone soldier can help making an unnatural mark on the terrain, as the Belgian farmer's angry outburst attests. This detail lends an ominous note to his assignment; we begin to sense the connections between a constructive knowledge of the land and its oblitera- tion. Tietjens plans to give the key to this mapped land to a "fat home general," who, we assume, will use it to plan barrages and attacks. The productive act of locating and positioning oneself in the surrounding world also involves, we see, the destruction of that very landscape. Tietjens's verbal map would have produced its own obsolescence, for it would have led to the erasure of the very geographical referents used in its creation.

The map reveals an essential element in this war order (or disorder): the very things that obscure a clear understanding of the world and of the mind paradoxically illuminate a new perspective and a new order. We can think of Franco Moretti's assertion that a map is a "connection made visible,"[32] since Ford's bloodied map certainly brings together spatial and literary form in its presentation. The map asserts the place-bound nature of this formal dilemma of how to represent the destruction of land and men, even while it embodies the very paradox that the war presents to writers: traditional forms (maps and narratives) that seem so inadequate may actually hold the key to representing the war. Tietjens's papier-mâché map both implies the order of the past, and simultaneously reveals how that order has been made obsolete – and, indeed (when we think of the use of maps in the implementation of the war), how that very order may itself have been an instrument of this destruction.

As Tietjens's mind rambles over his memory-scape, he continues his aestheticizing act – a movement away from the war – while, at the same time, he uncovers the war within the scene. In this outward and inward movement we begin to see the rhythm of *Parade's End* and further recognize the constructive and destructive aspects of memory's engage- ment with trauma. Moreover, Ford's interest in the relationship between a map and the transformation of land into art emerges here. The map's traditional omniscient bird's-eye view, now clouded by blood, resolves into the individual eye of Tietjens remembering the day he looked out over the view from a perspective that transgresses national boundaries:

> But, up there you saw the whole war. . . Infinite miles away, over the sullied land that the enemy forces held; into Germany proper. Presumably you could breath in Germany proper. . . . Over your right shoulder you could see a stump of a tooth. The Cloth Hall at Ypres, at an angle of 50° below. . . . Dark lines behind it. . . . The German trenches before Wytschaete! . . .

That was before the great mines had blown Wytschaete to hell.

But – every half-minute by his wrist-watch – white puffs of cotton-wool existed on the dark lines – the German trenches before Wytschaete. Our artillery practice.... Good shooting. Jolly good shooting! (*No More Parades*, 239)

Tietjens gazes out over the fields in Belgium, a section notorious for the unrelenting mud in the trenches. Even though the June 1917 attack on the Messines/Wytschaete ridge has not yet occurred (one of the few well-planned assaults that resulted in a limited gain for the Allied forces),[33] the ground would have been thoroughly marked by the past three years of war. Tietjens's mental eye attempts to organize a landscape cluttered with signs of war. From his vantage point the objects in the view are at first unfamiliar, but he quickly locates them in a military syntax. Gazing out over the expanse like an appreciative tourist enjoying a view, Tietjens sees the Cloth Hall of Ypres as the "stump of a tooth," reading the land as a wounded body and reinforcing the link between the devastation wrought on the land and the mutilation of men and women in the war. Yet Tietjens quickly moves away from this visceral image to a language of art, erasing bodies and substituting the more basic elements of form – lines, shapes, shadows, and color. With this he reveals an eighteenth-century sensibility in which, according to John Barrell, a "landscape" is automatically infused with pictorial meaning, and all images of land are "mediated through particular notions of form."[34] Like his view of the front as a map, this pictorializing emerges from an enlightenment perspective that orders and categorizes. Yet, again like the map, this aestheticization actually emphasizes the incongruity and banality of war's violent enterprise by juxtaposing it with painterly concerns. The German trenches become "dark lines," simply a painter's marks on the ground. The explosions of shells are seen as "white puffs of cotton-wool" that sit "on the dark lines." This play of light and dark – indefinite roundness on definite lines – facilitates Tietjens's appreciative recognition of the referents behind the images and his (ironic) exclamation "Jolly good shooting!" Indeed, this scene is one that Ford describes in his 1916 preface to Violet Hunt's novel, *Three Lives*, and stands, as Max Saunders notes, as an example of the distressing concurrence of "aesthetic pleasure" and violence.[35] The war becomes distant and safe, and the scene suggests visual harmony with its pleasing blend of aesthetic elements, rather than jarring horror.

The landscape becomes more thoroughly abstracted as Tietjens's mental gaze reaches further into the distance:

> Miles and miles away to the left ... beneath the haze of light that, on a clouded day, the sea threw off, a shaft of sunlight fell, and was reflected in a grey blur. . . . It was the glass roofs of a great airplane shelter!
>
> A great plane, the largest he had then seen, was moving over, behind his back, with four little planes as an escort. . . . Over the vast slag-heaps by Béthune. . . . High, purplish-blue heaps, like the steam domes of engines or the breasts of women. . . . Bluish-purple. More blue than purple. . . . Like all Franco-Belgian Gobelin tapestry. . . . And all quiet. . . . Under the vast pall of quiet cloud! (*No More Parades*, 239–240)

Light becomes the most powerful force in this passage, directing his gaze to reflections and colors. The light that creates this whole scene is not the light of a clear, sunny day, but rather a secondary and reflected light produced by the sea on a cloudy day, recalling Ford's assertion in his essay "On Impressionism" that the writer should aim to "render those queer effects of real life that are like so many views seen through bright glass" that not only frame the scene, but also reflect the present moment and the viewer.[36] Like the blood above the map, an apparent blankness and opacity actually illuminate the signs of war, even while inscribing them in an aestheticized representation of space. The airplane hangar seems just a "grey blur" – part of this play of light. The movement of the airplane, instead of recalling the use to which it might be put, directs Tietjens's attention to the glistening colors of slag-heaps – piles of metal refuse from military construction or destruction. His comparison juxtaposes, shockingly, two very different symbols of beauty – the modern machine in the steam domes and the breasts of women – and thereby signals the devastating effects of the encounter of machines and bodies in war, when bodies are fragmented and broken. Yet only a meditation on color emerges from this comparison; the machines and bodies become designs on tapestry from another time. We seem far from an empathetic vision of the tragedy of the bombings. Ironically, the tapestries are Franco-Belgian, recalling another moment of cooperation between these two beleaguered countries and turning us back to the time at hand.

Action and movement in the quiet scene – "White vapour rose and ran away" – recall Tietjens to the violence of war. The vapor comes from shells that the Germans are dropping on Poperinghe, a small village five miles behind Ypres. He remembers:

> There were two girls who kept a tea-shop in Poperinghe. . . . High colored. . . . General Plumer had liked them . . . a fine old general. The shells had killed them both . . . Any man might have slept with either of them with pleasure and profit. . . . Six thousand of H.M. officers must have thought the

same about those high-colored girls. Good girls! . . . But the Hun shells got them. . . . What sort of fate was that? . . . To be desired by six thousand men and smashed into little gobbets of flesh by Hun shells? (*No More Parades*, 240)

Leaving the temporary safety of an aestheticized landscape, Tietjens confronts the problem of bodies in a battlefield, both reading through and reading directly the blood that has obscured his map. The breasts that had previously been bloodlessly made part of the view suddenly accrue new resonances with the introduction of the tea-shop girls. Victims of the war, the girls change from objects of admiration and desire to "little gobbets of flesh," a fragmentation that blows to bits the previous static image of the slag heaps. War's effect on bodies causes problems with imagining others not only because so many others are the enemy, but also because it becomes so difficult to imagine other bodies as anything other than discrete and vulnerable collections of parts – the individual anatomized in horrifyingly literal ways. This memory provokes Tietjens's own frustration with his mapped landscape, which is out of the control of his "uppermost mind" (241). Yet his thoughts again turn to the green papier mâché map stained with the blood of O Nine Morgan, recalling afresh the trauma he has experienced.

The defacement of Tietjens's map, paralleling that of the land, allows the space of war to be read and recognized. Thus, like the ellipses (which punctuate all of these descriptions), the defaced map enables Ford to represent by means of partial erasure. Tietjens's map works as a synecdoche for the project of *Parade's End*, which involves the creation of a restructured narrative form that will represent the unrepresentable, thereby allowing the characters and narrative to progress beyond the moment of trauma. Tietjens thinks despairingly that his map-vision is a sign of "having lost so much emotion," but it is exactly this shaping of emotional response that allows him to maintain a conversation while experiencing a kind of mental breakdown. He realizes in the middle of this scene that "I've complete control of my mind" (*No More Parades*, 241), and the second novel can end a few pages after this transition from inner despair to a proclamation of order.

Imagining Effaced Experiences

Ford's larger experiment with representation and memory in the novel's narrative structure is apparent in the silences – a type of narrative ellipsis – that occur throughout the tetralogy. For example, neither the events immediately after the declaration of war nor the experience of August 4, 1914, the day war was declared, ever appear in the text. In narrative time, the war begins in the space between Part One and Part Two of the first novel, *Some Do Not*. Part One ends with Tietjens's night drive through the mists many months before the war begins. The existence of the war only comes out two pages into Part Two, with Sylvia Tietjens's offhand comment about her seduction of men "in the early days of the Great Struggle" (*Some Do Not*, 182). The temporal leap does not signal avoidance of the events of war; instead, it suggests that this war requires memory as a mediator between trauma and narrative. Traumatic events can only be viewed in the narrative, *Parade's End* proclaims, through a retrospective lens of memory. The beginning of the war takes place in the tetralogy not as part of an ordered, chronological sequence, but instead at two poles that flank the "historical" moment – a "before" and an "after" that transform the actual event into a narrative blank spot, made eerily concrete by the physical division of these moments – an empty space *between* the two parts of the novel.[37]

The effaced beginning of World War I not only enters the text through a retrospective reconstruction, but also through Tietjens's prediction of the catastrophe. Early in the first novel he prophesies the outbreak based on a prescient reading of the history and nature of Britain. "All the same," he remarks, "when the war comes it will be these little snobs who save England, because they've the courage to know what they want and say so" (*Some Do Not*, 27) His friend, Macmaster, ridicules his forecast, but Tietjens continues with his lecture:

> "War, my good fellow," Tietjens said – the train was slowing down pre-paratorily to running into Ashford – "is inevitable, and with this country plumb centre in the middle of it. Simply because you fellows are such damn hypocrites. There's not a country in the world that trusts us. We're always, as it were, committing adultery – like your fellow! – with the name of Heaven on our lips."
> "Yes, a war is inevitable. [...] It's like you polygamists with women. There aren't enough women in the world to go round to satisfy your insatiable appetites. And there aren't enough men in the world to give every woman one. And most women want several. So you have divorce cases. I suppose you won't say that because you're so circumspect and right there shall be no more divorce? Well, war is as inevitable as divorce. ..."
> (*Some Do Not*, 27–28)

The strength of this prediction not only impresses the reader (who, of course, knows that Tietjens is right), but also impresses itself on the shape of the narrative. His prescient vision of war – as well as of the battle of the sexes that will ensue in his own life – is the first example of the displaced knowledge and understanding that haunts this book. It is fitting that elliptical knowledge and narration should be so linked to Tietjens, who is consistently identified as a character more at home in the eighteenth than the twentieth century; the long literary tradition of retrospective moments of realization returns us to literary touchstones such as Wordsworth's account in *The Prelude* of the crossing of the Alps. Unaware of having done so until a peasant affirms it, the moment is characterized by a sense of loss and disappointment until, finally, imagination locates and enriches the experience so that Wordsworth can note it – "But to my conscious soul I now can say– / 'I recognise thy glory'"[38] – and ascribe meaning to the event. Yet while Ford's ellipses could be seen as a continuation of this long tradition of retrospective knowing, the mastery felt by Wordsworth is absent in the face of these war-caused gaps. The narrative ellipses suggest the inability of the characters (except for Tietjens) to understand in the actual times of crisis, instead relegating their grasp of trauma to the periphery of historical time. Tietjens's prediction resurfaces in Part Two of the first novel almost flippantly, for example, when Sylvia remembers how he had pinpointed the moment of war down to the very season – "about the time grouse-shooting began, in 1914, a European conflagration would take place" (193).

The end of the war occurs in a similarly elided space in the novel, but this time the elision is experienced by a character, not just by the reader. In the first pages of the third novel, *A Man Could Stand Up* – (1926), Valentine Wannop runs through an underground passage to answer a school telephone, missing the siren that signals the end of the war: "So she had not heard the sound. She had missed the sound for which the ears of a world had waited for years, for a generation. For an eternity. No sound'" (10). Through the static of the phone line and the half-heard words of the woman on the other end, Valentine learns of Tietjens's return. Understanding and recognition arrive in a belated and sputtering fashion ("Good . . . *God!*" she exclaims when she finally realizes what is being said [23]). In narrative space, the end of the war occurs not at the defined historical moment, but in the circuitous and errant movements of the mind. Even when the event related to the war does not involve an immediate trauma, the narrative cannot present it as a moment of lived experience. With the obvious parallel between the Valentine's underground passage and the trenches, Ford shows that loss and erasures haunt the home space as much as they do the front line. This moment gives us the first sign of the difficulties after Armistice Day in moving beyond the war – problems that will become overwhelming in the last book of the tetralogy.

Indeed, narratively, the historical end of the war exists only in that frustrated London minute, between two poles of after (Valentine's phone conversation) and before (back in the trenches with Tietjens several months before the fighting ends). Framed by Valentine's thwarted experience of the Armistice siren and a surreal Armistice celebration at the end of the novel, the narrative carries us back into the most violent battle scenes that appear in the tetralogy. This abrupt movement in *A Man Could Stand Up* – reveals the messiness of a war's end, especially for the soldier. Critic Samuel Hynes remarks on this disparity between the celebrations of Armistice and the experience of soldiers on the front:

> In the streets of London and Paris and New York people danced and cheered, but the end of the war didn't feel like that at the front. For the soldiers there, the end was an unraveling of order in their lives and the beginning of a life that most of them had not known – the civilian adult's life of decisions and obligations. For four years, war had given their lives meaning and direction; now that it was over, *who were they?* Every young soldier must feel that at the end of his war. Life will never be so simple again, or so exciting.[39]

Hynes's reading of the soldier's connection to the war omits some of the real ambivalence felt about life on the front, but it does point to the gap between the historical meaning of the moment as a triumph of the war's end and the actual experience of the event.[40] This is the gulf that *A Man Could Stand Up* – explores in its narrative structure, with the space of mud, gore, and death as the most vivid present for those who were a part of the war.

Yet a return to the map image might offer another way to think about Ford's ellipses and narrative strategies, for the map complicates our assumptions about the forms and representational strategies that enable or create empathetic engagement, whether with other people or with one's self (for that "other" perspective is here Tietjens's own, radically severed by shell shock, war trauma, and marital strife). Ford's use of this defaced map also suggests the need for an elaboration and revision of Worringer's thesis about realist art as the source of empathetic engagement. Gilles Deleuze and Felix Guattari provide one such insightful rereading of Worringer, arguing that abstraction is not always a function of distance and alienation, as Worringer would have us believe. In essence, they propose that we must expand the definition of abstract art from the one used by Worringer, who only examined abstraction as a manifestation of what Deleuze and Guattari labeled the "geometrical imperial Egyptian form" that works in a "rectilinear" fashion.[41] Thinking through the question of whether abstract art can promote an urge to empathy rather than the urge to alienation, Deleuze and Guattari use the terms "smooth" versus "striated" for the forms of art and the types of spaces that embody, respectively, connective and nomadic versus cartographic modes of being in the world. "Smooth" space is an "*amorphous*, nonformal space"[42] in which any sort of line is "a vector, a direction" rather than any kind of "dimension or metric determination."[43] Thus, longitude and latitude represent the measurement-based striated space that is imposed upon the smooth spaces of the ocean. We might think of this in terms of Michel De Certeau's differentiation between the pedestrian "speech acts" that make up the individualized, on-the-ground movement of the pedestrian in the city, versus the totalizing view from above.[44] When we move to aesthetics, we move into a binary between the "close vision" of the artist versus the distant vision of the viewer. Deleuze and Guattari write:

> The law of painting is that it be done at close range, even if it is viewed from relatively far away. One can back away from a thing, but it is a bad painter who backs way from the painting he or she is working on. Or from the "thing" for that matter: Cézanne spoke of the need to *no longer see* the wheat field, to be too close to it, to lose oneself without landmarks in smooth space. Afterward, striation can emerge: drawing, strata, the earth, "stubborn geometry," the "measure of the world," geological foundations," "everything falls straight down" ... The striated itself may in turn disappear in a "catastrophe," opening the way for a new smooth space, and another striated space.[45]

Thus, within smooth or what they also call "nomad" art, a single orientation and consistency in representation is not important, because the art represents the experiences of embedded individuals (it is from the perspective of the nomad rather than that of the cartographer). Contrastingly, striated or cartographic art and spaces are defined by their need for a coherent orientation and a sense of a central, defining perspective; the modern map can function as an exemplar of this. And, indeed, in Ford's novel and his representation of the maps of the war space, we see a version of that "catastrophe" – the overwhelming presence of war (broadly) and the death of O Nine Morgen (in the specific moment) – transform the striated space of the imagined contour map of the front into a smooth space of affective experience.

While Worringer was only looking at the organizational and cartographic modes of abstraction exemplified by geometric art, Deleuze and

Guattari claim that we must think about a nomad and connective visual art that is "abstract in an entirely different sense, precisely because it has a multiple orientation and passes *between* points, figures, and contours: it is positively motivated by the smooth space it draws, not by any striation it might perform to ward off anxiety and subordinate the smooth."[46] Abstract art, in this reading, *can* facilitate empathy because it creates new connections via the nomad lines that move through different spaces, objects, and perspectives. As our eyes follow the lines, we quite literally explore the effects of occupying other perspectives, not allowing one viewpoint to dominate. While nomad art does not allow for empathetic engagement through identification with recognizable representations, it does create connections by manifesting the very act and idea of forming relationships, presenting a structural example of how to move from space to space in a way that emphasizes the connective rather than the dissociative elements. The blood on Tietjens's map, therefore, can be read as a form of nomad abstraction that brings the inner trauma felt by Tietjens to the surface, rendering it legible and vivid. As Deleuze and Guattari define it, the "*abstract* in modern art" is a "line of variable direction that describes no contour and delimits no form."[47] They use ellipses to punctuate this claim; their ellipses function as a grammatical version of this absence of delimitation, and we will see how the ellipses perform powerfully in similar ways in Ford's narrative.

Thinking about this version of abstraction and its relationship to empathetic engagement helps uncover why the novels might work *formally* and why Tietjens's map image works *metaphorically* to promote not simply disorientation but also orientation. Thus, even in the middle of a scene in which the characters experience profound alienation from the minds of others, *No More Parades* itself might be seen as promoting empathetic experience. If we return to the first scene, we can see how the narrative "abstraction" of that opening and the oddly distanced perspective, while it disrupts our understanding of how to align our connections and affections, also forces us to establish new methods of connection with the events of war; our readerly alienation from the description aligns us with the disjunctive encounters of the soldiers. In *A Man Could Stand Up –*, the desire to connect emerges in one of the most unlikely of arenas: in the realm of military tactics. Tietjens reflects on what he calls his "mania" for "communication drill" when he takes over, mid-battle, a battalion to which he had been second in command (150). Appropriately, given the problems that always emerge, in the battalion of Tietjens, the organization of communications turn out to be the "heel of Achilles" (150). Yet for Tietjens, "it was perhaps the dominant idea ... perhaps the main idea that he got out of warfare – that at all costs you must keep in touch with your neighboring troops" (159).

What we must see in these novels is that, while Tietjens is right in his desire to connect, the only ethical method of doing so will be haphazard and enacted on the ground. While a "single command" is what the Allies need in order to win the war, organizational systems and bureaucratic perspectives are always suspect in these novels. The true crime in them is how the individual suffering of soldiers can become simply part of a game of war; reflecting on the inhumanity of it all, Tietjens thinks about how even the "war of attrition" could be "not an uninteresting occupation if you considered it as a struggle of various minds spread out all over the broad landscape in the sunlight" (152). Because the war had been put "into the hands of the applied scientist" (152), individuals can function only as part of a larger equation.

Yet even if the abstraction at work in the war machine is ultimately alienating in relation to the actual experience of the men, Ford's ellipses throughout the novels offer a way to create a nomad art that brings us into the individual minds of the characters. Tietjens's thoughts become perforated by these ellipses at moments of trauma. When O Nine Morgan dies on top of him, he realizes that "It was impossible to think in this row ... His very thick soles moved gluily and came up after suction ...." (*No More Parades*, 30). As he tries to keep ahold of himself at this stressful moment, when he is literally standing in blood, his "thoughts seemed to have to shout to him between earthquake shocks" (30). The ellipses emerge also as Tietjens frets about his inability to understand how Valentine might react to the scene, thus signaling the very literal gaps in his understanding, his mind's inability to move organically between different perspectives, and the potential lack of empathy between civilians and soldiers.

Yet these ellipses can *enable* movement between perspectives, even in moments of trauma. Sylvia's mind also becomes punctuated by ellipses at a moment of sexual and emotional tension, as she gambles on whether she will let Christopher go or try to lure him back. She remembers whipping a bulldog whom, it turned out, had been poisoned: "And I got the rhinoceros whip and lashed into it .... There's a pleasure in lashing a naked white beast .... Obese and silent .... Like Christopher .... I thought Christopher might .... That night .... It went through my head .... It hung down its head ...." (*No More Parades*, 154). These leaps and gaps bring the singularly self-centered Sylvia into a state where both Christopher's martyrdom and her own pain at his lack of interest in her ("It went through my head") become connected to the dog's suffering ("It hung down its head"). The ellipses here and elsewhere in the novel emphasize movements of the mind and the attempts to leap between perspectives, moments, and places. They are about connections and the disruption of a dominant perspective as much as they are about signaling gaps. As manifestations of syntactic erasure – a blotting of narrative, a shedding of words – the ellipses call attention to the very *idea* of movement.

Indeed, Tietjens's shell shock (which, we learn in an elliptical fashion, has taken place in the gap between the first and second parts of *Some Do Not*) proves a form of psychological ellipsis that jolts Tietjens out of his sometimes infuriating omniscience (he can no longer correct the encyclopedia). Thus, he reaches a state in *A Man Could Stand Up –* in which he cannot abstract himself from the tiresome and often terrifying business of the war: the question of whether or not an attack would come at his point in the line "was wearisome nowadays, though once it would have delighted him to dwell on it and work it out with nice figures and calculations of stresses" (156–157). This is a form of redemption in *Parade's End* that identifies Tietjens as a figure who is able to reject the instrumentalizing perspective that wants to view the world from a distance. Instead, he enters into the connective abstraction of the elliptical narrative, which both allows the readers to enter into the mindsets and experiences of the characters and forces the characters to break out of their limited perspectives and imagine the experiences of others. Thus, Tietjens ends up appearing as the Christ-figure that Sylvia, in her attempt to sabotage his standing with General Campion, his godfather and superior, has declared he wants to be ("'He desires,' Sylvia said, and she had no idea when she said it, 'to model himself upon our Lord . . . .'" [*No More Parades*, 148]). While Sylvia says this out of a half-insightful maliciousness, and while General Campion takes it as a sign of Tietjens's instability, the image works not simply because Tietjens sacrifices his own reputation and wealth for others, but because he moves away from instrumentalization and toward a more empathetic mode of being.

We get in *No More Parades* and the other volumes, therefore, some insight into how experimental, abstract, and defaced literary and visual forms might enable movement into other perspectives. Though Tietjens first appears as an exemplar of the statistical thinker who abstracts himself from the messy realm of empathetic engagement, the novels chart his painful emergence from this mode of being. Moreover, Ford does more than simply represent an individual movement into empathetic perspectives; he offers a narrative form – punctuated by syntactical and narrative ellipses, defined by disorienting shifts in perspective, and populated with metaphoric images like the blood-stained map – that suggests how narrative forms of abstraction might work to engage empathy in the same way as visual forms do in Deleuze and Guattari's formulation. Yet Ford's narrative empathy is defined by and emerges from war trauma; it also highlights, therefore, the difficulties and the dangers of moving outside one's own perspective, both for the soldier and, even if less overtly, for the reader. His tetralogy might thereby provide an illuminating case study of a "modernist empathy" that is defined by Miall's idea of the "dehabituating power of literary forms."[48]

Limiting Perspectives in *The Last Post*

The danger of this elliptical form of thinking – and of inhabiting it too fully, even for those who did not experience the bloodied space of war first hand – comes to the fore in the final volume of the tetralogy, which turns to postwar England. Ford was pessimistic about England's response to the war's end, declaring to Wyndham Lewis:

> "When this War's over," [Ford] said, "nobody is going to worry six months afterwards what you did or didn't do in the course of it. One month after it's ended, it will be forgotten. Everybody will want to forget it – it will be bad form to mention it. Within a year 'disbanded heroes' will be selling matches in the gutter. No one likes the ex-soldier – if you've lost a leg, the more fool you!"[49]

The forgetting will continue, Ford suggested, except this time it will take the form of a social amnesia. The guilt of those who stayed at home will lead them to carry on as if the bloodshed and horror had never happened.[50] Indeed, at one Armistice Day march, protestors passed out pamphlets entreating the public to "revere the memory of our class who fought, bled, and died, BUT DON'T FORGET THE UNKNOWN WARRIORS LIVING."[51]

This project of grappling with the oppressive effects of this national desire to forget motivates the narrative of *The Last Post*, and the novel achieves a perverse kind of success in its representation of the difficulties in both remembering and carrying on in postwar England – perverse because this success results in a text that is itself stuck in a deadly silence. Ford searches for a narrative form that will represent the nation's attempt to mourn the losses of war, and the formal difficulties of this project signify the failure of these mourning practices and the uncanny return of the repressed trauma. In manifesting the thorny politics of the postwar era, the novel has seemed an aesthetic failure to many readers – a narrative that circles endlessly, even to the point of boring the reader – and yet we could also read that as a successful experiment in representing the problematic politics of remembrance and repression facing a postwar world.

In a striking move away from the rowdy, nationwide celebration of the Armistice that occupies the final pages of *A Man Could Stand Up –*, in *The Last Post* the tetralogy collapses into a mute and isolated perspective, thereby transforming the narrative silences from potentially therapeutic "moments of silence" into unspoken brooding. The paralyzed Mark Tietjens, Christopher's older brother, functions as the horrific embodiment of this silence. A victim of a stroke caused by the shock of the Armistice terms of surrender (the war, we see, even injures the bodies of those at home), Mark cannot speak. Mark does not view his physical and verbal paralysis as an unwanted result of his illness, but as a chosen act of resistance against the Allies' decision to halt the advance against Germany: "He was finished with the world. He perceived the trend of its actions, listened to its aspirations and even to its prayers, but he would never again stir lip or finger. It was like being dead – or being a God."[52] His desire for silence is in part what makes it so difficult to transform such isolation into something productive. Indeed, although Mark's body is actually the prisoner of this silence, he still dictates the speech and actions of those around him. His reminiscences consume the first part of the book, while his mute presence directs the thoughts of the other characters. Even when the perspective shifts in Part Two to Sylvia's bitter musings, Mark's silent form reasserts itself as the dominant force as he "lay beneath the thatched roof beneath her eyes" (139). The characters and the story inevitably return to a painful revisiting of their personal and national traumas when they confront this figure who acts as a reminder – the sign of what has been repressed – of the continuing effects of the war.

Like the patient who resists speech in the analyst's office, characters in *The Last Post* remain silent about the effects of war, and therefore remain stuck in an endless cycle of remembering. Unlike other postwar British fiction, the novel does not act as what Christine Froula calls a "communal postwar elegy" that engages in "a dynamic, eventful working through of loss."[53] Instead of allowing narrative movement in the face of trauma, the ellipses have taken over the narrative to the extent that they now prolong the isolation and horror created by the war. Christopher Tietjens is summarily silenced by his absence from all but the last few pages of the novel, and Valentine denies herself both speech and thought for fear that even thinking of past traumas will harm her unborn child: "She must not think of that dreadful night because of the little Chrissie deep within her" (*The Last Post*, 186).

In its setting and time frame, *The Last Post* promises movement beyond the war into a time and place full of potential – a promise given in the celebratory ending of the preceding volume, *A Man Could Stand Up –*. Indeed, the basic situation of the characters, however socially complicated, suggests such a return to domestic normalcy: Christopher Tietjens has established a new career as an antique dealer, he and Valentine now live together, and Valentine will soon be a mother. They have established a new order based on mutual love rather than a legal marriage contract. Yet, within the first pages of *The Last Post*, the narrative voice and the perspective that refuses to engage in the reconstruction of the world dash these expectations of a novel focused on a healthy regeneration. The limits of the bed-bound Mark Tietjens's perspective emerge in the first lines. Lying on his back in an open-air hut, Mark is "staring at the withy binders of his thatch shelter; the grass was infinitely green; his view embraced four counties; the roof was supported by six small oak saplings" (*The Last Post*, 9). Just as the view is syntactically contained by descriptions of the hut, so do the withy binders limit Mark's vision. Unable to move himself, he must stare straight ahead. A few lines later we learn that, in fact, from his present angle a looming hill blocks the sight of the four counties; the hypothetical commanding perspective is never realized. This paralysis precludes the restorative ordering – one that brought the effects of war onto the abstraction of cartography – achieved by Tietjens in his imagined battlefield map. The thwarted narrative movement and the static perspective effectively keep the story from breaking out of its cycle of muted mourning. The new geographic, social, and narrative orientations in the aftermath of the war do not signal a fresh or progressive vision; instead, they expose the ways in which the war still haunts the nation.

If the first three volumes of *Parade's End* are, in some ways, a triumph of modernist empathy – in that the devastation of war, the disorientation of the life in the trenches, and the ellipses in the narrative stimulate, paradoxically, both the protagonists and the readers to form connections, even as they realize the ephemerality of these connections – the final volume represents its apotheosis and its demise. Narrative ellipses transform into actual muteness. The characters pivot inward: Tietjens and Valentine turn to their home, Mark retreats into his limited physical and self-focused mental world. In this face of these movements, many readers stop caring

about or trying to adopt the perspectives of any of them, perhaps accounting for the frequent dismissal of the final book.[54] Postwar England seems
a land in which the empathetic imagination occurs from within a state of
radical disconnection and silence.

It is within this turn to home – to the *heimlich* – that the suggestion of
the *unheimlich* also emerges; by rooting the perspective of the final novel in
the traumatized body of Mark Tietjens, the book suggests that the war,
even when ostensibly over and distant, may linger and erupt in undesired
ways. Mark's body, though never physically in the war spaces we have seen
in the preceding novels, becomes the body on which the effects of the war
emerge most frighteningly. There is a haunted movement in this seemingly
static rural world, because the war will return – and does return – through
the minds of those who are mute, silenced and damaged by the war. Rather
than the empathetic ability to occupy another perspective, we instead
experience the unwanted and uncontrollable return of the repressed via
Mark's mute body, which acts as a rebuke to all who would like to forget
the unpleasantness of the war. Ford's final book thus brilliantly depicts
a body that in its very presence will not let us leave the war behind, in the
same way that the body of the text enacts its own reminder of the
continued presence of the war.

Direct Address and the Poetics of War Writing

Ford's novels have an expansive scope; though World War I is at the center
of them, they are about the nature of British life and citizenship, about
domestic dramas brought into the broader social context. Thus, Walter
Benjamin might have been talking about Ford's novels – perhaps particularly *The Last Post* – when he described an author whose work "has as its
center a loneliness which pulls the world down into its vortex with the force
of a maelstrom," giving us "the sound of society plunging down into the
abyss of this loneliness," where we can perceive the "silence at the bottom
of this crater."[55] Mark Tietjens may function as that silent bottom point of
the crater where society comes to rest. The quotation, however, comes
from Benjamin's essay on Proust; Benjamin uses this crater to illustrate
Proust's inability to "touch" the reader; the crater in question is
a metaphoric one that speaks to Proust's essential alienation and isolation,
as well as the source of his literary fecundity.

I bring Benjamin's lines up not only because they highlight several of the
elements that have emerged in Ford's novels, but also because they lead us
to Mary Borden and her very different use of quiet in the lyrical spaces in

The Forbidden Zone. Benjamin's essay was first published in 1929, just over a decade after the last explosions of World War I and at a moment when a range of novels about the war burst on the scene. This war book out-pouring included *All Quiet on the Western Front* (1928; 1929 in English translation), *A Farewell to Arms* (1929), and *Her Privates We* (1930), to just name a few; Ford's *The Last Post* came out in 1928, and Borden's book of short stories and vignettes, *The Forbidden Zone*, arrived the next year.[56] Benjamin's crater is the product of a deafening maelstrom, like the noise of a world exploding and imploding during World War I, like the deadly explosions that produced the craters on the battlefields. Yet at the bottom of Benjamin's crater is a space of silence, of isolation and lack of inter-personal engagement, and we can see Mark Tietjens as both a sign of the postwar crater afflicting England and a victim of it. Benjamin's image resonates with Judith Butler's evocative description of the double nature of loss, which I will explore more fully in Chapter 4: the loss of the other involves a simultaneous loss of the self; the social catastrophe precipitates a personal one.[57] If it is not simply the individual, but also society that plunges into the silent abyss, the problem becomes interpersonal. We lose faith in the easy, above-ground transitions between perspectives; we are all isolated, together.

While concerned with this sense of isolation, Borden's text brings us back into the noisy realm of war, where she explores how certain stylistic techniques and choices might carve out quiet zones within a space of auditory bombardment. These are spaces that I would call uniquely lyric, recalling Culler's argument that poetic language can estrange us from our normal modes of perception, thereby heightening and sharpening percep-tion. I am not simply talking about the actual moments of silence that we can find in war texts, though those moments are productive starting points; I am instead focusing on how a text can create a silence, and why and how it might do so, even in the noisiest moments – in other words, how it can bring us down into that crater, and perhaps also can show us the way out. We are in the "now" of the lyric moment in Borden's book – it could be exemplified by such images as the "captive balloon" in a half-page story of that name, which "never moves. It never comes down or goes up . . . It is an oyster in the sky."[58] This observing oyster is that estranged organ of perception, "tied by a string to a cabbage field" (15), but more ominous than the passing planes. The world viewed by the captive balloon is the one brought to us through Borden's pared-down description and moments of direct address – whether the singular "you" or the plural "we" – which engender, often counterintuitively, zones of silence even in the midst of violence and the bombardment of war. Especially when connected with the effects of direct address, the "silence at the bottom of the crater" becomes the silence at the bottom of the text – or, quite literally, the subtext. It is in this space at the bottom of the crater that Borden looks for connection – for the possibility of empathetic engagement from an audience removed from the war by both time and space. During the moment of estrangement, Borden's text posits, we might be able to both recognize otherness and attempt an imaginative leap of perspective-taking.

Borden's *The Forbidden Zone* therefore shows how silence, so often theorized as a gap, a moment of obscurity, or a sign of absence, can play a powerful and disturbing connective function. In so doing – in making silence part of the method and a "gesture," to borrow poet Rae Armantrout's words[59] – Borden creates a poetics of silence that allows us to see silence as having a textual function, rather than simply indicating an empty space. Or, more accurately, the empty space of the silence becomes part of a sign system that engages the reader and allows for an attempted empathetic experience across boundaries of space, time, and experience.

Before idealizing this silence, however, we might usefully think about the "muteness envy" that Barbara Johnson's essay explores in relation to readings of Keats's "Ode on a Grecian Urn." Johnson examines the description of the urn and its depiction of a "scene of male sexual violence" as "a scene of general ecstasy," arguing that "an 'aesthetics of silence' turns out to involve a male appropriation of female muteness as an aesthetic trophy accompanied by an elision of the sexual violence."[60] When the silence becomes an ideal, it conceals the difference between "the two things women are silent about: their pleasure and their violation."[61] Johnson's text warns the critic about accepting silence as an ideal without interrogating the ways that the silence might serving a perverse function, in this case enacting a patriarchal censorship that works to keep women "constantly subject to the Miranda warning."[62]

The violence that has been depicted in *The Forbidden Zone*, however, is on mutilated male bodies observed by the speaker, who is sometimes identified as a nurse. We see Borden creating a space of aestheticized silence that does not celebrate the "silent form" of Keats's urn that only says "Beauty is truth, truth beauty";[63] rather, the quiet spaces of Borden's text point to the physical and mental wounds of war and the difficulty of trying to both elegize and empathize with those who are the victims. At the moments when the ravaged male body is most fully silenced – by death, of course, but also by amputation – the silence becomes uncanny. We begin to see how attempts to take the perspective of the lost figures and lost parts might be acts that verge on the uncanny for both reader and character. As Borden notes in her short introduction to the book, her text is dedicated to the *poilus* – the French common soldiers who fought and fell in such great numbers – and they and their wounded bodies hover around this text like a repressed and familiar absence that is made eerily present.

Yet Borden's slim volume seems at first more concerned with noise than silence; the sounds that herald the war and destruction are presented as assaults on the narrator and the spaces, and we exist in a soundscape that emphasizes the noisiness of war and the plentitude of auditory stimulation. In the first piece, "Belgium," we begin with the "cataracts of iron" (7) in the distance, and then the assault of the music of the military band – it is the sound of allies, true, but horrifically figured as an aural overload: "the noise, the rhythmical beating of the drum, the piping, the hoarse shrieking" (8). Similarly, in the second piece, "Bombardment," in the wake of a bombing "a scream burst from the throat of the church tower" (11). The noise signals destruction, and yet it is embedded within a text that presents a meditative and, in many ways, deeply quiet *experience* of reading. How can a war book so concerned with the front-line experience, we might wonder, create for the reader such a sense of stillness within the space of the text, and is this connected to the kind of imaginative engagement that Borden works to establish between reader and text? The first two stories begin in silence. In "Belgium," the steadily falling rain and thick mud "muffle the voice of the war that is growling beyond the horizon" (7). "Bombardment," on the other hand, begins with a perfectly calm day: "the sun was about to rise in stillness: no wind stirred" (11). In both cases, the silence is broken by the shrieks of shells and the activity of soldiers; silence and the chaos of war occur within the same spaces, but not at the same time. Yet, even in the midst of descriptions of noise and destruction, there is a sense of quiet pervading the text that is structural – a function of *how* the story is being told, rather than of the circumstances of action and setting.

The first narrative strategy to create this quiet space occurs on the level of the sentence; it is a linguistic muffling through an emaciated description – specifically, description at a remove. In one of the longer stories of the collection, "The Regiment," we are positioned as if we are viewing from afar the landscape, the villages, the roads, the distanced movements of the armies and the airplane in the sky: our distance is emphasized as we see windmills rendered as "grizzled dwarfs squatting on pedestals in fields" and

regiments of soldiers as "swarms of men" (21); the inanimate becomes
personified, while the humans lose their individuality. "The
Bombardment" brings this sense of remove to a more formal level, with
the world displayed like an "unconscious map" (11), but it is the descriptive
statements themselves that provide the essential abstraction. In
"Sentinels," however, this defamiliarizing description pervades the whole
story. Borden begins:

> All these little men coming out of their boxes along the road.
>   The boxes are oblong. They stand on end by the ragged ditches. The men
> pop out of the boxes into the middle of the road. They are blurred and
> shapeless. They wave dirty flags in weary warning. A motor car slows up and
> stops before the box. The languid menace of these figures stops it; their
> joyless power holds it with its engines panting. (19)

With short, declarative sentences, Borden's stark statements give us a set of
images that resemble a child's drawing of a scene; it is the line drawing
rather than the image with a full palate, it is the visual equivalent of the
noise-dampening rain. We are in the realm of "knowledge by description" –
Bertrand Russell's term, which Dora Zhang has usefully explicated in
relation to Woolf – where the limits to this description serve to highlight
both the narrator's and the reader's remove from that scene and the
impossibility of moving into the realm of "knowledge by acquaintanceship," or direct relationship to the thing.[64] Without the identifying title,
our level of knowledge would be similar to that of a child, interpreting the
image without prior knowledge; we see the shapes, but we are not given the
identifying nouns.

More graphic description does take place in some of the other stories,
where we see the patients in the wards and hear their suffering. But other
even quieter, abstract pieces engage the reader with a frightening calm that
may give us a different and deeper understanding of the Western Front
experience. Rajini Srikanth's argument about the importance of avoiding
the sensational in human rights narratives and language is relevant here:
narratives with heightened descriptions and graphic images of suffering
certainly stimulate shock and outrage, she notes, but "in the interstices of
descriptions of the everyday lies the potential for transformative understanding of readers and for mobilizing our inner resources toward
action."[65] In other words, we need those small spaces of narrative quietness
in order to move from passive receptivity to action. Thus, while Borden
apologizes in her prefatory note to those who might find the stories
"unbearably plain," noting that "I have blurred the bare horror of facts

and softened the reality in spite of myself, not because I wished to do so, but because I was incapable of a nearer approach to the truth" (3), Srikanth's insights help us realize that there is a power to plain language that may reach beyond the shock value of the graphic description.

The fiction writer Charles Baxter's discussion of defamiliarization clarifies this theory: when the "object is stripped of its usual meanings," it is then "desymbolized," which "removes the tyranny of meaning over event."[66] The event that is highlighted in the scene quoted from "The Sentinels" is not the action of the sentinels stopping the motor car, but the broader event of survival in a war space – numbing, boring, and yet essential. The setting has been so trimmed down that it becomes, we might say, pure atmosphere, and it is the atmosphere of weary repetition, which suggests that life itself is without a clear sense of meaning and joy; it is a zone of stillness. As Baxter has noted, "in a moment of stillness, the atmosphere supplants the action."[67] The quietness is broken only by the arrival of the outside element. With the halt of the car, everything briefly changes: the sentence structure becomes more complex, with a semicolon introduced in the final line of the paragraph. The language similarly is varied; we get more complex adjectives and nouns ("languid menace," "joyless power") to describe the men, who had formerly been devoid of such descriptors.

Borden's prose becomes more vivid as she describes the uncanny nature of war wounds in "The Beach," even as this story presents the terrible estrangement that the war creates – an estrangement from the self as well as between those who fought and those who did not. The two characters in the story are not named; they are simply called "The man" and "The woman," and we witness their conversation and their thoughts with disturbing clarity, since what characterizes their interaction is the alienation that they feel from each other, as well as the lack of knowledge of their own selves and states of mind. The woman wonders whether she will continue to love her wounded and disabled fiancé, while he wonders whether he will let her go. The moments of connection that they do experience are more threatening than reassuring; he muses, for example, "What shall we do about it?" (34), and sees the same question in her eyes, giving him knowledge of her thoughts that he does not want to have and cannot use wisely. Access to his thoughts, as well, is more to be feared than desired: she "closed her ears to his tiny voice and listened desperately with all her minute will to the large tranquil murmur of the sea" (35). The horror of his perspective is rooted in its lack of wholeness; as he describes it to her, his body is both vividly present and absent in the same moment, for his foot "goes on throbbing" although "they cut it off two months ago" (34). The town is full of convalescent soldiers who have lost limbs, parts of their bodies, portions of their faces. The truly terrifying part of the war in this story is the presence of the absences that mark the men and shock the women.

Even in this story of life-altering wounding, Borden uses quiet description; the traumatized men and women have "tiny" voices and "minute" wills. The use of this kind of description would seem to coincide with Benjamin's vision of a stillness at the bottom of the crater that separates us and testifies to our inability to know our experiences. Yet this is not the only style Borden deploys; these moments of descriptive abstraction and quiet are embedded within some forms of address that function, on one level, to erase the distance between the reader or addressee and the events of war. Most striking is her use of direct address, both implicit (for example, when the use of imperatives implies a listening "you") and explicit, when the reader is directly interpellated by the narrator's use of "you." In the center of her text – the stories that begin "Part II: The Somme" – stand three vignettes where the first-person voice engages in a direct and almost shocking dialogue with a "you." We already have had a brief glimpse of this kind of direct address in the first piece in the book, "Belgium," where the speaker seems to be responding to an unseen listener's questions, which are questions that we as readers might have: "On our right? That's the road to Ypres . . . Ahead of us, then? No, you can't get out that way. No, there's no frontier, just bleeding edges" (7). The unheard questions continue, and then the "you" of the text is brought in even more emphatically: "This is what is left of Belgium. Come, I'll show you" (7).

With that "Come, I'll show you," Borden points (both literally and figuratively) to the kind of textual relationship that she works toward here; direct address brings the reader both onto the page – for we are called to being, even if reluctantly, by that "you," rather than engaging with narrator at a distance – and into the "now" of lyric address. We can see these moments of address as attempts to break through the narrative distance of fiction and force us out of our complacency and into a direct experience of anticipation and wonder; we may see the King along with the other people in the town: "If we wait we may see him. Let's stand with these people in the rain and wait" (8). The distance of fiction dissolves into a shared (though imagined) personal experience of war space.

Yet the politics and the ethical possibilities that emerge when you stand with the people are not so easily parsed; it turns out that we are not such astute listeners – "Yes, I told you, this is the army" (8), the narrator says.

We have not clearly understood what it is we are doing or what we will see. Nor do we see very well, though we are caught, by the end, in the hopeless rhetorical questions of the narrator, and have to be told more than once, "Come away, for God's sake – come away. Let's go back to Dunkerque. The King? Didn't you see him? [. . .] You didn't notice? Never mind. Come away" (9). The addressee's failure to pay attention and to understand what is going on becomes the focus in these final lines; the story is about the attempt to make the visitor – who may also be the reader – understand the space of war, which is characterized here not by immediate scenes of violence and action, but by the physical devastation of the land and towns, and the static despair of the army. Access to the interior of those soldiers is not granted here; we are given only hints about their state of mind by their interactions with the space: "stumbling along the slippery ditches" and "leaning in degraded doorways" (8). We must be astute readers, but even so we may simply remain in a state of spectatorship.

These moments of direct address in the story recall apostrophe – that turn to the absent (lost) figure so often encountered in elegiac fiction and poetry. Yet the absent figure is not a lost soldier; instead, it is the reader or addressee. Indeed, Borden suggests in her introduction that she is trying to figure out how to represent this experience of war to those who were not there themselves: she dedicates the book to the *poilus* because "I believe they would recognize the dimmed reality reflected in these pictures. But the book is not meant for them" (3). Borden asks the reader to acknowledge his or her absence from the experience of war and the importance of trying to understand this experience, even if it ends in frustration and bewilderment. Borden both offers and withdraws direct address as a way to bring the addressee and the reader into the text. We are interpellated by the "you" and become an actor in the story, gaining some sort of imagined empathetic relationship with the other figures, though perhaps only if we are a receptive reader of this lyric space. In our "estrangement from the prosaic perception"[68] we sense our responsibility and our implication in the event. As Borden states in her note to the text, speaking to those who "find these impressions confused," their disorientation is a product of the confusion of the war, and an "attempt to reduce [the fragments] to order would require artifice on my part and would falsify them" (3). Just as the addressee in "Belgium" is asked to engage with and understand the place on its own terms by the use of direct address, so is the reader – for the addressed "you" could be reader or another addressee; the distinction is rarely clear. Rather than suggesting that the distance from an event allows a corresponding distance from responsibility, Borden's direct address suggests that both reader and addressee must be immersed in the "now" of the war space.

Yet Borden does not want to let us off with a sense of an adequate engagement, of having done enough, seen enough, understood enough. Instead, the emphasis is on how the reader is part of these events in ways that we might not have anticipated, and how there will always be that distance (and therefore the complicity that comes with not having tried to help or alleviate the suffering), and we need to respect and reflect that distance in our own understanding of this experience of war. We experience this particularly when Borden reverses the position of the "you" and the narrating "I" in the first story in Part II, "The City in the Desert," thereby foregrounding this question of how to understand and describe the war to an uncomprehending observer. The story begins with questions; the narrator seems puzzled by the scene that is in front of her: "What is this city that sprawls in the shallow valley between the chalk hills? Why are its buildings all alike, gaunt wooden sheds with iron roofs?" (73) are just the first questions. We learn in the third paragraph that these are not just rhetorical questions; there is a "you" who is listening: "You tell me that there is no sea over there. But the roar?" (73). The "you" has knowledge of the scene, it appears, and seems to be aware of the violence that the narrator wants to avoid. With this kind of address, the story is a narrative of continuous small revelations of information (it is not the sea that makes that roar, but what could be so unending and relentless, if not some massive natural force?). The story is a revelation of the horrors behind this barren scene, a coming into a knowledge that must be painful and frightening since it involves the kinds of violence being done to the bodies and minds of the men fighting. This reversal of authority between the "I" and the "you" in the story (unlike in Belgium, the "you" is the one with the knowledge, rather than the speaking "I") thrusts the reader into an uneasy state of realizing the limits to any sort of understanding in this war space. When the reader is engaged in the narration through direct address, she becomes the narrator as well as the audience and, therefore, a potential actor faced with the consequences of her decisions.

We experience this sense of complicity not just in stories such as "The City in the Desert," with its speaker's accusation that the "you" of the story has knowledge – perhaps false knowledge, since the "I" cannot accept that the roar is anything but the roar of the ocean – but also in stories that are more familiarly lodged in the intimacy of the first-person narration. In "Moonlight," we immediately enter into a much more specific first-person perspective, with the narrator identifying as a nurse in a front-line hospital, who is in her cubicle resting and hearing "the little whimpering voice of a man who is going to die in an hour or two" (39). This narrator is not confused, like the one in "The City in the Desert," nor attempting to educate, like the one in "Belgium"; instead, she exhibits an epistemological confidence, even in the face of the impending death in the ward and the looming causes of death suggested by the rumbling of guns in the background. She assures us, "The section is quiet. I know. I can tell. The cannonade is my lullaby. It soothes me. I am used to it" (39). These short declarations, most with "I" as their subject, suggest both authority (through the forceful claiming of the subject position) and anxiety (through the repetitive assertion of calmness). As she lies on her bed listening to the sounds of the wind and the blowing grasses, which frighten her because all she can understand and be reassured by are the familiar sounds of war, the narrator becomes progressively more agitated and torn between duty and fear: "The sick man is still mewing. I must go to him. I am afraid to go to him. I cannot bear to go across the whispering grass and find him in the arms of this monstrous paramour" (43). The "paramour" is "Pain," the "mistress of each one of them" who comes to the hospital. In the midst of the narrator's description of Pain "plying her trade" (45) with promiscuous abandon, the barriers of the story break and the narrator speaks to someone, perhaps the reader: "Listen. Do you hear him?" (45). The "you" is now beside the speaker, who is attuned again to the sounds of war and the sounds of the man's suffering outside, until his sounds finally stop, and the narrator urges, "Quick! Be quick! In a moment a man's spirit will escape, will be flying through the night past the pale, beautiful, sentimental face of the moon" (46). These are the closing lines of the story, and we therefore end with the voyeuristic sense of having witnessed a man's suffering and death. The act of reading becomes a project of listening; the quiet that emerges at the end signals a moment of respite through death from the sound of suffering.

In the midst of the quietness in these stories, a paradox – that, as Baxter notes, "silence is an intensifier . . . it strengthens whatever stands on either side of it"[69] – comes to the fore. Rather than softening the trauma, the stillness makes the turmoil at the edges even more distinct; the thundering guns in the background start to roar in our imaginations with the destruction they portend. The silence that death brings highlights the sounds of suffering that precede and will follow it. Thus, moments in "The City in the Desert" that may seem descriptively quiet, plain, and even empty are actually reverberating with the unsaid and with the unspoken answers to the questions asked by the "I": "You say that those bundles are the citizens of the town? What do you mean?" (75) asks the narrator, and the lack of an adequate answer resonates: how can we be in a world where numberless brown-wrapped bundles are bodies of fellow citizens? The narrator muses that this hastily constructed city of sheds will be washed away by the torrent of the tide, for she is still embedded in the fiction of the background sound and is still imagining the sea, even as we readers know it is the sound of guns. And yet she also acknowledges her extreme perplexity; the "you" appears to pose this question of where the city will go and the narrator replies "Down where? How do I know? I'm lost. I've lost my way. The road was slippery. There were no landmarks. The village I used to know at the crossroads was gone" (74). The question thus leads to other questions and to the slow accrual of description – the epistemology of the war space is characterized by disorientation. From that moment of complete admission of confusion – "I'm lost" – the sentences slowly build; the paragraph continues with further description, but it reveals only an inability to make sense of this landscape that defies normal human organization and the natural rhythms. The paragraph ends with a flagrant misinterpretation by the narrator: "You see those intersecting bands of wire, looking like a field of tangled iron weeds and iron thistles? That is evidently to keep the mud from slipping away" (74).

For the interpellated interlocutor in this conversation, the quiet, distanced view of the scene inspires engagement more thoroughly and deeply, I think, than does another story, the "Enfant de Maleur," in which we read a description of the agonizing and resisted death of the eponymous character. Borden writes that "Foul odours, foul words, foul matter swirled round him, and always there was that terror in his eyes, and the sweat pouring down his body that was greenish now as if covered with slime" (53); we are horror-stricken and disgusted by that image. Yet the repetitive banality of death is hidden by this graphic description; our horror is attached to this one man's singular experience. Just as the nurse-narrator is helpless to assuage his suffering, despite her medicines and training, so we are also firmly on the outside; the first-person narration assures us that we are not in that place and not part of that horror: she observes the death-bed confession of the *Enfant de Malheur* to the exhausted priest, noting that "I knew that I must not miss the last act of the drama that was playing itself out so quietly on that ugly narrow bed. I knew that I would never again in this world see anything so mysterious" (60). The narrator is a clear spectator; the death is the show. The reader too has access to the show, but it is not a performance into which we can intervene, or even one that can be comprehensible to those outside this duo of priest and dying sinner; we cannot even listen to or hear the words of the *Enfant de Malheur* as he whispers to the priest. There are no gaps in the narrative or clear break-downs of narrative understanding that could allow some sort of readerly work or action to occur. The first-person narrative and direct address can create a space of listening that often is a function of the division between the "I" and the "you," between writer and reader. Here, however, the kind of listening that occurs for the reader is more indirect – we know that the confession has been listened to officially by the priest but only briefly and unofficially by the narrator, and hence the reader. The drama of the story and its vivid description results in narrative distancing, rather than the sense of immersion felt in those stories with barren descriptions. Empathy is both mobilized and revealed as partial and unattainable.

The reader only rarely is allowed to remain in one narrative position in Borden's text. The roles are switched in the story "The City in the Desert," because the reader is put in the odd position of the one who knows. The narrator is simply describing the scene; we are the ones who give meaning to those descriptions in this war world. Thus, the moment quoted above – "You say that these bundles are citizens of the town? What do you mean? Those heavy brown packages that are carried back and forth, up and down, from shed to shed, those inert lumps cannot be men" (75) – rests in fact upon knowledge any reader of a war text would have: of course, here, the bundles could indeed be men. The effect of this rhetorical question is not, therefore, to make the reader complicit, but to emphasize the radical strangeness of the banal and repetitive presence of dead bodies. Rather than being overwhelmed by a given number – 1,000 dead, 10,000 dead – that, in its immensity, strains the limits of our imagination, even if it is based on starkly realistic counts, we are instead made aware of the shocking nature of a world in which *we can know* that bundles are not merchandise, but bodies; the fact of this assumed knowledge highlights the horror of our own assumptions about the stakes of the war. The narrator's shock and refusal to accept the information she requests, information that would defy logical assumptions in any other context, foregrounds this horror.

This question of knowledge is even more prominent in the next story, "Conspiracy," because not only do we have the "you," but also there is now a "we." We enter into a vision of the war as part of a conspiracy to kill off a generation of young men. Again the language is deliberately subdued, veiled in the beginning, with metaphors that shock with their banality: "It is all carefully arranged. Everything is arranged. It is arranged that men should be broken and that they should be mended. Just as you send your clothes to the laundry and mend them when they come back, so we send our men to the trenches and mend them when they come back again" (79). The horror lies in the metaphor: the men as the dirty, ripped laundry, the cycle of being sent out and brought in. By using "we," the speaker makes us part of the conspiracy, unwillingly complicit in the process of mending men so that they can go back into the battlefield where they will destroyed again. The "we" in this text is not an identity that we would claim willingly, at least based on the description given here. The bitter logic of the front-line hospital, which makes the men well enough to return to the war, transforms even nurses and doctors, whose business is to relieve suffering and to heal, into agents of pain and destruction. The writing in this piece becomes part of an experiment in truth-telling, in finding a language to express the logic of war and the injustice of healing. The zones of narrative silence existing in the space carved out by direct address – the silence brought about by the necessity to listen when called on – point to the possibility of both recognizing ourselves as part of the "we" implicated in the violence described and coming to an understanding of our relationship to narratives of trauma and war.

Thus, Borden's text brings us back to a view first imagined in the examination of Hardy's elegies: that modernist empathy emerges in the estranging linguistic spaces cultivated by the lyric in which the empathic imagination crosses subjective boundaries and challenges the inviolability of the individual perspective. Perspective-taking within this war-scape – a space of trauma – highlights the sense of loss and alienation that defines the modernist empathetic imagination. Ford and Borden remind us that this endeavor to stretch outside of the safe zone of individual experience will confront us with our own inability to understand or make sense of an other's perspective, but that such a confrontation still may point the way to a more ethical form of engagement with the unimaginable.

CHAPTER 4

Elegizing Empathy
Eliot and the Subject–Object Divide

In T. S. Eliot's 1953 play, *The Confidential Clerk*, the well-meaning but oblivious Sir Claude explains that his youthful dream was to be a potter, not the businessman that he became. He admits:

> – And as for me,
> I keep my pieces in a private room.
> It isn't that I don't want anyone to see them!
> But when I am alone, and look at one thing long enough,
> I sometimes have that sense of identification
> With the maker, of which I spoke – an agonizing ecstasy
> Which makes life bearable. It's all I have.
> I suppose it takes the place of religion.[1]

This revelation of aesthetic empathy is surprising in a play that is more of a farce in the tradition of *The Importance of Being Ernest* than it is social or aesthetic commentary, and this moment is equally farcical in that the "maker, of which I spoke" is none other than Sir Claude at a younger age. Yet the "agonizing ecstasy" is worth noting here; it foregrounds the pain and pleasure at the heart of the act of identification with the art object even in this ironized moment, as well as the way, in this case, it is overtly born from a sense of loss. The agony of no longer being that maker, the ecstasy of being able to inhabit (and having been able to inhabit) that maker's perspective, the way that this act of identification emerges from an experience of perception – these are all themes and ideas that define Eliot's earlier and less humorous explorations of the empathetic imagination.

This chapter examines the elegiac nature of modernist empathy, and it also takes up the question posed by Borden's book at the end of the preceding chapter: can lyric estrangement give us the template for a more nuanced and ethical form of engagement with others? Eliot's poetry will provide an example of one particular version of how empathy might evolve as both an aesthetic and an ethical practice. On the one hand, Eliot's theories of perception and empathy contain a certain confidence at their

core, since he ultimately views as deep and worthwhile (even if futile!) the
attempt to see beyond the boundaries of the self. On the other hand, this
attempt to engage becomes tied up with an elegiac project of recording the
losses that might occur with every movement outside the self. I argue that
while Eliot reveals the self as a prison, he also raises the possibility of
breaking free from the boundaries of selfhood through acts of empathetic
imagining. Yet this path leads to self-dispersal and disorientation, which
the empathizing subject must guard and defend against. This is the classic
paradox of the empathetic imagination: it is precisely in the moment of
attempting to know another that we realize both the impossibility of that
project and the potential unknowability of the self.

Whereas Chapters 2 and 3 focused more on the perspectives of the reader
and the literary protagonist or poetic voice, this chapter and the next
explore the objects of perception and the subject–object dynamic; in
particular, with Eliot we see the self objectified and made strange.
The spatial (on an internal and even microscopic level, rather than geographic) and the formal elements of empathy are central to this chapter,
while the uncanny nature of objects is considered more fully in Chapter 5
on Virginia Woolf. I start by looking at Eliot's engagement with both the
seventeenth-century mathematician and philosopher, G. W. Leibniz, and
the late nineteenth-century philosopher and subject of Eliot's dissertation,
F. H. Bradley; their writings provide the route into understanding Eliot's
theory of subjects, objects, and empathetic engagement. This section, with
its focus on the movement between perspectives, engages with questions of
orientation and the place of empathy, worked through on the minute level
of the monad. I then shift to Eliot's poetry, examining both unpublished
drafts and the final published version of *The Waste Land* (1922), in which
we can see empathetic identification at the center of the elegiac enterprise.
The question of how and whether we can occupy other perspectives
becomes especially pressing when confronted with the loss of others and
of self. Reflection on the empathetic act becomes, in this case, an elegiac
project *in and of itself.* If Hardy gave us a prosody of loss and a rationale in
his novels for the aesthetic and social necessity (if danger) of empathetic
engagement, Eliot gives us a theory of empathy that makes perspective-
taking and loss inextricably linked. Finally, I turn briefly to Eliot's later
long poem, *Four Quartets,* which, I argue, we can and should think about
as reverberating with concerns that emerge from Eliot's early Bradleyian
theory of how we might be able to break through our own individual
perspectives, but which ultimately presents a world in which perspective-
taking means first and foremost the submission to a belief in one

overarching perspective that can perhaps never be attained – and thereby suggests a world without empathy.

The Place of the Monad: Leibniz, Bradley, and the Psychological Point of View

For a figure so often described as stiff and cold – Virginia Woolf calls him "pale, marmoreal Eliot ... like a chapped office boy on a high stool, with a cold in his head"[2] – Eliot is concerned to a surprising degree with the possibilities for engagement outside the solipsistic individual perspective, and this interest manifested itself in his early studies on Leibniz and Bradley. Eliot's early essays reveal the key elements from the writings of both philosophers that would reverberate in his later prose and poetry: namely, that the individual point of view is the substance of what it means to be a subject, and that part of the project of the individual is a concentrated and unrelenting attempt to break free from the limits of the individual point of view, even in the face of the probable impossibility of this project.

The challenge of theorizing the dimensions of subjectivity emerges in early essays written while Eliot was at Harvard, where he pursued first a BA and then a PhD in Philosophy, ultimately writing a dissertation on Bradley, but also doing work on Leibniz, among other philosophers. Of the psychologists that Eliot was reading in his spring 1914 seminar at Harvard, he finds Theodor Lipps – the German psychologist and aesthetician who was the first to coin the term *Einfühlung* (empathy) – and his theory of subject–object relations the most compelling. Eliot noted in the seminar in May 1914:

> Best theory that of Lipps, *Inhalt und Gegenstand*: Things given. We are conscious of thing. Self and its objects form one whole. Get psychological objects by turning in direction of Self (*Ich*). Mental states are relations which in one reference are external. Properties not things but experience with respect to a point of attention ... Appearance in relation to self would demand a whole universe of sciences. Lipps has mind essentially related to world. Abstract self and world along with it.[3]

The self here is a part of a whole that includes its "objects," both external and internal; it is "a point of attention" plus "experience" of outside and inside. More interesting is Eliot's focus on how any act of turning perception onto the mind shows that the self is an "it," an object, when it shifts its focus inward. The world, therefore, has substance only through and within our own acts of perception; the self is only an "experience with respect to"

the observing point of view. On the one hand, this is a deeply alienating –
as in othering – view of the mind and the self; on the other hand, Eliot
appears to see this as a way to reunite the self and the world; we are all
objects in the face of perception, even when the perceivers are ourselves.
What Eliot seems drawn to is the way in which we can still theorize a mind
and a world that are essentially related, and a theory in which the self and
the objects of perception are deeply united. The world and the self are all
experiences of perceiving consciousnesses, and that is simultaneously unifying and alienating.

Eliot's most intense engagement with the structure of the self, at this
point, was through Leibniz's *Monadology* (1714), an exploration of what
Leibniz views as the fundamental units of being – monads. These monads
are, Leibniz describes, "simple substances which have perception only,"[4]
which he distinguishes from souls because souls have memory, and therefore have a way of defining and ordering perceptions. The mere monads are
instruments of perception, and these perceptions are always changing
through internal shifts in perception. Although they are all different
from each other, each "has relations which express all the others," and,
consequently, "is a perpetual living mirror of the universe" (point 56; 248).
Leibniz goes from this fundamental unit of perception to that which he
describes as the ultimate monad – God – who "alone is the primitive unity
or original simple substance, of which all created or derivative monads are
products" (point 47; 243). The monad therefore epitomizes Leibniz's claim
that perception is the basis of all being, and that these perceptions,
although all separate and unable to be shared between monads, point to
the larger and unifying force of God. Concomitantly, the universe exists
only as monadic perception; even what we would consider nonsentient
objects are monads and have a base level of perception, though without the
reflective capacity that occurs within life forms. Leibniz therefore gives us
a vision of a world made up of and based upon perception at the most
fundamental and basic level – the monad – that highlights both the ever-
shifting nature of perception (within monads), the ordering method of
memory, which higher order beings (animals, people) use to make sense of
the shifting perceptions, and the ultimate inability to move between
monadic perspectives, except through the unifying concept of God – an
idea that we will see emerge again in Eliot's *Four Quartets*.

This idea of a unifying vision implies that there is something beyond
the self, but Leibniz's adherence to the limits of the monad leaves little
room for fusion or extension.[5] It was this part of Leibniz's monadology
that first drew Eliot's critique, as well as revealed a seed of Eliot's

optimism in a paper he wrote in February 1914 on "Description and Explanation" for a Harvard graduate seminar with American idealist philosopher Josiah Royce. In it Eliot offers a critique of Leibniz's monadology, arguing that Leibniz is wrong to focus on the substantive element of the monads and to define them first and foremost as physically separate entities, because the *act* of perceiving is, in fact, the defining element of this smallest unit of being. Once we understand that we can never occupy more than one point of view at a time, Eliot notes, we enter into a world that "suggests a monadology, differing from Leibniz in that the centres are points of view and not consciousnesses" (*Complete Prose I*, 125). Eliot elaborates on this idea in a slightly later essay written in the fall of 1914 while at Oxford, "Objects: Content, Objectivity, and Existence," in which he explores the consequences of this focus on point of view:

> A point of view cannot be said to be identical with an individual human mind, or with any cross-section of a mind. It is the total state during which the object or group of objects present to that consciousness remains totally identical, and may vary in extent according to the interest involved, which dictates how far the identity need go to be considered total. The discrimination of these points of view has a certain value inasmuch as we are apt, when we have passed from one point of view to another, let us say, more critical point of view, to forget that the first retains its own rights and is not absorbed. (*Complete Prose I*, 167)

The autonomy of each point of view is reiterated here: the object exists through a particular point of view, and each point of view is distinct; and, although movement between points of view is not only possible, but normal, points of view remain distinct ("not absorbed"). In so far as an object is known through only one point of view, Eliot writes, it is "identical with the point of view" (167); we only see it as an object when it is compared with the original perspective through another point of view. Eliot connects this epistemological method with language: it is through use that words get their meaning, he writes, and this is both how we can gain some sort of common understanding, and why we realize that our worlds are all different – the world of the "man of genius . . . is not the same world as that of the plowboy or the jellyfish" (167). Yet Eliot defends this view against the charge of solipsism because, he says, though we can know only our own world, we never intend to know only our own world – we intend simply to know *the* world. It is an unintentional solipsism at the most, he suggests – and we can understand that there are other versions of the world, even if we do not (or cannot) share them.

Eliot's response to Leibniz and his monads reflects, in one sense, what Robert Chodat has described as the essence of modern literature: a deep suspicion about the primacy and transcendence of human agency – the ability to act toward an end, to be in control – and a challenge to the idea of the unified, objective, and omnipotent "I."[6] This is also what both drew him to and allowed him to critique Bradley, whose idea of "finite centres" and the Absolute bore resemblances to Leibniz's theory of monadism. One of Bradley's primary claims in his 1893 *Appearance and Reality* (which became the focus of Eliot's dissertation) was that what he calls "immediate experience" is at the center of reality, and that the "Absolute" provides a resolution of the incredible isolation and separation of each experience.[7] Eliot is probing this question of how to bridge these immediate experiences when he claims that "Description, unless otiose, is always more than description, for it involves a change of point of view; and explanation never really explains, because it involves the maintenance of one point of view (an act of will, so to speak) and this maintenance is impossible" (*Complete Prose I*, 122). Let me emphasize those final words – "this maintenance is impossible" – because I think they anticipate the nature of Eliot's future engagement with perspective-taking. The mind, Eliot argues in the contemporaneous "Finite Centres and Points of View" (1914) – an essay in which he examines Bradley's idea of finite centers (which Eliot describes in this piece as a version of the monad) – is made up essentially of the objects it perceives; structurally, "The mind, then, is nothing more than the system of objects which appears before it; and only by an extension of the term can we speak of "individual minds"; the phrase is properly a contradiction" (*Complete Prose I*, 176). It is hard to imagine a more definitive rejection of the idea of the inviolable agency of the individual, for it dissolves any sense of impermeable boundaries between the mind and the world, the self and the objects around, and it speaks to the essentially multiple nature of the mind (the phrase "individual minds" is "a contradiction"). Eliot continues to develop this idea in a later published piece on "The Development of Leibniz's Monadism" (1916), in which he argues that Leibniz provides an early example of a conception of the relationship between subject and object: "In Leibniz we find the genesis of a psychological point of view; ideas tend to become particular mental facts, attributes of particular substances" (*Complete Prose I*, 447). What the monad sees is "the substance" of the world (as we will see when we examine the Tiresian vision in *The Waste Land*);[8] as critic Donald Rutherford describes it, "the being or reality of material things consists solely in the fact that they are perceived."[9] Yet it is more than this – not simply the being of material things, but also that of the self, is created through acts of perception. We are, perhaps oddly for misogynistic Eliot, veering toward a conception of a performative subjectivity of the sort theorized by Judith Butler in relation to gender.[10]

While destabilizing and potentially terrifying in one sense, there is also a positive element in this vision of the troubled nature of the "I" and the material world; Eliot's adoption and revision of both Leibniz's monadology and Bradley's finite centers point to the more generative implications of this vision for understanding the engagement between individuals. As Eliot concludes in his essay on Bradley:

> In this way, only, a finite centre is exclusive, in that you cannot go in or out with impunity. You cannot, without completely abandoning your own point of view, completely understand that of another. I do not say that a point of view may not be transcended, or that two points of view may not melt into each other; but in this transformation the ingredients have ceased to exist. (*Complete Prose I*, 175)

This is a touchstone point, for its effects reverberate beyond the boundaries of this particular essay; this question of mobility between and transformation of the finite centers and monads reappears in *The Waste Land* in clear ways. Points of view are, in this formulation, more or less exclusive, since as units of perception they cannot simply shift into another perspective.

The idea of complete understanding of another perspective is a fiction; yet, that final sentence suggests some room for transformation – indeed, there are two different types of transformation Eliot identifies here: melting and transcendence. Readers of *The Waste Land* will recognize phrases from the final sentence quoted above reappearing in Eliot's claim that Tiresias unites all the characters: "Just as the one-eyed merchant, seller of currants, melts into the Phoenician Sailor, and the latter is not wholly distinct from Ferdinand Prince of Naples, so all the women are one woman, and the two sexes meet in Tiresias. What Tiresias *sees*, in fact, is the substance of the poem" (*Collected Poems*, 72). Notably, the imbrication happens within a figure who embodies two perspectives that not only are different, but are so often portrayed as irreconcilable (by Eliot as well as so many others): the male and the female. The poem posits this unique merged perspective as the source of its material; it is through a perspective born of a double vision that the poem comes into being. Tiresias' predicament will emerge with all of the pathos and sense of loss embedded within the seer – as well as with the problematic power dynamics that allow this poem to render the experience of the empathizing seer more worthy of attention than that of the lower-class figure in this poem.

If we go back to this early articulation of melting, the dangers of this merger become clear; in that act "the ingredients have ceased to exist" (*Complete Prose I*, 175). Eliot's willingness to posit this risk as viable suggests the attraction to masochistic self-destruction that we will see played out in poems such as "The Death of Narcissus," as well as in *The Waste Land*.[11] Destruction defines that movement into another perspective, and an inevitable loss occurs when trying to see the world through new eyes. If the world is composed or understood only through our perception of objects, and this perception by others cannot be understood or "seen" by another, then in order to move into another perspective, some kind of transformation must occur: melting or transcendence, a dissolution or a rising above. In the act of taking on another point of view, the original perspective ceases to exist.

Yet perhaps an insistence on the isolation of each perspective results in a situation in which it is pointless even to try to understand others. Eliot writes in an essay that brings together "Leibniz's Monads and Bradley's Finite Centres" (1916):

> The point of view from which each soul is a world in itself must not be confused with the point of view from which each soul is only the function of a physical organism, a unity perhaps only partial, capable of alteration, development, having a history and a structure, a beginning and apparently an end. And yet these two souls are the same. And if the two points of view are irreconcilable, yet on the other hand, neither would exist without the other, and they melt into each other by a process which we cannot grasp. If we insist upon thinking of the soul as something *wholly* isolated, as *merely* a substance with states, then it is hopeless to attempt to arrive at the conception of other souls. For if there are other souls, we must think of our own soul as more intimately attached to its own body than to the rest of its environment; we detach and idealize some of its states. We thus pass to the point of view from which the soul is the entelechy of its body. It is this transition from one point of view to another which is known to Mr. Bradley's readers as transcendence. (*Complete Prose* I, 468)

Eliot's focus on needing to move beyond the "*wholly* isolated" vision of the soul appears as a push to reach beyond the isolated, solipsistic "I" that has been so central to our understanding of the modernist subject; this is one of the moments where I think we see the optimism that we do not normally associate with Eliot's vision of the world.[12] "Melting" is the term that emerges most powerfully in poems such as "The Death of St. Narcissus" (1915), in that previously quoted note to *The Waste Land*, and more metaphorically in terms of a fascination with and horror of transgressed boundaries and changed states. Melting implies a change from solidity into fluidity – a movement from a state of concrete edges to one of diffuse and disordered limits. It is both a scientific term and a metaphor with erotic overtones.[13] Transcendence, the term Eliot reaches in that final line of the passage, renders more problematic the question of the *place* of empathetic experience, for it implies a shift into a more metaphysical form of perspective-taking. In so doing, it suggests a movement outside of perspective-taking in general, and perhaps a move away from the empathetic imagination.

Melting Saints, Seers Seeing Double

Perhaps we can see the pleasures and dangers of melting as the operative metaphor most overtly in Eliot's poem "The Death of Saint Narcissus." It was one of the poems that Eliot thought about including with *The Waste Land* (and it was eventually published in *The Waste Land: A Facsimile and Transcript*, after it had appeared in the 1950 *Poems Written in Early Youth*). The poem raises questions about parsing the subject–object divide of empathy in ways that recall Eliot's focus in his early essays on perception itself as the fundamental basis of meaning-making. It begins with lines that we immediately recognize from the first section of *The Waste Land*, though the color of the rock is different:

> Come under the shadow of this gray rock –
> Come in under the shadow of this gray rock,
> And I will show you something different from either
> Your shadow sprawling over the sand at daybreak, or
> Your shadow leaping behind the fire against the red rock:
> I will show you his bloody cloth and limbs
> And the gray shadow on his lips.[14]

We begin with an invitation that recalls Mary Borden's insistent speaker; we are in the realm of the "I" and the "you," though this moment of intense identification and self-awareness of the reader is almost immediately left behind as we switch to the account of Saint Narcissus. Yet this brief, somewhat clunky moment of asking us to look past ourselves (our own shadows) and at another highlights the act in which this poem is most interested: the question of what it means (and what kind of destruction may ensue) when we try to step outside the self. "The Death of Saint Narcissus" presents to us the saint as a figure entering into an extreme state of self-awareness – one that becomes consuming when all he can perceive is his body as an acted-upon object. This self-knowledge is presented as an understanding of the edges of and the limits to the perceptual organs ("His eyes were aware of the pointed corners of his eyes / And his hands aware of the tips of his fingers" [95]). Through the sharpening of eyes and fingers into instruments that can sense not only the surrounding world, but also themselves, Saint Narcissus – whose name recalls the mythic origins of this fascination of man with himself – renders himself an object of experience and knowledge, just as much as the surrounding people and things. Saint Narcissus is both perceptually over-aware and deeply isolated; these experiences of extreme self-awareness hinder, rather than enable, communal engagement: "Struck down by such knowledge / He could not live mens' [*sic*] ways, but became a dancer before God" (95). His state is thus dysfunctional, but his narcissistic turn ends up allowing him to experience and understand, indeed to become, beings other than himself, ranging from trees ("First he was sure he had been a tree") to another person ("Then he had been a young girl") (97).

   In each of these states, the horror of being able to feel into a self that is not oneself, but that becomes oneself, is intensified and leads to a kind of knowledge that ultimately turns violent. In the saint's second stage, for example, "he knew that he had been a fish / With slippery white belly held tight in his own fingers, / Writhing in his own clutch" (97). Eliot underlines in his manuscript the "his" of the grasping hands; it is essential for the drama of the poem to emphasize that the saint's exquisitely refined self-perception renders both the self and the "other," the human and nonhuman, as objects and, more specifically, as manifestations of the trauma that the perceiving self can do. Saint Narcissus simultaneously becomes the fish and the fingers that clutch this fish, object and actor, the prey and the hunter. Similarly, as a young girl, violated by a drunken old man, the speaker knows both the trauma of the victim and the desire of the drunken rapist:

> Then he had been a young girl
> Caught in the woods by a drunken old man
> Knowing at the end the taste of his own whiteness,
> The horror of his own smoothness,
> And he felt drunken and old.   (97)

This is the self objectified to an extreme level. Such double and internalized knowledge is too much, and the saint must leave other people: "So he became a dancer to God" (97). This decision leads to his ultimate immolation and melting away through a form of torture that ends in death; with eroticized violence, the arrow-tips penetrate the boundaries of the skin from the outside, and blood escapes from the interior and stains the skin. The saint's submission to God leads to a final breaking of boundaries, not only between inside and outside of the body, but also in his embrace of death. The shadow, which had before been the shadow of man (of ourselves, the readers, but also presumably of any human), that necessary accompaniment to the self-conscious and self-aware state of being human, is no longer projected before or after Saint Narcissus. Instead, it has been consumed – or lingers in the orifice connected to consumption ("Now he is green, dry and stained / With the shadow in his mouth") – and Saint Narcissus's awareness of self and other has fused and then been drained away.

"The Death of Saint Narcissus" thereby performs the kinds of elegiac empathy that Eliot embraces later in *The Waste Land,* by depicting the trauma involved in an imaginative habitation of another body. Knowing another perspective seems to mean and to lead here to a dual understanding of victim and aggressor, masochist and sadist, object and subject. Such knowledge is self-destructive, both because it involves a transmogrification of the self that leads to a continued slippage and dissolution of the individual perceiving subject, and because the only resolution seems to be the death of both body and soul – that moment in which melting becomes a kind of transcendence, as the quotation from Eliot's essay describes. If the soul could be the entelechy of the body, as Eliot had written, it has no place to inhabit or to energize when the body becomes "green, dry and stained" (97) – a literal shell of the self. Thus, this final moment of perspective-taking indicates a movement out of perceiving perspectives, rather than a proliferation of them. Indeed, this profound empathetic stretching seems to lead to an emptying of identity and knowledge of others and, at the same time, of life.

"The Death of Saint Narcissus" darkens our understanding of Eliot's vision of selfhood and conception of individual autonomy,[15] and can be read in terms of the elegiac homoerotic desires at work in the text (as Colleen Lamos does),[16] but it also can foreground how imagining others involves a simultaneous self-dispossession, and this dispossession has consequences for the very body of both subject and object of empathy. The conservation of energy functions here as in other closed systems; with each movement of psychic energy into another perspective, an equal amount must be taken from the starting perspective: knowledge and understanding cannot be simply increased. While the amount of insight or knowledge may remain the same, what Eliot's poetics reveal is that omniscience is the ultimate fiction.

The kind of relationship embodied in "The Death of Saint Narcissus" gestures to the ambiguity of the idea of an autonomous "I" in Eliot's poetry, and *The Waste Land* provides a compelling canvas on which to extend this analysis and to chart Eliot's double-sided version of literary empathy. Indeed, it is in *The Waste Land* that we can see one of the essential elements of modernist empathy: while we may be able to shift perspectives and "stand in someone else's shoes," this ability, even as it promotes the possibility of seeing through another's eyes, also defeats the positive aspects of that act by highlighting the fragmentary and alienating nature of the process. The coherence of the self is lost – or is revealed as the fiction that it has always been – in this act of perspective-taking, although an awareness of an existence outside the self is gained. Yet perspective-taking may still function as the necessary core of making sense and meaning outside of the solipsistic "I" if – and perhaps only if – we can see self-shattering in the light shed by theorist Leo Bersani's critique of the sanctity of the autonomous self: "The self is a practical convenience; promoted to an ethical ideal, it is a sanction for violence."[17] The dissolution of the self would be, in this case, the necessary step in achieving a more ethical vision and set of relationships with the world. Moments of loss might be the ones that most tellingly reveal the problems with our vision of the stable subject. We might recall Judith Butler's description of the way that mourning exposes the fallacy of assuming an autonomous subject: "It is not as if an 'I' exists independently over here and then simply loses a 'you' over there, especially if the attachment to 'you' is part of what composes who 'I' am. If I lose you, under these conditions, then I not only mourn the loss, but I become inscrutable to myself. Who 'am' I, without you?"[18] The fact that it so often takes moments of great loss to compel this understanding of the dependent nature of the individual subject reveals the difficulty of imagining the self as anything less than whole. In *The Waste Land* the fragmentation of the self is given; the question of what this means for imagining others is what is at stake.

The Waste Land has been examined for its elegiac tendencies by numerous critics, most often as a response to World War I and to the death of Eliot's close friend, the French medical student Jean Verdenal, who was killed in Gallipoli in 1915.[19] In an elegant reading of the antipastoral mode of the poem, Sandra Gilbert describes it as a kind of elegy for elegy itself – a "ravaged terrain littered with the shards of the English elegy,"[20] even as the poem also attempts to rework many of the conventions of the elegy form. For my purposes, I'd like to focus on the project of perspective-taking in relation to this elegiac mode.

Unsurprisingly, if we are thinking of it as an elegy, *The Waste Land* signals in the very first lines both the importance and the problematics of perspective-taking.

> April is the cruelest month, breeding
> Lilacs out of the dead land, mixing
> Memory and desire, stirring
> Dull roots with spring rain.
> Winter kept us warm, covering
> Earth in forgetful snow, feeding
> A little life with dried tubers.   (*Collected Poems*, 53)

The spatial and perspectival disorientation we get here is key to understanding the poem as elegiac in tone. We begin in the first person, but detached and without a clear identity; it is a voice that seems to comment with authority on those most appropriate of poetic topics – nature, memory, desire – in a varying but easily established tetrameter that suggests a kind of metrical consistency. And yet we are asked to reorient ourselves almost immediately; the shift to the "us" of the fifth line, and its authority of a shared perspective, is immediately disturbed by our realization that this perspective seems to be underground; what kind of sight and knowledge can exist, we might ask, when occupying such a perspective? The repetition of the gerunds at the end of each line not only suggests the unfixed temporality of the actions (they have no clear beginning or end), but also seems purposefully alienating, leaving us literally hanging at the end of each line. The title of the section, "The Burial of the Dead," alerts us that this voice might be that of the dead – not an unusual choice in modern elegies, where ghosts such as Hardy's Emma or Wilfred Owen's mangled soldiers proliferate. Yet this dead body seems to multiply in disturbing ways; the frightening aspect is not that the dead might speak, but that the dead might shift and transform, that there is always an other within, and that the constant change proclaimed by Pater in his "Conclusion" – "This at least of flamelike our life has, that it is but the concurrence, renewed from moment to moment, of forces parting sooner or later on their ways"[21] – is not just a function of life, but also of death. The seeming contradiction that Diana Fuss notes in her exploration of the "corpse poem" holds true here, as well: "A dead body and a poetic discourse are mutually incompatible, two formal states each precluding the other. A poem implies subjective depth while a corpse negates interiority. A poem signals presence of voice while a corpse testifies to its absence."[22] The voices of this first stanza not only speak to an absence, but to a multitudinous and shifting set of absences; "us" points to multiplicity, not unity – it is not about a shared vision, but a constantly changing one. This multiplicity is affirmed when the voice emerges from the ground and into the Hofgarten in line 10, becoming multilingual and strangely intent on claiming in German (translated here): "I'm not Russian, but Lithuanian, a real German" (*Collected Poems*, 53). The compacting of three national identities into a line that declares only one is true rings of a deluded and false sense of national coherence; we might wonder if it is the coherence that can only emerge in death. Even a movement back in time in the final lines of the stanza, a seeming turn to origins and the definitive starting point of childhood, offers instead an explosion of personal pronouns (I, we, me, you, he) that reaffirms our sense that perspective-taking in this poem will be defined by dispersal, not coalescence. The meter, too, engages in a shifting that Margaret Holley describes as a movement "from one metrical basis to another and in and out of meter itself from line, stanza, or section poem to the next," which allowed Eliot to "turn their various echoes and reverberations loose in the poem like a cultural accompaniment."[23] Both pronouns and prosody work against desires for cohesion and unity.

What, Eliot forces us to ask, does it mean when we must deal with two frightening poles of identification: the torpid dead stuck in the mud, and the mobile dead who seem to move from past to present perspective with jarring suddenness? So far we are simply on the level of understanding perspective-taking as both frightening and unproductive. From this sticky mud, however, we move to the next part of "The Burial of the Dead" with lines that foreshadow the arid and sterile landscape of red rock in "What the Thunder Said":

> (Come in under the shadow of this red rock),
> And I will show you something different from either
> Your shadow at morning striding behind you
> Or your shadow at evening rising to meet you;
> I will show you fear in a handful of dust.   (*Collected Poems*, 53–44)

How, we might wonder, is the fear in the dust connected to the shadows at dawn and dusk? While the image of shadows suggests an ability to conceptualize, even to perceive, one's self as outside the self, the reference to fear in the dust brings us back to the idea of self-loss and absence; ashes to ashes, we might think as we are propelled into the terrifying realm of nonbeing, of death. Is it fear of absent selfhood or fear of a world without religion or other ways to explain (and justify) existence after death? Eliot leaves us hanging, suspended like the shadows with an uneasy sense of the limits of our understanding. He reinforces this experience with the meter, for every other line in this hexameter set of lines has a dangling ghost beat – the completion of a final foot in the hexameter pattern. Such a ghost beat allows for, Eavan Boland has argued, the resonance of an "emotional silence made by earlier noise"[24] – a moment when we expect the sound that would continue and complete the rhythm of the line, but which in its absence produces a haunting space of foreboding.

This missing beat points to the prosodic embeddedness of loss in Eliot's poem, and brings us to critics' discussions of modernist failures of consolation in the face of grief and loss, as well as of the potentially ethically necessary nature of this failure. As Patricia Rae notes, philosophers such as Jacques Derrida reject "so-called normal mourning" because they see "all such reconciliation to loss as unethical, an act of infidelity toward lost loved ones and a failure to respect what death really means."[25] This challenge to Freud's claim in "Mourning and Melancholia" (1917) that we can make a distinction between successful and unsuccessful responses to loss (mourning versus melancholia) is reframed as a question of whether "successful" mourning – successful in the sense of being true to the trauma of the loss – should ever end in reconciliation to that loss. As Rae argues, Freud himself offers a formulation of this argument in "The Ego and the Id" (1923), describing how melancholia may be "a necessary part of ego-formation."[26] Melancholia is characterized, he argues, by an "object-cathexis" whereby the ego internalizes the attachment to the lost object so that the loss then becomes rooted in the self, rather than in an exterior object that could be replaced.[27] Yet in "The Ego and the Id," Freud notes that this substitution within the ego "makes an essential contribution towards building up what is called its 'character.'"[28] What first is characterized as unsuccessful and leading toward a dysfunctional melancholia is reformulated as constitutive of the healthy modern subject.

A parallel approach can help us understand the Janus-faced nature of modernist empathy, as well as reframe the movement between subject positions in ethical terms. The manifestation of modernist empathy that we see in *The Waste Land* neither assumes that there is something inherently laudatory or ethical about the act of occupying another perspective (as we often assume in our discourse today), nor suggests the inverse – that a shift of perspective is only an act of self-gratification or the colonization of another. Stephen Spender, however, found Eliot's presentation of other minds and voices troubling; he brings up the pub scene in the second section of *The Waste Land*, "A Game of Chess," as an example of a conversation that "does not objectively present the people it describes; it merely exists in the mind of the reader, who is made to imagine that he is sharing the life of the people. But what he is really seeing and hearing is a part of his own mind."[29] This brings us back to the focus on melting in the early poems, where perspectives blend and blur; to Spender, the voices in the pub seem part of the reader, rather than of their speaker, and his critique reveals the problem of other minds that Eliot insists upon so vigorously in *The Waste Land*. We switch abruptly from the poetic voice, which has just intoned "And we shall play a game of chess, / Pressing lidless eyes and waiting for a knock upon the door" (*Collected Poems*, 58), and into the gossipy voice of the pub-goer recounting a conversation: "He's been in the army four years, he wants a good time, / And if you don't give it him, there's others will, I said. / Oh is there, she said. Something o' that, I said" (58). In making this shift, Eliot allows us to question the social valences of perspective-taking; indeed, this reliance on different voices is both a symptom of and an answer to the problem of how we can imagine others.[30]

First and foremost, Eliot's multilayered approach to voice allows for a complex negotiation between perspectives. *The Waste Land* is a document that, unlike many other poems (whether by Eliot or others), has been defined by the voices that have gone into its making and the parts that have been lost. From its early stages it was characterized by literal shifts in voice – Eliot's, Pound's, and Vivienne Eliot's – visible on the draft pages in the comments, marginalia, and marks upon the text itself. As Michael Levenson argues in his classic reading from *A Genealogy of Modernism*, Eliot's vision of poetic creation "involves selection, suppression, control, and order,"[31] and we can see this aesthetic of selection in Eliot's process of culling in *The Waste Land*. Such suppression and control provide a counterbalance to the messiness of multi-editorship. We also cannot ignore the original title of the poem, "He Do the Police in Different Voices," which references the unexpectedly dramatic abilities of the young Sloppy in Dickens's *Our Mutual Friend*, who is indispensable to his elderly guardian and employer because of his ability, as he reads her the newspaper, to "do the police in different voices."[32] From its inception, therefore, the poem is framed as an example of this ability to *perform* other voices. Whether or not this focus on performance behind *The Waste Land* illuminates a way to enter other perspectives, however, is something that remains up for debate over the course of the poem.

A small set of changes between the drafts available in the facsimile manuscript and the final published versions points to Eliot's refinement of how he would control and perform these voices in the poem. Madam Sosostris, the "famous clairvoyante," seems both charlatan and seer; the poem mockingly calls her both "the wisest woman in Europe" (*Collected Poems*, 54) and a consummate businesswoman, who quickly switches out of her prophetic mood, with its visions of the Hanged Man and circling crowds, to a business mode, where she notes that "I bring the horoscope myself, / One must be so careful these days" (54). As a clairvoyant, she is an example of someone who can see, perhaps more "clearly," in ways that are obscure to the rest of us. Her visions bear a weight in the poem, for she is our first introduction to the drowned Phoenician Sailor, whom she here identifies with the listener and to whom she attaches a parenthetical remark: "(Those are the pearls that were his eyes. Look!)" (*Waste Land Facsimile*, 7). Eliot cared about this line, for though Pound crossed it out, Eliot kept it in, which suggests that the prophetic voice is key here. Yet the most interesting revision in terms of a shifting point of view involves a later parenthetical from that same stanza that Eliot did excise: "(I John saw these things, and heard them)" (*Waste Land Facsimile*, 9). This moment is difficult to parse: are we hearing the voice of the unnamed interlocutor with Madame Sosostris, or the voice of the poet, or are we hearing one of the dead figures Madame Sosostris has herself entered into, one who has seen the crowds circling? The perspective is unclear, though the effect is blunt: we are thrust out of our comfortable focalizing standpoint and into one that intrudes upon the scene in an uncomfortable way; we become *too* aware of this shift in perspective. Eliot took out this line in the published version, but its presence in the drafts shows how much the question of how and whether we can actually see and enter into other points of view was central to the poem from its inception.

The textual tapestry of always-occluded perspectives emerges even more in "A Game of Chess," the second part of *The Waste Land*, and it is particularly ripe for an exploration of voicing, as Spender made clear. Tim Dean notes that "impersonation may represent a way to inhabit other existences – a way to transform oneself by becoming possessed by others":[33] the kind of act that we have been primed for by Madame Sosostris, and one that points to the uncanny nature of such movements into other perspectives. While this formulation sets up a dynamic that is quite different from empathy – we don't equate feeling *with* someone as being *possessed by* them – Eliot productively blurs the line between these two methods of how to step outside an isolated, autonomous, individual viewpoint. The scene is set in a room that provides access to the intimacy of the boudoir – the woman's chair seems to be at a dressing table, covered with her jewel boxes and "vials of ivory and colored glass" (*Collected Poems*, 56) that infuse the air with their "strange synthetic perfumes" (56) – and the man's appearance is signaled by the sounds of "Footsteps shuffled on the stair" (57). Already the poem reveals an elaborate sense of formality and artifice. The danger of intimacy is foretold in the picture on the wall of the rape of Philomel.

Yet in the conversation that follows, the poem illustrates what Marshall Brown called the "essential mystery of the lyric," which is "its way of being of two minds."[34] Eliot reworks this aspect of lyric by emphasizing how these two minds are barely able to occupy the same physical space of the poem, let alone the same mental space. Throughout the first long scene-setting stanza, Eliot's lines, though changing between tetrameter and pentameter, manifest a certain rhythmic consistency, a regularity that recalls the conversational tone of blank verse (which Pound critiqued in his marginal comments as "Too tum-pum at a stretch" and "too penty" [*Waste Land Facsimile*, 11]). This poetic regularity is brought to a climax in the final four lines of the stanza:

> Footsteps shuffled on the stair.
> Under the firelight, under her brush, her hair
> Spread out in fiery points
> Glowed into words, then would be savagely still.
>
> (*Collected Poems*, 57)

In the manuscript Eliot had started with two rhyming couplets for the final four lines, with the third line above originally written as "Spread out in little fiery points of will" – a line Pound critiqued as a "dogmatic deduction but wobbly as well" (*Waste Land Facsimile*, 11). With the revision of that line, Eliot changed not just the meaning, but also the rhyme; the expectation of a second rhyming couplet, created by the first, is immediately confounded. Indeed, "Spread out into fiery points" has no end punctuation, yet the enjambment with "Glowed into words" is jarring; we expect a pause between "points" and "Glowed," for they act like phrases in a list, rather than a continuous sentence. The missing words, the missing rhyme – these create a space in the text that is further emphasized by the unexpected shift into the conditional verb form; we are moving from the realm of past tense to that of possibility, but that possibility is followed by the almost oxymoronic "savagely still," which mirrors the "stumps of time" and the brutal silencing of Philomel referenced in the lines above. The stilling of words – a gesture to a present absence, just as the "Jug Jug" of Philomel creates its own marker of the words that are no longer voiced – points to the fragility of spoken words, as well as to the way that they linger even in the spots of silence and inarticulate sound.

With Eliot's introduction of speech, we enter into a moment in which the poem becomes multiply voiced, a movement into the subjective realm so often seen as the defining element of the lyric. We get two voices: the first is given quotation marks that help us see it as speech that is heard, not simply the traditional "overheard" voice of the lyric.[35] Counterpointed with this clearly spoken voice is another, not marked by the quotation marks, that seems to respond to the first voice, though we are not sure if it is the metaphorical voice of the poem that reveals itself only to the reader, or if the voice is engaging in actual conversation. Is it heard or overheard? This ambiguity creates some of the challenging dynamics in this section, for the relationship between the two voices – the lyric enunciation and the narrated character enunciation – creates a tension in how we read and hear these lines. Here are what Marshall Brown calls the "two voices" of the lyric made literal and apparent;[36] indeed, there is a sense of schizophrenia in the shifts between the minds, since the voices shift from hysterical to depressive. We are no longer in the surface conversation of the superficial but charming world of the "conversation galante" that Eliot explored in early poems, from "Portrait of a Lady" to his poem named "Conversation Galante" itself. Instead we are echoing those interactions between speaker and woman, with the underlying hysteria and despair laid bare.[37] The first stanza of speech presents the essentials for meaningful engagement:

> "My nerves are bad to-night. Yes, bad. Stay with me.
> 'Speak to me. Why do you never speak? Speak.
> 'What are you thinking of? What thinking? What?
> 'I never know what you are thinking. Think." (*Collected Poems*, 57)

Stay. Speak. Think. These are three basic prerequisites for connection: presence, conversation, and thoughtful engagement. While the hysterical speaker has the order somewhat off (putting speaking before thinking), the imperative of these lines is clear: this is someone who is looking for, hoping for, demanding a kind of meaningful connection. Immediately, however, we realize that the possibilities for conversation between these two voices, not to mention for empathetic engagement, are slim, not only because it is unclear whether the "response" of the second voice is actually voiced and heard by anyone other than the reader, but also because the thought that the voice expresses reveals a mind far away from the room filled with perfumes, focused instead on the horrors of a World War I trench, the "rats' alley / Where the dead men lost their bones" (57). The reader engages in a delicate balancing act between the immersion in the intimate thoughts of the (possibly silent) second person and the voiced thoughts of the woman; the very possibility of the second person's silence makes the reader's insight into the thoughts all the more moving and personal – perhaps we know more than the woman at the dressing table about what the other might think, for she does not seem to respond to the haunting response to her question about what he is thinking, instead asking another question: "What is that noise?" (57). Yet this also suggests a frightening impenetrability within the scene; we are witness to a failed act of communication and connection; the attempt of the woman to "know" her companion's thoughts is thwarted not only by his remove, but also by her distraction and inability to settle and focus on the other person. Noises, irritation at being unanswered, worries about what to do with life – these hinder her understanding; she can't stand in his shoes because she is too unsettled in her own.

This lost attempt to connect creates some of its pathos, perhaps, because the world of the speakers is familiar to Eliot; he is writing the scene about a class and a couple that reflect his own experiences. This is not the case in the pub scene that follows in "A Game of Chess," though the dynamic is curiously similar: we see conversations that are in fact not conversations; the scene in the drawing room is the one-sided questioning by the woman, met by the seemingly unvoiced thoughts of the second person; the conversation in the pub is a monologue account of a conversation – one voice dominates both sides – except for the conversation-ending interjection of "HURRY UP PLEASE ITS TIME" (*Collected Poems*, 58). Yet perhaps it is because the verses in the pub scene do not present a thinking mind, but only a speaking voice, that Spender criticizes this section, saying that the "psychology of his people is . . . crude," for they are "all part of the world of *things.*"[38] The problem may be that Eliot's use of voices animates subjects who have been objectified, which does not allow for empathy with them. "A Game of Chess" reveals the kinds of damage that the perspective-taking of the poetic voice can do, owing in part to its uncanny power to simultaneously objectify and animate.

With the third section, "The Fire Sermon," we reach the most overt example in the poem of the empathetic imagination, as well as of the transformation of both body and mind caused by entering into another perspective. Tiresias, the figure who has attracted the most attention in the poem because of Eliot's note describing him as the central personage, provides the template for the toll exacted by perspective-taking. He has lived as both man and woman, and now seems doomed to have "perceived the scene, and foretold the rest" (*Collected Poems*, 61) – a kind of second sight that far surpasses that of Madame Sosostris, both in its understanding of the other and in its infliction of trauma on the perceiving body and mind. Tiresias, who has "foresuffered all" (62), now suffers through the scene of sexual indifference and aggression – yet his pain is blunted, and he seems more weary and inured than traumatized by viewing the assault on the typist. The class and gender complexities of empathetic imagining begin to emerge. His dual-sex body exemplifies the two perspectives that have melted into each other (indeed, his "wrinkled female dugs" suggest a general melting of the body); the scene then moves to the liquid space of the river that "sweats / Oil and tar" (63) and shows the melting act of sex in one of the boats. Yet, as A. David Moody emphasizes, Tiresias is oddly, disturbingly, without feeling; he seems to view the typist and the "young man carbuncular" (60) impassively, as if he truly takes on the mechanistic perspective that is implied by the first metaphor of the section, where he is "throbbing between two lives" like a "taxi throbbing" (60). He functions as the apotheosis of the poet's perspective, able to move fluidly between the perspectives and achieve the kind of omniscience that might seem more imagined than lived. In his lack of feeling, in his ability to unite the perspectives without actually feeling their pain, he serves, in Moody's words, as "the final expression of the poet's anti-self" because, "from the point of view of poetic life, which is immediate feeling, Tiresias means death" – Tiresias is only dissociated, distanced perspective, not immediate feeling.[39] The stakes of perspective-taking come to the fore: Tiresias' empathetic vision can exist only within a subject devoid of feeling.

Yet we should push Moody's assertion further; if there is a disassociation from sensibility required or enabled by perspective-taking, how does that get manifested within the lyric or by the lyric subject? Rather than seeing Tiresias' impassive double vision as antipoetic, we might think about how *The Waste Land* offers a particular way of thinking about the subjective mimesis of the lyric: it reflects the experience of the individual subject, but it is a modern subject, who is singularly disassociated from him or herself. Rather than being a presentation of poetic death because of the absence of feeling, Eliot's Tiresias voices one of the central difficulties of the subject who is split, who can see the split, and who cannot see how to reconcile it.

In the final section, "What the Thunder Said," we go from the blurred boundaries of a world that seems too fluid to a space that has been sucked of all moisture; the ambiguous boundaries are the result of the crumbling of this dusty landscape. Here we are confronted with an arid "wasteland" landscape, a scene of barrenness akin to the world of the Western Front ("After the agony in stony places / The shouting and the crying / Prison

and palace and reverberation / Of thunder of spring over distant mountain" [*Collected Poems*, 66]). The thunder intervenes with its reverberating
"DA," – which the speaker then translates into a set of moral and ethical
imperatives. Rules and boundaries enter into this desiccated scene, and
they provide the possibility of coherence and order.

If we return to the teachings of Leibniz's monadology in which, as
Daniel Tiffany puts it, "perception is substance,"[40] the interpreted words
of the voice of the thunder begin to embody not just a prescription for how
one should live, but also an enactment – as the footnote suggests, what
Tiresias sees becomes the substance of the poem. The "DA" of the thunder
is rendered into words; the poet transforms these words into the ordering
structure for the poem, a structure based on interpretation *as* the substance
and requiring an explanatory note, which gives Eliot's translation of the
terms and describes the fable of the Thunder. We have, in fact, returned to
Leibniz, who also argued for the simultaneous obscuring and "expressive"
aspects of language: "The very name of any thing will be the key to all that
could be reasonably said or thought about it or done with it."[41] Eliot seems
to take up this idea in his reference to a story that is, in its essence, about the
way that humans engage in language-making when confronted with
sound. We can see this productive nature of language in the "DA" of the
thunder (*Collected Poems*, 68); within that one sound is contained a system
of Indic philosophy and a key to how to interpret and live. The DA gives us
three words – *datta, dayadhvam*, and *damyata* – which Eliot translates in
his notes to the poem as "give," "sympathize," and "control," in accordance
with the Sanskrit story from which he drew. I have written elsewhere that
this middle term is a sign that, even in this stony and unforgiving land that
seems to offer little hope of community and continuance, it is still necessary to try to stand outside one's own perspective.[42] Reading those three
commands in the context of Leibniz's assertion, however, brings out
another layer. If the "DA" contains all three of those dictums for how to
live one's life, then we have to think about giving, sympathizing, and
controlling as elements that not only coexist, but also that depend on
each other.

This raises the question of what this triad might reveal about Eliot's
vision of empathy.[43] The "*Datta*" presents a giving that resembles
a sacrifice of the self: "blood shaking my heart / The awful daring of
a moment's surrender / Which an age of prudence can never retract"
(*Collected Poems*, 68) – a dangerous act of breaking free from convention
and code that comes from the heart, that organ of desire and emotion.
The poem describes a giving that is striking for its physicality, but it is the

physical draining of the self that allows a "we" to exist: "By this, and this only, we have existed" (68). The self shatters here in ways that allow for a move from "I" to "we" – and yet, since the experience does not end with just this imperative, the surrender of the self does not lead to a thanatological dissolution into nonexistence. Yet this image recalls the bloodied Saint Narcissus who sacrifices his body in his attempt to become one with others; we return to the self-destructive nature of attempting to reach outside the boundaries of the self.

Similarly, the control implied by "*Damyata*" (*Collected Poems*, 69) has several connections to the perspectival shifts that we associate with empathy, despite the apparent discordance between control, which suggests a dominant and directing perspective, and empathy, which we think of as an opening up and a relinquishing of control. The description of control in these lines articulates this tension between choice and coercion:

> *Damyata*: The boat responded
> Gaily, to the hand expert with sail and oar
> The sea was calm, your heart would have responded
> Gaily, when invited, beating obedient
> To controlling hands   (69)

The repetition of "Gaily," emphasized by its placement at the beginning of two lines, yet also distanced from its corresponding verb, "responded" (itself a repeated word), illuminates the strain: the object of this control is acted upon and responds, and we must wait for the time it takes to move from one line to the next to learn that the response seems willing, happy. This beat of time is enough to make the "Gaily" seem less persuasive, more wishful; the state is further emphasized by the change in tense between the first and the second response: we go from the active past tense of "responded" to the conditional past of "would have responded." The translation of the metaphors – from sailor to lover, from boat to heart – requires a shift into a conditional space that can only be imagined, like the move into another perspective. Thus, control is desired, but not enacted; the willingness of the heart is hoped for, not experienced.

In between these two moments – one of which is characterized by the actual daring of the moment of surrender, the gift of the self and the body, and the other of which exemplifies the hoped-for yet unachieved control – we have that middle term, "*Dayadhvam*." Sympathy here is defined by imprisonment: the lines describe a state in which we are trapped, the key having turned "once only" (68) – therefore remaining in a locked position. It is within the confines of our mind that we feel, the lines suggest, most solitary and confined: "We think of the key, each in his prison / Thinking of the key, each confirms a prison / Only at nightfall" (69). In these successive moments of the surrender of the heart (*datta*), the caging of the mind (which paradoxically makes us realize the existence of other minds – *dayadhvam*), and the wished-for responsiveness of the other's heart (*damyata*), we shift from heart to mind to heart again. The mind makes us realize our solitude, and yet it also blunts the rough desiring and controlling power of the states of *datta* and *damyata*.

The final lines of the poem portray the difficulty and the potential of perspective-taking:

> London Bridge is falling down falling down falling down
> *Poi s'ascose nel foco che gli affina*
> *Quando fiam uti chelidon* – O swallow swallow
> *Le Prince d'Aquitaine à la tour abolie*
> These fragments I have shored against my ruins
> Why then Ile fit you. Hieronymo's mad againe.
> Datta. Dayadhvam. Damyata.
> Shantih shantih shantih (69)

The potential lies in the opportunity to make meaning on a larger scale: by escaping the solipsistic self – that self seemingly stuck, "each in his prison / Thinking of the key, each confirms a prison" – Eliot suggests the possibility of entering into a more inclusive perspective. The ending is thus a version of what Levenson described as the poem's method of development, which works "not by resolving conflicts but by enlarging contexts ... by widening."[44] The fragments in the last stanza move from one scene of grief and absence to the next: from the protocultural level of the nursery rhyme (London Bridge) to Dante's *Purgatorio* ("*Poi s'ascose nel foco che gli affina*"); from Greek myth (the swallow in the myth of Philomela) to the Prince of Aquitaine; and, finally, to the Renaissance tower of Babel ("Why then Ile fit you") in Thomas Kyd's play. The return of the "Datta. Dayadhvam. Damyata" in the penultimate line does not present a joyful triumph of what giving, sympathizing, and controlling will lead to, but may posit a kind of sober success. Fragmentation in and of itself suggests an attempt to transcend the solipsistic self, and this seems both necessary and potentially productive. We are left with a modernist empathy that, uncertain of the possibility of escaping a sense of absence, loss, or alienation even when occupying other perspectives, still seems ultimately committed to embracing and following through with this move into others. The turn to the "peace that passeth understanding" in the final line – Eliot's gloss of "Shantih" – suggests that some resolution within a state of unknowing may be the ultimate end.

Four Quartets **and Transcendent Empathy**

Yet Eliot did not stop thinking about the question of subject–object relationships and perspective-taking after *The Waste Land*; the refrain from *Four Quartets* that "in my beginning is my end" (*Collected Poems*, 184) resonates, since we see in this poem cycle a return to Eliot's early interest in Leibniz – in particular, in his vision of a unifying monadic experience arrived at through, and only through, God. God and religion come back in Eliot's exploration of perspective-taking and the empathetic imagination, and this time Eliot moves away from a sense of inevitable fragmentation and dispersal and toward a vision of a unifying transcendent perspective. While I focused on melting as an analogy for the elegiac empathetic experience in *The Waste Land* and other early poems, the more appropriate term in Eliot's later work, I would argue, is "transcendence." Unlike melting, which describes a chemical and a physical transformation, transcendence implies a movement in space – though often an immaterial space. In the Oxford English Dictionary definition, transcendence is defined as a "surmounting or rising above"; when the term refers to "the Deity," it involves "being above and independent of the universe."[45] Transcendence, according to Eliot's reading of Bradley, involves a shift, a *transition* between points of view; it is, in many ways, closely connected with our ideas of empathy and perspective-taking, though it does not deal with the aftermath of such a transition – what happens when you have changed points of view. Transcendence renders more problematic, as well, the question of the *place* of empathetic experience, for it implies a shift into a more metaphysical form of perspective-taking. This raises a question in Eliot's later poetry about where empathy exists when an individual attempts to transcend his particularities in service of a Christian vision.

A very short poem Eliot considered publishing alongside *The Waste Land* provides an interesting transition between these two terms, directly referencing melting within a framework defined by ideas of transcendence. Not yet an official Anglican – the conversion did not occur until 1927, though the process leading up to it took place over many years – Eliot is still concerned with whether Leibniz's God or Bradley's "Absolute"

provides a satisfying answer to the question of whether we can break free
from our isolated singular perspectives. He writes:

> I am the Resurrection and the Life
> I am the things that stay, and those that flow.
> I am the husband and the wife
> And the victim and the sacrificial knife
> I am the fire, and the butter also.   (*Waste Land Facsimile*, III)

This voicing of God's words, in which the god is both presence and
absence, life and death (and life through death), points to the complexity
of trying to narrate another perspective, and to a seeming ability to override
that complexity through the figure of God. Yet the inherently opposing
nature of the identities presented in the poem – the pairing of the victim
and the sacrificial knife is only the most overt of the five – suggests the
tension that can emerge. Like Tiresias with his experience of both male and
female visions, the voice of this God emphasizes the destructive nature of
this sort of double vision: the poem moves from opposing forces that carry
no positive or negative valence to, just after the line about "the husband
and the wife," binaries that do suggest the trauma of movement between
these poles. The final line, "I am the fire, and the butter also," has brought
us back to melting from what we might consider the ultimate act of
transcendence in the first line – the Resurrection. The butter will change
shape and nature upon contact with the fire; it will melt, and we can see the
tension and difference between the vision of sacrifice as melting versus as
transcendence.

   This poem, therefore, balances uncomfortably between these two different ideas of what it might mean, when approaching the world from
a Christian perspective, to move from one point of view, one state, to
another. The first lines suggest that instead of seeing sacrifice as a shift
from being into nothingness, we must think of the Resurrection: it is
a transcendence, in the Bradleyian style, between points of view. As noted
earlier, Eliot foregrounds how the "transition from one point of view to
another" (*Complete Prose I*, 468) defines Bradley's idea of transcendence,
closely connecting it, therefore, to the idea of empathy as a passage between
points of view. The question is, however, whether Eliot's later poem, *Four
Quartets*, explores not only religious belief (its first and foremost goal, as John
Whittier-Ferguson reminds us[46]), but also the empathetic imagination.
In other words, how does empathy connect to religious experience?

   In the short "I am the Resurrection and the Life," Eliot cannot yet rest
easily with transcendence. While melting implies a blurring of boundaries

between two entities on an extreme level – both molecular and tangible – transcendence suggests entrance into a realm outside of – above, in fact – the original state. Transcendence implies an original starting point, and the question that lingers is whether one could, or would want to, return to the origin, especially given the caveat in Bradley's vision of the shifts between points of view as leading to the erasure of the starting point: the original point of view will have "ceased to exist" (*Complete Prose I*, 175). Ultimately this movement suggests, I will argue, how empathy is not a term that makes sense in Eliot's later world of faith. This is not to say that empathy does not play a central role in both practices and theories of religious experience, but instead that the idea of the individual subject in relation to an "other" loses its resonance when the goal is union with God, thereby rendering the question of perspective-taking and movements outside the solipsistic self almost moot in the face of the "Christian pilgrimage"[47] that is the work of the *Quartets*.

At first it may seem that Eliot is all about perspective-taking on even a literal level, for the poem consistently situates us in specific geographies and places. While not concerned with cartography in the same way as Hardy or Ford, Eliot's poem takes us on a journey from "Burnt Norton," the English country house that Eliot had visited with his longtime friend and almost lover, Emily Hale, in the early 1930s; to "East Coker," the small English town that had housed some of Eliot's ancestors; to "The Dry Salvages," which Eliot takes the time to identify at the start of the poem, as the "small group of rocks, with a beacon, off the N.E. coast of Cape Ann, Massachusetts" (*Collected Poems*, 192); and finally to "Little Gidding," a small town in southeast England known for its church. All four poems are eminently located and locatable in a topography made meaningful by Eliot's personal and ancestral histories. The journey that Eliot proposes starts on the ground; we must place ourselves in the garden, in the open field, next to the ocean, or on the path to the church. The movement to and between these spaces both enables and requires acts of pilgrimage; to be a pilgrim is to be displaced, a wanderer – to be rooted no longer in one viewpoint. The pilgrimage requires a journey and, more specifically, a journey that is an act of devotion that brings you to some better, blessed (and inevitably changed) state. We can see it as performing the movement toward transcendence that Eliot has gestured to in his early writings as part of the necessary project of reaching outside one's own perspective. So far, therefore, it seems that these poems propose acts of perspective-taking on these more literal, geographic levels.

Yet the literal and material spaces, while they may provide the granular level of detail from which this poem starts, are not the terrain that Eliot is interested in traversing now; indeed, they quickly merge into abstraction: the souls from "Burnt Norton" Part III, which are "Driven on the wind that sweeps the gloomy hills of London, / Hampstead and Clerkenwell, Campden and Putney, / Highgate, Primrose and Ludgate" do not settle in any of these mappable terrains, but instead move into the "world of perpetual solitude / World not world, but that which is not world" (*Collected Poems*, 180–181). Similarly, one of the few moments where empathy seems to come up – in the second section of "The Dry Salvages," as part of an explanation about the backward glance of memory – is quickly transformed from the act of understanding another's suffering to a look that reveals the universal "primitive terror" or "moments of agony" (195). This agony is part of a larger pattern, Eliot says, and provides our way into an understanding of time and the eternal that we cannot get from our own experiences and our own pain. He elaborates: this agony, like "past experience revived in the meaning / Is not the experience of one life only / But of many generations" (195). The moments of terror are

> . . . likewise permanent
> With such permanence as time has. We appreciate this better
> In the agony of others, nearly experienced,
> Involving ourselves, than our own.
> For our own past is covered by the currents of action,
> But the torment of others remains an experience
> Unqualified, unworn by subsequent attrition.   (195–196)

Eliot points to the apprehension of a meaning and an understanding that can be accessed only if we stop clinging to a narrative of progress and a belief in chronology, and instead look for an underlying pattern – one of those unchanging patterns that reveal the possibility that the end and the beginning are one and the same. With the descriptor "nearly experienced," Eliot pushes us to imagine a strange proximity – it is through the recognition of the other's suffering that we can most closely understand the permanence and the pattern; our own moments of pain become blurred and attenuated by the proliferation of events, but if we can look at the suffering of others, we understand how "the agony abides" (196) in ways that transcend the individual. We arrive at the paradox that connects to the ethical challenge and imperative at the heart of occupying another perspective: it is only through the experience of others that we may come to know ourselves, for it is this very experience that reveals how unknown to ourselves we are.

Our first response might be to see this as a moment where Eliot suggests that empathy can be mobilized through seeing the suffering of another.

We could describe this possibility in terms used by Judith Butler when she reflects on Emmanuel Levinas's discussion of an encounter with the face of the other: the face for Levinas, Butler explains, stands as "the wordless vocalization of suffering"[48] that brings us into awareness of the need to protect the other, even as it also reveals the possibility of harming the other. We are in the realm of God's commandment, "Thou shalt not kill," because the face here "bespeaks an agony, an injurability, at the same time that it bespeaks a divine prohibition against killing" (Butler, 135). Yet this moment of understanding in Eliot's poem is useful because it allows us a full experience of an other from which we can return, enriched by a greater understanding, to the self. Nor does it do what I have argued is characteristic of modernist empathy, and what we can see so clearly in Eliot's earlier poetry; it does not challenge our idea of the autonomy of the individual subject and reveal the loss that follows from every attempt at empathy, as well as the trauma to the perspective of both subject and object. The individual subject is not of interest to Eliot here; the question of return to an autonomous subjectivity is not at stake in the movement toward greater faith. Transcendence from one's particular perspective in this case means a recognition that the starting point is always part of that larger pattern – that "the future is a faded song" (*Collected Poems*, 196), as the speaker muses just a few lines later at the start of Part III. The pain of others recalls to us the omnipresence of that node of pain in our own experience. This seems far from the prison of the self – which can be escaped, but only to recognize the fragmentation that will ensue – that was manifested in Eliot's earlier poetry; instead, there is a stability to the structure Eliot proposes here, a world in which past and future no longer operate on a chronological continuum, where the mind must not think of the "fruit of action" (197), but instead of the state in which "right action is freedom / From past and future also" (199).

We could get at this change from another angle: as Whittier-Ferguson notes, by the 1930s and '40s, "what the first person denominates ... is, theologically, simply not very important to Eliot."[49] Moody concurs that, for Eliot at this point, understanding the perspective of others and sharing their experience is not about interpersonal connection: "There is no sense of the value of its being a shared experience, or one suffered in common with other men in other times."[50] Instead, he notes, when "the poet is at one with others, then it is only in the universal."[51] In an anecdote recalled by Stephen Spender, Eliot says that belief and acts of belief, like prayer, are attempts to think outside and be outside the self. When asked by Leonard and Virginia Woolf, "What are your feelings when you pray?," Eliot tells them it is "the attempt to concentrate, to forget self, and to attain union with God. The striving."[52] This "striving" that defines prayer, that defines union with the universal – with God – is a present participle; it is not an action that ends, nor one that can be contained in any neat chronology. If we return to the Liebnizian understanding of God as the point of unification of perspectives, then we can see this attempt to attain union as not the shift in perspectives that is definitive of empathy, but instead a movement into a state in which all perspectives are contained. There is no other in this shift, and therefore no movement that resembles empathetic imagining.

This movement outside the self requires immense concentration and a desire to merge with the universal that is God. But other moments seem to point to a more moderate form of engagement – moments when the poem addresses a "you" and we have a sense, as Whittier-Ferguson notes, that we "have more in common with one another than we might have thought."[53] In the second poem of the cycle, "East Coker," the poetic address blurs the boundaries of not only perception but also time: the poem addresses a "you" who observes men and women "daunsinge" (*Collected Poems*, 185). Yet the use of the archaic spelling and quotation from Eliot's ancestor, Sir Thomas Elyot,[54] already distances us from the apparent grammatical invitation to intimacy achieved by the "you." Even this implicit dropping of the veil, however, is not enough; the poem warns us that we can only watch from a distance: "If you do not come too close, if you do not come too close," the poem cautions (184). Thus, there is a paradoxical invitation and warning, entrance and barrier, indicating both the necessity and the complication of trying to let another perceiving subject in.

Four Quartets is about an absence with which we must all live as beings unable ever to merge fully with the Christian God. Despite offering a template for a future-focused elegy (mourning the loss of what will never come), *Four Quartets* avoids the elegiac tone that so thoroughly defined *The Waste Land*. The reasons for this can be found, I think, in the poem's vision of a circular, encapsulating sense of time. We might first see this in the musical prosody of the poem, which leans heavily on what Harvey Gross and Robert McDowell describe as "syntactical music" that "achieves qualities common to both music and poetry – the feelings of arrest and motion, of beginnings and endings, of striving and stillness."[55] This emerges most clearly in the repetitions – of words, phrases, and images – that pattern the sections; the focus on the enigmatic opening to "Burnt Norton" is a case in point: while the section gestures to the echoes of past moments that resonate in the mind, with its repetition of phrases about time, past, present, and future, and with its resolution on the "one end, which is always present," the tone escapes the elegiac, even when revolving around what has been lost. Similarly, "East Coker" begins with the proclamation, "In my beginning is my end" (*Collected Poems*, 184), and ends with its mirror image: "In my end is my beginning" (191). As reflection and repetition become the central theme in this section, we might ask if it is possible to have elegy without a linear chronology. We find ourselves deep into the essential meaning of the resurrection of Christ, where sacrifice becomes celebrated, rather than mourned, because the resurrection leads to an eternal presence in the face of absence.

Does this suggest a state not only beyond empathy, but also beyond elegy – a state in which there is ultimately no loss, since we are outside of a normal accounting of time? Loss depends on temporality; it cannot be charted without it, so if the beginning and the end are continuously present, there is no absence at all. And yet there may also be a near constant state of loss or feeling of melancholia, for there is never the possibility to move beyond some absence or trauma; we are always reliving, always aware of the circle around which we are turning. Our losses and traumas may, however, be in service of a larger good; as Eliot writes at the end of his 1939 essay "The Idea of a Christian Society," we must "recover the sense of religious fear, so that it may be overcome by religious hope" (*Selected Prose*, 291). Out of fear, then, comes hope; out of loss may come a sense of universal connection. Eliot, at the end, and despite his earlier resistance to the same movement in Leibniz and Bradley, arrives at a vision of overall harmony that encompasses and reconciles individual experiences of suffering and loss.

CHAPTER 5

Uncanny Empathy
Woolf's Half-Life of Objects

In "Modern Fiction," Virginia Woolf condemns the Edwardians H. G. Wells, Arnold Bennett, and John Galsworthy as "materialists" who "spend immense skill and immense industry making the trivial and the transitory appear the true and the enduring."[1] Here, as well as in other essays such as "Mr. Bennett and Mrs. Brown," she emphasizes the misguided attention that the Edwardians give to the material world, whether it emerges in Galsworthy's transformation of a character into a material object (Mrs. Brown, in Woolf's anecdote, would become in Galsworthy's story simply "a pot broken on the wheel and thrown into the corner"), or in Bennett's exhaustive consideration of every element of the setting, where he "would observe every detail with immense care," from the advertisements to Mrs. Brown's gloves.[2] In contrast, she writes, modern writers are interested in and strive to write about "the dark places of psychology" ("Modern Fiction," 162). She regards the Russian novelists in particular as models for her British contemporaries, for they have what she calls "an understanding of the soul and heart" and "sympathy for the sufferings of others" (163). Yet, as Woolf continues, though the Russians provide a version of what modern writers hope to create, they lack the humor and sense of contrariness that she sees throughout English fiction.

Part of Woolf's project, I will argue here, is to achieve this "Russian" ability to expose the hearts and souls of her characters, but without what she terms the "hopeless interrogation" and focus on suffering that she sees in their writing. This project is fraught, and Woolf grapples in early and later works with both the idea of empathy (getting an "understanding of the soul and heart") and the kinds of loss and suffering that one encounters and courts when searching for this sort of understanding. In the first part of the chapter I examine her early novel *Jacob's Room* (1922) and argue that, in this search, Woolf often returns to the object world that surrounds her characters, but in ways that try to reach beyond the "materialism" with which she labels the scapegoat Edwardians in her essays. Instead, Woolf focuses on what I'll call the half-life of the objects, a phrase that both connotes the partial life these objects seem to contain and emphasizes how they are defined by loss – by past owners, past uses, past meanings – and, like memory, carry the traces of the past in ways that inexorably fade. These saturated objects become, with their personified and surrogate status, objects of empathy – or, more precisely, objectified versions of empathetic imagining – that may offer the only way to understand the perspectives of the absent humans. These objects differ from those described by the Edwardians because they are not in service of setting a scene or articulating class differences; they are meant to do work that may be impossible but is yet critical for the writer who wants to reveal character, the work of accessing some essence of the object's user or owner. In doing so, the objects often enter into the realm of the Freudian uncanny, for they take on lives that challenge the autonomy and the authority of the subject.

It may sound, in the description above, as if Woolf is offering us a theory of object relations that is willfully blind to an object's role as mediator and an example of the hidden economic relations at work; is she instead, we might wonder, presenting a vision of a spiritualized object world in which the forces of production and the object's material origins are erased? Yet, because Woolf brings to the forefront the loss embedded in subject–object relations, as well as the essentially empty nature of object identification, I believe that in *Jacob's Room* Woolf asks us to interrogate our enshrinement of objects in order to reveal the way that they are gendered and classed. The critique changes in slight, though important ways, however, when Woolf is dealing with an art object, which we see her doing in *To the Lighthouse* (1927). Woolf's treatment of the art object, Lily Briscoe's painting – which figures so centrally in the book in general, and in "The Lighthouse" section in particular – recalls Walter Benjamin's discussion of the aura of art objects. Benjamin describes this aura as emerging from the accrued tradition of the work of art: "The uniqueness of a work of art is inseparable from its being imbedded in the fabric of tradition."[3] Benjamin's explanation usefully points to the messy outlines of such objects, with their web of connections to people, their blurred boundaries between those confused categories of "represented" and "real." A different kind of half-life is at work in *To the Lighthouse*, however – a half-life that points to the other lives this object illuminates, reveals, and also conceals. I say "conceals" because one of the lessons I take from both *Jacob's Room* and *To the Lighthouse* is the ultimate impossibility of ever escaping subjective experience, and therefore the impossibility of ever being able to see other than from a limited point of view. We will see a change in Woolf's

presentation of this problem of being stuck in our own subjective experience as we go from the shoes of *Jacob's Room* to the painting in *To the
Lighthouse* – a change from recognizing through "object empathy" the
futility of reaching epistemological certainty through perspective-taking,
to exploring a form of looking that, through its lack of an epistemological
imperative (the need to *know* something or someone), may offer another
way into knowing subjects and the world.

My choice of these two novels is not simply because in both Woolf
thinks about objects in interesting ways (although she does), nor because
they both question the possibility of understanding others, even as they
also pursue it as a necessary goal (though they do this as well). I also focus
on them because they are two of Woolf's most overt elegies – to Jacob, to
Mrs. Ramsay, and to the pre–World War I mindset – and, therefore,
provide a way to think about subject–object relationships within elegy.
The crucial relationship between object and mourning is an essential
element of the genre itself, where objects so often stand in for or remind
one of the lost beloved.

Lauren Shohet's analysis of Milton's *Lycidas*, a paradigmatic elegy, helps
to illuminate this relationship in Woolf as well. She posits that in *Lycidas*
Milton upended the previously "received notion of elegy as a profoundly
subjective genre," so that we can instead see two models of subject–object
dynamics at play in the poem: one is a "transcendent subjectivity" and the
other a "collective subjectivity."[4] As opposed to the transcendent subject
models, in which agency always returns to the subject in any subject–object
interaction, the collective models "show poetic subjectivity in constant
negotiation with objects: coming out of objects, returning to objects,
acquiring voice only when subject and object conjoin."[5] Woolf adopts
this collective version when she explores the possibilities of understanding
others when they are gone. As Ann Banfield argues, subject–object relationships are bound up with an elegiac impulse within what she describes
as the "monadology" of Woolf's fictional universe, "whose plurality of
possible worlds includes private points of space and time unobserved,
unoccupied by any subject."[6] Banfield describes how an "elegiac form" is
the "adequate response to a world revealed by science":[7] a world in which
objects may have existences separate from the perceiving subject, and yet
which we only know through that highly atomized and specific perception
as "sense-data."[8]

Woolf's ambivalence toward the interpretive and emotive weight that
objects can and do (and can't and don't) carry matches her highly ambivalent relationship with empathetic understanding. Two literary critics have

recently explored this ambivalence: Megan Hammond has argued that Woolf resists the project of "fellow feeling" as posited by Lipps, and that her late novels and political essays "work to further destabilize the already unstable project at play in literary modernism . . . troubling and sometimes even rejecting the kind of fellow feeling that aims primarily for 'feeling into', or 'feeling with', or oneness" (Hammond, 149). Hammond turns to the German phenomenologist Edmund Husserl and his former student Edith Stein in order to analyze this version of empathy that resists oneness and presents an awareness of the belated and distanced nature of all attempts to understand another's experience. Dora Zhang has likewise examined Woolf's intersubjective relationships, though she is interested in the question of representation – how "there is ultimately something about the what-it-is-like qualities of first-person experience that language fails to capture."[9] Zhang connects this focus of Woolf with the contemporaneous projects of William James and Bertrand Russell, in which they explore the connections between what Russell called "knowledge by acquaintance" and "knowledge by description,"[10] terms that can usefully help us think through the stakes of the empathetic imagination. Knowledge by acquaintance is direct and based on experience of the "thing," but it tells us only about that experience and does not give any knowledge of a truth or abstraction beyond it. Knowledge by description, on the other hand, is necessarily indirect and expressed "through inferences and generalization."[11] Knowledge by acquaintance cannot, in fact, be described or put into language, for it immediately loses its direct nature of knowing, and is no longer knowledge by acquaintance. This poses philosophical and literary questions about how to narrate a first-person experience and whether the immediacy of knowledge by acquaintance can ever be expressed in language.

Zhang's suggestive exploration of this dilemma hinges on Woolf's turn to deictic terms like "this." Zhang argues that such words are used both to gesture to and, on some level, to solve this problem of representation; I think they also help to illuminate the question of empathetic identification, as well as provide a reason why objects might be possible bridges between acquaintance and description. We can experience objects through direct sensory interaction with them; we can know other's experiences of objects only through their generalized description (and, therefore, according to Russell, we cannot actually "know" the objects seen by others at all). But one possibility emerges, suggested by Woolf's interest in a form of apperception – that through other people's descriptions of objects we might begin to know those people. In other words, even while it might be impossible to know some*thing*, some *object*, through a description of it, given the subjective nature of perception, we can begin to learn, through that description, something about the *viewer* – that some*one*. Thus, objects, as fiction writers have long acknowledged, enable character development; they enable knowledge of the other.

The writer Charles Baxter has made such a point in his essays about the craft of writing, contending that "objects become subjects" in fiction and thereby end up more expressive, at times, than the characters that surround and love them.[12] So often, Baxter notes, these uncannily alive objects are signposts of trauma, arguing, with humor, that "people in a traumatized state tend to love their furniture."[13] In the "Time Passes" section of *To the Lighthouse*, he claims, the house itself becomes the soul of the book in the face of the chilling trauma of World War I. While I spend more time on the art object – Lily's painting – his discussion of the summer house influences my reading not only of "Time Passes," but also of *Jacob's Room*.

These animated, half-alive objects suggest a further way to get past the binary of empathy versus abstraction that Worringer had made in his *Abstraction and Empathy* and that Hulme had then popularized in Britain; they offer the possibility of mobilizing empathy without, or beyond the boundaries of, a realist deployment of character.[14] Moreover, these half-alive objects reveal an abstracted empathy that does not involve the "self-enjoyment" that Theodor Lipps had seen as the center of the empathetic act.[15] Woolf's object-bound empathy thereby gives us a way to think about *empathy within abstraction* and also provides a template for understanding acts of perspective-taking beyond realist modes of representation. To understand this movement between the desire to feel into something and the simultaneous sense of alienation in the face of the world and the self, I will make use both of Freud and of the more traditional idea of the memento mori as a repository of loss and an aid to mourning. The empathy that we see in *Jacob's Room* and *To the Lighthouse* emerges from and reflects absence rather than self-enjoyment and psychic gain.

Before delving into Woolf's novels, I want to briefly look at one of her early short stories, "An Unwritten Novel," which she saw as an essential precursor of the book that followed it, *Jacob's Room*, and in which she briefly explicates the more subject-focused elements of empathy. This story, published in Woolf's volume of short stories, *Monday or Tuesday* (1921), verges on an exercise in entering into another's perspective. "Have I read you right?"[16] the narrator wonders, as she looks at the face of a woman sitting opposite her on a train. This is the premise of Woolf's essay "Mr. Bennett and Mrs. Brown," but here the movement into another's story is made into a physicalized melding of experience. After finally speaking with the woman, the narrator notes some of her idiosyncratic twitches and gestures and, without understanding why, begins to mirror and experience the same sort of things herself. The woman on the train "shuddered, and then she made the awkward angular movement that I had seen before, as if, after the spasm, some spot between the shoulders burnt or itched" (10), and then rubbed the window vigorously to try to remove a spot. Moments later, "Something impelled me to take my glove and rub the window ... And then the spasm went through me; I crooked my arm and plucked at the middle of my back" (10). The narrator attributes this involuntary assumption of the woman's movements and physical experiences to the woman having "communicated, shared her secret, passed her poison" (11). "Passed her poison": this phrase gets to the discomfort that such shifts in perspective and experience can bring, and the phrase brings the experience back to the body in very literal ways. We are in the realm of Vernon Lee's empathetic appreciator of art, who feels the rise of the column as a physiological sensation.

This physiological empathy leads, in this case, to an imaginative and emotional one; it is the precursor and the instigator of the creation of the narrative. For at this point the narrator enters into the fellow passenger's story, articulating it as if she was in the scene, experiencing the indignities of the woman's life herself. Strewn with dashes – which signify the hesitations and roadblocks facing the narrator as she tries to tell the story of the woman opposite, named Minnie Marsh by the narrator – "An Unwritten Novel" is about this very attempt to tell the story of another person, as much as it is about the imagined Minnie Marsh. The narrator's desire to get at the heart of the woman's experience seems futile; there is a "break" in the human eye that leaves you unable to grasp the essence of another, "so that when you've grasped the stem the butterfly's off" (15). Yet this urge to know another is so compelling that the narrator – perhaps everyone – is unable to escape it: "the eyes of others our prisons; their thoughts our cages" (15). The real jolt of the story, for both narrator and reader, comes when the woman finally disembarks and is met by her son; his existence topples the edifice of a lonely spinster life that the narrator had constructed.

The narrator remains undaunted after the initial shock of being so wrong about someone's story and, reinvigorated, returns to the project of story-making: "Wherever I go, mysterious figures, I see you, turning the corner, mothers and sons; you, you, you. I hasten, I follow" ("Unwritten Novel," 21). Yet the comment made here about the empathetic imagination *is* daunting, despite her jaunty nonchalance; we are left with an

experience that suggests the improbability of entering into and understanding another perspective. "An Unwritten Novel" reveals that we can
construct stories about others that turn out to be radically wrong in their
most fundamental premises. This is the act of storytelling that Woolf later
describes in "Mr. Bennett and Mrs. Brown" as the essential process of
character creation in novel writing; at that later moment she is less interested in whether the story gets it "right" or not, as long as it makes us see
something about the essence of the figure. The narrator here, too, pushes us
to view this need to enter into other consciousnesses as worthy of celebration and continuation; it is what connects her to the "adorable world" (21)
that she leaves us with in the final line. It is from this fundamentally
optimistic vision of empathetic imagination – that it is necessary to try to
shift perspectives, even when that shift is a failure – that we enter into
Woolf's decidedly less optimistic exploration in *Jacob's Room*.

Uncanny Letters, Empty Shoes

Nowhere is the need to move outside the self and the difficulty – impossibility, even – of doing so more immediately apparent than in Freud's own
topography of consciousness, where we encounter the ultimate and irreconcilable division of the subject. We see Freudian critics highlighting this
challenge in their readings of a variety of Freud's texts. Lacan argues in his
lectures on Freud's concept of the ego that Freud, in his description of the
ego in *Beyond the Pleasure Principle*, "wanted to save some kind of dualism
at all costs,"[17] and needed to assert that "the real *I* is not the ego," nor is it
"only a mistake of the *I*, a partial point of view."[18] Instead, Lacan argues,
the ego is "a particular object within the experience of the subject."[19]

  This idea of an ego that is objectified, and therefore able to be differentiated from the "*I*" of subject, accords with Freud's description of the
uncanny in his 1919 essay, "The Uncanny." In his exploration of the
phenomenon of the uncanny and how it is often felt in the presence of
a *doppelganger*, Freud explicitly describes the development of the "con-
science" that acts as a kind of authority, and "which is able to treat the rest
of the ego like an object" because "man is capable of self-observation."[20]
Philip Weinstein reads Freud's uncanny as foregrounding a "slippage" of
boundaries – in particular, a slippage that is "*spatial*: scenes supposedly
occurring 'out there' but actually being shaped from 'in here.'"[21] This
spatial movement recalls the trajectory followed when engaged in an act
of empathy, in which one moves outside one's own perspective and into
the point of view of another being. Important in Weinstein's idea of

slippage is the recognition that the uncanny involves disorientation – a sense of being lost – and then reorientation, though this reorientation is usually more disturbing than comforting. Freud himself describes reorientation as a kind of doubling or "telepathy"; the individual is not sure which ego is his or her own and may in fact replace his own ego with the ego of the double.[22] In this formulation, the doubling describes not the occupation of another self, but the loss of one's own self and its occupation by the other.

Although the idea of the occupation of the self by an other may seem to be the inverse of empathy, this formulation connects us back to Vernon Lee's explanation of empathy in *Beauty and Ugliness*, where she describes how, when feeling into an object (a "non-ego"), we are in fact returning to our selves: "Empathy, or *Einfühlung*, that is to say, the attribution of our modes to a *non-ego*, is *accompanied by satisfaction or dissatisfaction because it takes place in ourselves*."[23] Lee here firmly recognizes that, although empathy involves the assigning of "modes" to the other, that act is simultaneously one that occurs within the self – perhaps not quite the occupation of the self by an other, but certainly a blurring of the clear lines of attribution so that we can see the movements that go back and forth. As she states, "pleasure or displeasure in the subjective state which we recognize or imagine, is due to this subjective state *having been ours*, and becoming ours again when we thus attribute it."[24]

The link between uncanny and empathetic experiences helps clarify why empathy might seem a potential threat to the idea of the stable, indivisible self. Describing another psychologist's definition of the uncanny, Freud notes that "a particularly favorable condition for awakening uncanny sensations is created when there is intellectual uncertainty whether an object is alive or not, and when an inanimate object becomes too much like an animate one."[25] The uncanny object, in these terms, has violated certain boundaries; it moves into the realm of a subject. In this way the uncanny object confounds our norms and our own sense of control over our surroundings; it becomes a rejection of enlightenment rules in which human subjects are in charge of both animate and inanimate worlds. It is a quintessential modernist phenomenon because it reveals the lack, as Weinstein says, of a "free-standing subjectivity" and the subject's loss of "an orientational grip on others."[26]

If objects becoming subjects is a characteristic feature of the uncanny, what happens when subjects become objects, or when they enter into the transactional object world? Is there a similar move into the uncanny when empathy with objects – an attempt to enter into the object's perspective – is at play? Here is where a consideration of Woolf's *Jacob's Room* becomes useful; its emphasis on an uncanny nature to objects seems to have been deeply deliberate, for many of Woolf's revisions worked to emphasize how objects become repositories of human identity and meaning, taking on agency or import in ways that animate those objects, giving them an eerie life of their own. Jacob's shoes at the end of the novel might stand as the most memorable example of an object that takes on a haunted identity, and it is certainly one that Woolf highlighted, crossing off in her notebooks the potential final lines ("They both laughed. The room waved behind her tears") and ending it simply with "She held out a pair of Jacob's old shoes."[27] The most uncanny moment comes, however, in the middle of the book when the narrator focuses on the letter written by Betty Flanders to her son Jacob, and which, after having been delivered, is left lying in the hall while Jacob has sex with Florinda in the bedroom:

> The letter lay upon the hall table; Florinda coming in that night took it up with her, put it on the table as she kissed Jacob, and Jacob seeing the hand, left it there under the lamp, between the biscuit-tin and the tobacco-box. They shut the bedroom door behind them.
>
> The sitting-room neither knew nor cared. The door was shut; and to suppose that wood, when it creaks, transmits anything save that rats are busy and wood is dry is childish. These old houses are only brick and wood, soaked in human sweat, grained with human dirt. But if the pale blue envelope lying by the biscuit-box had the feelings of a mother, the heart was torn by the little creak, the sudden stir. Behind the door was the obscene thing, the alarming presence, and terror would come over her as at death, or the birth of a child. Better, perhaps, burst in and face it than sit in the antechamber listening to the little creak, the sudden stir, for her heart was swollen, and pain threaded it. My son, my son – such would be her cry.[28]

Woolf cushions this terrifying description with an "if" ("if the letter had the feelings of a mother"). But the salient point here is how the letter functions, in the final part of the quotation, as what the narrator describes just after as a "phantom of ourselves" (*Jacob's Room*, 92). We see first one version of how to understand the inanimate objects and spaces: they could be seen as the narrator describes the houses, simply saturated with human detritus, containing what we shed rather than any essential essence of identity. But quickly the passage shifts into the realm of possibility ("if" it had the feelings of a mother), and then begins to merge the letter and the mother so that they lose their boundaries: the paper heart is "torn." With the movement into a new sentence, even though Woolf continues with a conditional verb ("would"), we enter into a new syntactical field and seem to have pushed beyond the boundaries of the conditional and imaginary, and into the realm of actual effects on the mother when confronted with the "obscene" thing behind the bedroom door. We have one sentence that fully presents that shift – the letter has become the mother at this moment, object has turned into subject – and it switches from the conditional to the indicative: "for her heart was swollen, and pain threaded it." The final sentence from that paragraph above – "My son, my son – such would be her cry" – moves back into the conditional, but the emotive agency of the mother has been thoroughly channeled by this point; we do not question her presence.

In this exquisitely painful (and funny) and deeply unsettling vision of mother-love confronted by the adult desires of the child, Woolf explores not only the potential agency of the object, but also the loss that is embedded in the object as it functions as or for a subject who is not there. Indeed, a little later the narrator makes quite explicit the loss that occurs when identity becomes rooted in the object world:

> Let us consider letters ... to see one's own envelope on another's table is to realize how soon deeds sever and become alien. Then at last the power of the mind to quit the body is manifest, and perhaps we fear or hate or wish annihilated this phantom of ourselves, lying on the table. Still, there are letters that merely say how dinner's at seven; others ordering coal; making appointments. The hand in them is scarcely perceptible, let alone the voice or the scowl. Ah, but when the post knocks and the letter comes always the miracle seems repeated – speech attempted. Venerable are letters, infinitely brave, forlorn, and lost. (*Jacob's Room*, 92–93)

There is a violence in this description; in the attempt to move outside of the subject's body, a kind of amputation occurs: "deeds sever and become alien." Like the self that becomes unfamiliar, occupied in frightening ways in Freud's vision of the uncanny, here the letters become this terrifying double, a "phantom of ourselves" that reveals that we no longer are simply a unified whole. This is why these letters are "forlorn, and lost," for they are objects with no identity outside of their connection to the writer, and they are also severed, made alien, in their assumption of that voice that highlights the distance from the mouth that could utter the words. They are the disembodied words that point to the loss that occurs whenever there is a movement to a different state – the law of entropy applied to the realm of identity. The letters are not simply disembodied; they can negate the body that wrote them (when the meaning is banal, even the "hand in them is scarcely perceptible").

The letters thereby have their own uncanny agency, which we can see taking over as the paragraph moves forward. We begin with human subjects – indeed, the imaginatively present subjects of the writer and the reader ("Let *us* consider letters . . . to see *one's own* envelope"). But then, just as the narrator reflects on the split between mind and body – that "power of the mind to quit the body" – in those middle sentences, so too the human subject disappears by the end of the paragraph: the subjects are the objects by the end ("the post knocks and the letter comes"). What is lost is the human subject, the by-product of this personification. The letter seems to have taken the mind out of the body, leaving the writing subject diminished and impoverished, while the object itself becomes the subject.

Letters and disembodied voices also bring up the trope of prosopopoeia, which is closely connected to autobiography and, as I have argued in my discussion of Hardy (see Chapter 2), to elegy as well. I would like to push that idea further here by looking back at Paul de Man's resonant discussion of the link between the trope and autobiography. After examining Wordsworth's *Essay on Epitaphs* in the piece "Autobiography as Defacement," de Man leads us to the following conclusion: "As soon as we understand the rhetorical function of prosopopoeia as positing voice or face by means of language, we also understand that what we are deprived of is not life but the shape and the sense of a world accessible only in the privative way of understanding."[29] De Man is delving into the question of linguistic embodiment, how a trope can give us a face and name; the dilemma is that language is *always* metaphor: "not the thing itself but the representation, the picture of the thing and, as such, it is silent, much as pictures are mute."[30] Accordingly, we can see how language is always enacting a state of privation from the real; it is a sign of our distance, our loss, our constructed and imagined relationship with the world. We are back in the realm of "knowledge by description," which can never get at the acquaintanceship we may experience. Prosopopoeia thereby performs the loss that it is supposed to alleviate.

Woolf's reflection on letters in *Jacob's Room* presents this same vision of the language that manifests loss, always embodying the distance from the subject itself. And yet I do not want to get too caught up in the deconstructive project that de Man's argument demands, since I think that Woolf's text is not simply about performing its own loss. If we return to that quotation from *Jacob's Room*, we can see the recognition of the violence engendered by prosopoetic language. This confrontation with words that claim to give voice (or face or name) to us is unsupportable: we wish this other "annihilated," she writes (*Jacob's Room*, 92). In the manuscript Woolf made letters less immediately threatening, more diminutive, more playful ("this little phantom of ourselves; imp ~~this changeling, this imp~~" [*Holograph*, 124]). Indeed, there is a pathos to a letter, which is the "sheet that perishes," as opposed to published writing, which is the "sheet that endures" (*Jacob's Room*, 93). The sticking point here seems to be the "I" that Woolf so often wants to avoid – that "damned egotistical self" that she thinks ruins Joyce and others.[31] She rubs out some of that narrative "I" in her final draft, changing, for example, the "I" of the holograph draft of the typescript to a "we" in this sentence: "The world I seek hangs close to the tree" (*Holograph*, 126). Letters are gendered in this text, despite the acknowledgment that "Byron wrote letters. So did Cowper" (*Jacob's Room*, 93); the people who write the most letters here are the women: Mrs. Flanders, Mrs. Jarvis, Mrs. Durrant, Mother Stuart, Clara Durrant, and even Florinda who, "for some reason when she wrote she declared her belief in God" (94). Yet even this "sheet that perishes" has its formal value, helping writer and reader to abstract and reach outside the "I" in both the letter's appropriation of the writer's voice and its movement into the spaces of others. Letters can translate the self into a page, an imagined voice, and thus suggest the possibility of a more porous form of boundary between the self and others. Woolf's exploration of object-empathy resonates, therefore, with Vernon Lee's insistence on the enrichment to the empathizing subject's experience of the world; in that shift of the "*ego* into the *non-ego*"[32] the subject occupies and experiences things that the inanimate *non-ego* would not be able to experience, and the "experiences" of the object are translated back into the subject. Yet Woolf reveals how object-empathy is more damaging than affirming when the objects abscond with the subjects and the subjects are lost (to distance, to death).

It is not insignificant, of course, that the example I chose – the example that the narrator focuses upon – is a written object, for Woolf's whole novel could be seen as an attempt to explore the damages and the possibilities of entering into another subjectivity. On the one hand, it presents a classic example of literary empathy – you write (or read) yourself into another perspective, another consciousness. On the other hand, this attempt to do so is ringed with anxiety and doubt from the very beginning. By having Jacob first enter the book as a small child who immediately finds and clutches a sheep's skull – an animal memento mori – Woolf presents us with an object that speaks of death and loss, but in ways that are far from the literate and lyrical outpourings over Yorrick's skull (here we have a sobbing child, an animal skull). We are ushered in this first scene, therefore, into a world in which objects should mean more or less than they do: they have only a half-life in the sense that they are resonant, yet oddly mute (like the skull) or desperately verbose (like the letter); these objects seem either not to represent the subject, or to make off with the subject, to take control of the subject with their own wordiness.

In this recognition that subject–object relations may be much more fraught and threatening to the autonomy of the subject than we might first imagine, Woolf also explores the benefits of isolation from interpersonal relationships, resulting from the perhaps inevitable hierarchies at their root: gender, age, class, and education. Woolf will later call, in a more politicized way, for an "Outsider's Society" in *Three Guineas* (1938); here the productive nature of being on the outside, alone, emerges on the personal level.[33] A diary entry written just before the end of World War I in 1918, in which Virginia Woolf recognized explicitly how the war precipitated and necessitated reflection on the possibility (and the imperative) of perspective-taking, reminds us that *Jacob's Room* stands also as a kind of modern elegy for a young man lost to the war. Woolf noted in her diary, "The reason why it is easy to kill another person, must be that one's imagination is too sluggish to conceive what his life means to him – the infinite possibilities of a succession of days which are furled in him, & have already been spent."[34] This connection between violence and a lack of imagination highlights not only an individual, but also a social, national, and political need for empathizing. Yet Woolf is also aware of the necessity of safeguarding the autonomy of the individual, which emerges in an entry eight years later, in July 1926, as she reflects on her immediate (and biting) judgments of two young women seen walking through the countryside:

> These screens [of critique and judgment] shut me out. Have no screens, for screens are made out of our own integument; & get at the thing itself, which has nothing whatever in common with a screen. The screen making habit, though, is so universal, that it probably preserves our sanity. If we had not this device for shutting people off from our sympathies, we might, perhaps, dissolve utterly. Separation would be impossible. But the screens are in the excess; not the sympathy.[35]

While the need for empathy may have seemed most pressing during the mass violence of World War I, Woolf's further insight is not simply an entrenchment or rebuttal. The double-sided nature of the empathetic imagination is the key here: it is both necessary and threatening to the boundaries of the self; there is the worry, Woolf notes, that we might "dissolve utterly" should we have no screens to shut people off. This is a particularly pressing problem in a novel like *Jacob's Room*; here, the barriers between the narrator and Jacob are not only part of the general problem of imagining other minds, not only due to the difficulties of empathizing with the dead, but also a result of the gender barrier between the narrator and Jacob. This is presented most starkly in the Cambridge scenes, where Jacob's adolescent misogyny is reinforced by the layers of distance that sanctify the male spaces and keep the women out. "No one would think of bringing a dog into church . . . a dog destroys the service completely," the narrator muses, reflecting upon the distracting nature of women's presence in the King's College Chapel, before giving us one of the rare glimpses of Jacob's direct thoughts: "For one thing, thought Jacob, they're as ugly as sin" (*Jacob's Room*, 33). As with other moments when we move into a "Jacob thought" section, the paragraph ends with his thought; we are left with its echoes, almost as if the narrative voice, which is gendered female – "Granted ten years' seniority and a difference of sex, fear of him comes first" (94) – is given pause by the way that this thought so firmly shuts women out. The problem of understanding other minds is thereby exacerbated not only by that final divider, death, but also by the social barriers erected between the sexes; failures in imagination are therefore all the more likely.

Woolf's narrator is keenly aware of these failures; the moments of narrative intrusion most often reflect on the problematics of knowing another being: we may be, in her words, "surprised . . . by a sudden vision that the young man in the chair is of all things in the world the most real, the most solid, the best known to us," and yet, "the moment after we know nothing about him" (*Jacob's Room*, 72). Even earlier in the novel the narrator has baldly stated "It is no use trying to sum people up" (31), for "Nobody sees any one as he is . . . They see a whole – they see all sorts of things – they see themselves" (30–31). Both instances highlight the fleeting and futile nature of acts of empathetic imagination; we learn more about ourselves from our attempts to understand others than we learn about those others.

The kind of isolation implied by attempts to reach into objects and the various failures in trying to "know" Jacob suggest the sense of loneliness that pervades this novel and its quest to understand another human. Just as Betty Flanders's letters gesture to an essential and deep ambiguity about their double embodiment/disembodiment, so does *Jacob's Room* suggest the double nature of being alone. An unalterable distance between individuals remains even when intersubjective boundaries seem most thoroughly perforated, and even with an expressed desire to bridge the gap between subjects. Indeed, being alone appears to both instigate and be reinforced by the desire for empathetic engagement. The supposed ability to occupy another perspective and to "know" another's experience and emotions only illuminates what remains unknown. Yet rather than simply focusing on the futility of these attempts, in *Jacob's Room* Woolf recognizes, and perhaps even celebrates, the productive and pleasurable nature of both being alone (the physical state) and experiencing loneliness (an affective state), thereby giving us another way to think about the empathetic imagination.

The project of *Jacob's Room* is predicated, it appears, on a sense of the intrinsically lonely nature of humans; Jacob has the gloomy thought, while traveling on his own in Greece, that "it was not that he himself happened to be lonely, but that all people are" (*Jacob's Room*, 141). And yet, a few lines later, the benefits of this state emerge – "he had never suspected how tremendously pleasant it is to be alone; out of England; on one's own; cut off from the whole thing" – a feeling that the narrator attributes to "the wild horse in us," which allows us to experience "a rush of friendship for stones and grasses, as if humanity were over, and as for men and women, let them go hang" (141). In the holograph version of the novel, where we see Woolf's early draft, this embrace of solitude is even more pronounced because "everyone he thought is completely selfish & alone" (*Holograph*, 213). In the published novel, however, Jacob makes the distinction between the loneliness of all people and the pleasure of being alone; to be alone turns out to be oddly productive in ways that ultimately challenge the centrality of the human subject and the human as subject. We see aloneness as both short-circuiting an understanding of other people ("let them go hang") and opening up a broader fellow feeling for the natural world.

Thus, we can begin to parse Jacob's thought more carefully. Loneliness is something that he sees in all people – the essential Paterian idea of the unscalable thick wall of personality that rings each individual. Only far away in Greece, with the absence of other people and, concomitantly, of these reminders of our fundamental distance from other perspectives, can Jacob imagine himself into another perspective – in this case, that of the rocks, trees, and natural world. As critic Amelia Worsley writes in "Ophelia's Loneliness," Shakespeare used what was then a relatively new word to describe a state that was related to the physical idea of being alone, but that offered up a whole new dimension of the concept. Worsley shows that, "unlike these other terms[,] 'loneliness' can describe an experience that occurs in company as well as when people are alone."[36] Loneliness is therefore is a state of mind, rather than a statement of physical relationality. As such, it implies an isolation that would preclude occupying another perspective, or even, perhaps, being able to imagine that another perspective exists. It allows Jacob to imagine a new set of relationships with the natural world, even as he wishes to sever those with people. Even in this state of solipsistic loneliness, it seems, there is a hope of connection with that which could be utterly foreign and distant.

The fallacy of trying to take on a perspective outside of our narcissistic viewpoint seems to be emphasized in the very next shift in the novel, however, when we enter into the perspective of a new character, Sandra Wentworth Williams. She thinks, with melodramatic intensity, "I am full of love for everyone. . . – for the poor most of all – for the peasants coming back in the evening with their burdens. And everything is soft and vague and very sad. It is sad, it is sad. But everything has meaning" (*Jacob's Room*, 141). But as soon as she speaks the words "Everything seems to mean so much," then "with the sound of her own voice the spell was broken. She forgot the peasants" (142). With this voicing – the reminder of her own physical body – Sandra Wentworth Williams loses interest in the peasants. She becomes aware of her own beauty, reflected in the mirror, and this reflection banishes thoughts of others outside of the mirror frame. Thus, Woolf foregrounds how attempts at perspective-taking seemed destined to fail, returning to the narcissistic gaze contemplating itself.

Yet the project of understanding others continues as the necessary, if doomed, quest of the novel, and Woolf gives us no choice about maintaining resilience in the face of an uncommunicative subject. It is a novel that takes shape, Tammy Clewell has pointed out, between two scenes of absence, as it tries to respond to the calls – "Jacob, Jacob," – that are voiced by his brother Archer in the beginning and by his friend Bonamy in the end.[37] In between are the myriad moments at which other characters try to understand Jacob, a project that often becomes, for both the narrator and the other characters, a process of extrapolating feelings and thoughts from his face, his bearing, his room. These characters experience a stalemate in their attempts to know Jacob; in the final pages, when we might expect to have a better sense of Jacob, we and the characters are still searching. We see in succession, for example, the various women who love him trying to conjure him from a stranger in a restaurant, a character in a Molière play, or the statue of Ulysses in the British Museum.

Alongside the narrator's frequent musings about the difficulty inherent in understanding another person, these examples seem to suggest a failure of both the empathetic imagination and the realist project, and the inherently inadequate or unsetting nature of any attempt to animate an absent figure. Jacob is irrevocably gone; the need to cross the barriers of death, time, and sex is both imperative and doomed, as the narrator repeatedly reminds us. Jacob is an almost silent figure in the book – at one moment the narrator muses about his state of mind, but then draws back, noting that "whether this is the right interpretation of Jacob's gloom ... it is impossible to say; for he never spoke a word" (*Jacob's Room*, 49). The fate of the observer, of the writer, is to be shut off irrevocably from others: like the choice of where to sit at the Opera House, the narrator reminds us, life is based on choices that involve shutting off other possibilities of understanding: "the difficulty remains – one has to choose. For though I have no wish to be Queen of England – or only for a moment – I would willingly sit beside her; I would hear the Prime Minister's gossip; the countess whisper ... But no – we must choose. Never was there a harsher necessity! or one which entails greater pain, more certain disaster; for wherever I seat myself, I die in exile" (69). It is an inevitable drifting from possible knowledge of another – a moment of clarity and solidity – into what Woolf describes as the partial and ephemeral "manner of our seeing ... the conditions of our love" (72). Yet even more than this, the half-humorous claim that "I die in exile" brings together both the solitary nature of human life and the feeling of loneliness that pervades it – one always is imagining the things one cannot experience. To see and to love – the "manner of our seeing ... the conditions of our love" – are acts that make apparent our distance from others.

The final image in the novel makes this failure of the empathetic imagination concrete. Mrs. Flanders bursts in and, holding out Jacob's shoes, asks, "What am I to do with these, Mr. Bonamy?" (*Jacob's Room*, 176). The repetition that occurs throughout the book and, in particular, in this final one-page chapter, keys us into how elegizing *and* perspective-taking depend on the repetition of structures, perhaps even of hollowed-out forms, in order to make meaning. Earlier in the text the description of his room was followed by an effort to pin down Jacob: "'Distinction' – Mrs. Durrant said that Jacob Flanders was 'distinguished-looking.' 'Extremely awkward,' she said, but so distinguished-looking'" (70). And yet, as we see the narrator ask a page later, why are we surprised that at one moment we feel "the young man in the chair is of all things in the world the most real, the most solid, the best known to us," and "the moment after we know nothing about him" (72)? Jacob's empty shoes in the last line express this ultimate lack of knowledge – the inability of outside forms to do more than project a shell of the person. With their literalizing of the loss, of the inability to imagine Jacob in them, the shoes show how the commonplace phrases ("distinguished-looking") that have suggested connection to Jacob are ultimately hollow and disposable.

While Betty Flanders's letter was uncannily animated, absconding with its subject, these shoes are deafening in their silence – their inability to embody their absent owner. What they do embody, however, is the emptiness, the lack, the way in which they are not filled. "To stand in someone else's shoes" is that familiar trope of empathy, and the image at the end of *Jacob's Room* gives a certain kind of lie to that vision: to stand in them would be to put them to a different use; the shoes would no longer be able to stand for Jacob, since the meaning of Jacob and the meaning of most objects divorced from their owners in this book is the very fact of loss, pure and simple. If we attempt to embody an object, an inanimate non-ego, either we are left in a transactional limbo, like with the letter, or we are trespassing on the very life that used to animate those objects. These last lines thereby highlight the uncanny nature of objects in *Jacob's Room*, for they leave Bonamy, Mrs. Flanders, and the reader in a state of disorientation about the agency that we should and could ascribe to those objects that surrounded Jacob. Death brings a kind of closure to this indeterminacy: there is no longer the need for a defense against death, which Freud identified as central to the kind of "doubling" that occurs within the uncanny. With actual death, the objects become no longer uncanny since the life they took on is no longer in need of protection. Thus, the room around which the narrator hung quivering so often is no longer a site of making meaning; the repetitions that characterize this final page – the descriptions of the eighteenth-century building and of the listless air of an empty room – are no longer in service of insights into the nature of their occupant; indeed, the word-for-word repetition when the room is described throughout the book highlights the failure of objects and spaces to lead to insight and knowledge of others. The narrative perspective withdraws now that the central character is gone. In the failure of the empty shoes to bring to life their former owner, the ending of the book seems to point to a form that can represent the loss occasioned by the war.

The Fringes of Consciousness in *To the Lighthouse*

Questions about the link between loss or mourning and insight or productivity become all the more resonant when we turn to Woolf's later elegiac novel, *To the Lighthouse*, and think about the self-sacrifice tied to one form of understanding others, as well as the possibilities for other forms of empathetic understanding that might be at work in this novel. On the one hand, this novel reveals a deep distrust of the project of what Woolf calls "sympathy," for sympathy becomes linked to the aggressive neediness of Mr. Ramsay and the rapturous, yet draining acquiescence of Mrs. Ramsay. As Hammond has discussed, this novel critiques the one-way movement of "sympathy," which is demanded by men and given by women (Hammond, 152). Yet looking at the objects that hover between the realms of the abstract and the material will give us some ideas, I argue, about how Woolf might develop a productive and ethical form of empathetic engagement, and how she might also be doing what Hammond identifies as one of the projects of the modernist novel – to enact "the separation between sympathy and empathy" (7), in this case in service of representing character and exploring loss.

In a novel that is defined by questions about how to bridge divides – temporal divides (the chasm caused by the war, deaths, physical change), spatial divides (Lily's picture, as well as the space between the house and the lighthouse), and social divides (in particular, the divide between men and women, which Mrs. Ramsay both crosses and reinforces) – one type of divide stands as central: the intersubjective divide, or the question of whether we can ever know or feel with another person. As in *Jacob's Room*, Woolf here explores the question of this "subjective" knowledge through the more "objective" realm of ordinary objects and art objects. The close relationship between objects and human feeling emerges in the very first lines of the novel; little James Ramsay, who is described as belonging "to that great clan which cannot keep this feeling separate from that," transfers to the pictures of furniture he is cutting from a catalog his excitement about possibly visiting the lighthouse: the refrigerator becomes "fringed with joy."[38] The fragility of this mode of relating is immediately apparent, however, as his father's discouraging "it won't be fine tomorrow" (*TTL*, 4) vanquishes any joy James projects onto his paper cutouts; he can only, when his father comes around again, try to "make him move on; by pointing his finger at a word, he hoped to recall his mother's attention" (37). In this instance we see the projection of the self onto the surrounding world – that version of the pathetic fallacy that Ruskin abhorred, describing it as belonging to "men who feel strongly, think weakly, and see untruly (second order of poets)"[39] – presented as a kind of inversion of the empathetic experience, since here "feeling oneself into" an object means endowing it with the subject's feelings, not experiencing the object's. Young James's fringes recall William James's statement in *Psychology: A Briefer Course* (1892): "Let us call the consciousness of this halo of relations around the image by the name of 'psychic overtone' or 'fringe.'"[40] For William James, one's knowledge of "things" involves knowledge of the relations that surround them; there are always "fringes" to the things around us; our perception is always different and our experience of the object world is always shifting from moment to moment.

As a member of that tribe who does not see a clear distinction between self and other, subject and object (Woolf here implies that there are those who do see this distinction), James Ramsay's joy at the prospect of going to the lighthouse creates that aura around the picture of the refrigerator.

William James belongs to the group of radical empiricists who challenged the idea that the subject was a stable, unified entity. Instead, as Judith Ryan explains, for them "the only admissible evidence for the existence of something was that of our senses; the only reality was that of our consciousness."[41] This theory breaks down the barrier between subject and object, for the "self was no longer firmly enclosed in the body but in consciousness itself, and this was no longer a discrete unit but included everything that was within the individual field of perception."[42] In the very first lines of the novel, indeed, we see Woolf engaging with similar questions about the relationship between subject, object, and perception, though not simply with questions at the heart of empirical psychology and philosophy, but also with questions about how to think through the representation of a perceiving subject whose boundaries are expansive in ways that do not fall into the template of the pathetic fallacy.

Thus, little James Ramsay's porous boundaries between self and other not only suggest his individual experience of the object world – still in the less mediated state of childhood – but also signal Woolf's ambivalent and varied relationship to the pathetic fallacy. This has intimate connections with the questions of perspective-taking that are at the heart of empathy. Critic Satoshi Nishimura analyzes this from a narratological perspective, arguing that many of Woolf's explorations of the inanimate world are examples not simply of personification, but also of "inanimate focalization."[43] Inanimate focalization is in essence another way of describing the pathetic fallacy, for it indicates when the language of thought and emotion are attributed to inanimate objects, thereby creating a "form of displaced subjectivity."[44] Nishimura claims that this version of the pathetic fallacy is a reminder that even though focalization tends to be viewed as a "psychological concept," Woolf's use of it in *To the Lighthouse* illuminates the linguistic question of how to create a seeing subject within an narrative – who or what is this seeing eye/I? The implications of this in terms of thinking through empathy in general, and through object-oriented empathy in particular, involve asking how perspectives are occupied and what sort of relationship emerges between the occupied perspective and the occupier. Woolf is attuned to the nuances of this movement, as will be seen not only in the second section of the novel, "Time Passes," but also in scenes like this first one with James.

Even though James's transference of emotion to the paper cutouts is both innocent and poetic, it is also linked to a larger suspicion in the novel about the way that characters relate to others. More specifically, James's projection of his own feelings onto the object world is a more benign version of the imposition of self that we see operating in such a repressive fashion with Mr. Ramsay. Yet an alternative to this – the act of taking the perspective of some other being or object – is also not without its problems. A danger in this novel is not with perspective-taking, per se, but with the *kind* of sympathy we see Mrs. Ramsay give to both Mr. Ramsay and to other men in the book; most problematically, the gift of sympathy becomes deeply gendered. The term "sympathy," which is the word that Woolf uses throughout the novel, embodies aspects both of what we would call sympathy today and also of empathy: sympathy has in the twentieth century been differentiated from empathy because it involves, as Robert Katz wrote, a reinforcement of one's own self-consciousness: "we become even more sharply aware of ourselves," while the "empathizer tends to abandon his self-consciousness" and the divide between subject and object disappears.[45]

The balance between self-consciousness and an awareness of others is complicated in this novel because Woolf explores the benefits and the dangers of many different modes of perspective-taking. Mrs. Ramsay stands as the classic empathizer who gives herself over to those around her – specifically to her husband, but to others as well. We see the most striking scene of this early on when her husband stands near her, "demanding sympathy" (*TTL*, 37) because of his anxiety that he is not as important a philosopher as he would like to be. In the process of assuaging this need, Mrs. Ramsay must empty herself of her own energy, and when Mr. Ramsay goes away, comforted, "there was scarcely a shell of herself left for her to know herself by; all was so lavished and spent" (38). In expending this energy, Mrs. Ramsay pushes against what William James calls that "minimum of selfishness in the shape of instincts of bodily self-seeking in order to exist."[46] And yet, while this seems to take a huge toll on the self, there is also a way in which Mrs. Ramsay's sense of self is reinforced, not simply drained, by giving sympathy. Mr. Carmichael's presence makes Mrs. Ramsay uncomfortably aware that perhaps "this desire of hers to give, to help, was vanity" (41). Indeed, though Mrs. Ramsay is a creative and life-giving force, the characters are not uncritical of how her urge to give sympathy is what allows Mr. Ramsay to need it, to demand it. As Lily reflects ten years after her initial visit to the summer house, and when she has returned after the death of Mrs. Ramsay, "Mrs. Ramsay had given.

Giving, giving, giving, she had died – and had left all of this. Really, she was angry at Mrs. Ramsay" (149). The dynamic of an unbalanced male–female sympathetic exchange that Mrs. Ramsay enables is at odds with the more balanced gender relationships that we see developed in this novel, between figures like Lily and Mr. Bankes, for example, and with the idea of artistic autonomy. This is the case even as Mrs. Ramsay is also celebrated for her creative prowess, both procreative (eight children!) and artistic, as at her dinner party that acts as social symphony, sparking moments of connection and communion.

Mrs. Ramsay is our touchstone for the idea of moving into another perspective, and she herself feels a deep connection to the central object of the novel: the lighthouse or, more specifically, its beam of light. In her moments of solitude she muses about this connection, as well as about how empathetic identification may emerge most readily in the absence of other people. She reflects, "for watching them in this mood at this hour one could not help attaching oneself to the one thing especially of the things one saw; and this thing, the long steady stroke, was her stroke. Often she found herself sitting and looking, sitting and looking, with her work in her hands until she became the thing she looked at – that light, for example" (*TTL*, 63). This time alone, at the reflective evening moment, enables her extension outside of herself that allows her to shed her identity and occupy that of something else. Important here is how this transformation occurs: it is through the act of looking – a gaze that is not figured as aesthetic here, but that is concentrated and intense – that Mrs. Ramsay becomes the other, becomes the light. With the focus on looking, we can again recall Vernon Lee's theory of aesthetic empathy, but Mrs. Ramsay's kind of looking is important to differentiate from the observation that Woolf elsewhere connects to the probing, object-oriented, materialist mind. With characters such as Mrs. Ramsay, Woolf shows her interest in both the centrality of the material world and the importance of engaging with it in a way that is *not* focused on labeling or naming or "knowing." Instead, using a character like Mrs. Ramsay, who is short-sighted and unable to read easily the billboard advertising a circus on her walk into the town (11), looking becomes about creating both an "aesthetic relationship"[47] and also, I would argue, an empathetic one. Mrs. Ramsay's vague and inclusive form of looking leads to connections to the natural world; as she puts it, "It was odd, she thought, how if one was alone, one leant to inanimate things; trees, streams, flowers; felt they expressed one; felt they became one; felt they knew one, in a sense were one; felt an irrational tenderness thus" (63). Her form of vision is short-sighted in a literal sense, but expansive in its scope and interest.

On the one hand, therefore, Mrs. Ramsay's connection to the inanimate world seems an apt pairing with Mr. Ramsay's work, which is described by his son Andrew as concerned with "subject and object and the nature of reality" (*TTL*, 23). On the other hand, the key element of Mr. Ramsay's philosophical project is to think about an object *without* a perceiving subject; Andrew clarifies his description of his father's work by saying to Lily, "Think of a kitchen table then ... when you're not there" (23). Woolf makes this description comic when the visual Lily imagines a "scrubbed kitchen table ... lodged now in the fork of a pear tree, for they had reached the orchard" (23). Objects without perceiving subjects become decontextualized; the kitchen table takes flight and absconds from the kitchen and ends up in the orchard with "its four legs in the air" (23). Mr. Ramsay takes the subject out of this triad of subject, object, and the nature of reality, but Lily's vision shows how this is a form of abstraction that proves ridiculous, if not impossible. This is not a rejection of abstraction in general, but of the kind of abstraction that yearns for an "objective" vision. Not only does the object thus lose its bearings, ending up literally up in the air, but the viewer loses sight of any emotional content or connections. Hence, Mr. Ramsay is able to "pursue truth with such astonishing lack of consideration for other people's feelings" (32).

It is not surprising, therefore, that Mr. Ramsay is defined by his selfish inability to step outside of his own egotistical perspective – his double lack of vision, we might say. Mr. Ramsay not only cannot see into other perspectives; he actually does not see the world around him at all: "He never looked at things" (*TTL*, 71). Such blindness is inexcusable, for it turns him into a tyrant with his family, needing constant sympathy and attention not only from his wife, but also from any other woman who might be around. He sees without seeing: he

> looked once at his wife and son in the window, and as one raises one's eyes
> from a page in an express train and sees a farm, a tree, a cluster of cottages as
> an illustration, a confirmation of something on the printed page ... so
> without distinguishing either his son or his wife, the sight of them fortified
> him. (33)

The kind of abstraction that occurs here involves the reduction of the human to a concept; individual identity, feeling, and perspective are erased in the process of looking.

In the face of the Ramsays and their differing methods of defining the subject, the object, and the nature of reality, Lily stands as a corrective and presents a more productive method of seeing and form of vision. Exemplifying neither Mr. Ramsay's blindness and desire for an elusive "objective" reality nor Mrs. Ramsay's self-immolating fusion with people and objects around her, Lily is the character most keenly aware of the power of perception, as well as a sometimes unconscious practitioner of an empathetic vision. Her role as a visual artist immediately proclaims her as concerned with how and what to see; her own reflections on the act of perception in the early parts of the book refine this role. Seeing becomes connected to a kind of personal reality and truth that Lily, as an artist, must uphold. Thus, she thinks to herself that "She would not have considered it honest to tamper with the bright violet and the staring white, since she saw them like that, fashionable though it was, since Mr. Paunceforte's visit, to see everything pale, elegant, semitransparent" (*TTL*, 18–19). Vision is linked to being; "this is what I see; this is what I see" (19) is Lily's mantra to uphold the integrity of her own way of seeing the world in the face of self-doubt and the demands of the external world. Both observation and being observed are therefore intensely personal acts; Lily must steel herself when, as Mr. Bankes examines her painting, she reflects on the traumatic scrutiny of "the residue of her thirty-three years, the deposit of each day's living mixed with something more secret than she had ever spoken or shown in the course of all those days" (52). For Lily, what she sees constitutes a "vision," and this kind of vision is distinct from other forms of looking. Lily is not able to give the "sympathy" that Mr. Ramsay demands because it involves a subjugation of the self, an immolation of her own needs in the face of his, but she is able to see into the heart of Mrs. Ramsay better than anyone else. In her first painting of the scene with Mrs. Ramsay and James as focal points, Mr. Bankes is interested to notice that she has portrayed them as simply a "triangular purple shape" – the mother reading to a child "reduced, he pondered, to a purple shadow without irreverence" (52). Not only is this reduction without irreverence, but the reader learns soon after that it indeed represents the core of Mrs. Ramsay's being more truthfully than any other, more seemingly realistic depiction, for when alone Mrs. Ramsay realizes that "one shrunk, with a sense of solemnity, to being oneself, a wedge-shaped core of darkness, something invisible to others" (62). Lily's vision, while not accurate in terms of the exterior, is deeply accurate in terms of Mrs. Ramsay's interior experience.

Lily's form of vision has its recognized limitations, and yet is still profoundly concentrated; it is impersonal, yet full of emotion. In the final section Lily finally regains the mood necessary for painting and seeing; she determines to hold onto it, for

> One must keep on looking without for a second relaxing the intensity of emotion, the determination not to be put off, not to be bamboozled. One must hold the scene – so – in a vise and let nothing come in and spoil it. One wanted, she thought, dipping her brush deliberately, to be on a level with ordinary experience, to feel simply that's a chair, that's a table, and yet at the same time, It's a miracle, it's an ecstasy. The problem might be solved after all. (*TTL*, 201–202)

We might note Lily's use of "One" to start three sentences in the passage above. Not only does it suggest her desire to step outside the personal, it also emphasizes the unifying project that this book revolves around. This kind of looking, this kind of vision, also requires the deep effort characteristic of modernist theories of aesthetic labor – the bending of language to the curve of the meaning that Hulme describes in his essay on "Romanticism and Classicism."[48] Yet such looking also demands an awareness of the extraordinary, the visionary, the exaggerated and miraculous, which are qualities that become associated in the novel with the artist rather than the philosopher or scientist; it is a an act that Woolf later reflects upon in her diary, while in the throes of writing *The Years*, when she thinks of the laborious nature of bringing together disparate visions: "Its [*sic*] obvious that one person sees one thing & another another: & that one has to draw them together. Who was it who said, through the unconscious one comes to the conscious & then again to the unconscious?"[49] Woolf connects this fluctuation between conscious and unconscious states to her project of drawing together different visions; this is the task of the writer and artist. Mr. Ramsay's perseverance is admired, his intellectual fortitude noted ("Qualities that would have saved a ship's company exposed on a broiling sea with six biscuits and a flask of water – endurance and justice, foresight, devotion, skill, came to his help" [*TTL*, 34]), but his inability to *see* means that he ultimately fails to understand others or to achieve a knowledge of the world around him.

In contrast, in the first section, "The Window," Lily begins to achieve the kind of union she desires thanks to her painting's purple shadow, the wedge of darkness, even if she fails to connect deeply in actual interactions. Lily wondered,

> What device for becoming like water poured into one jar, inextricably the same, one with the object one adored? . . . Could loving, as people called it, make her and Mrs. Ramsay one? For it was not knowledge but unity that

she desired, not inscriptions on tablets, nothing that could be written in any language known to men, but intimacy itself, which is knowledge. (*TTL*, 51)

Lily sets up a complicated set of connections here. She begins with a vision of merging – a unity in which the boundaries between the two substances, between the adored "object" and the adoring subject, are erased. This kind of "unity" and intimacy are Lily's goal, and she begins by differentiating one kind of "knowledge" (that which can be inscribed, collected, and preserved; those "inscriptions on tablets") from another, that is not in the "language known to men." Though "men" here stands for humans, we might assume, there is a gendered nature to such collection and codification of knowledge, as we have seen with Mr. Ramsay, Mr. Bankes, and Charles Tansley. Here we have again a dichotomy central to this novel, in which there are different (and gendered) ways to know and to see. Lily, with her desire for unity, acts as the figure who gives us the kind of vision and knowledge that seems most enduring and productive.

Yet the desire for union might not be possible or even desirable; Lily is unable to merge with Mrs. Ramsay ("Nothing happened. Nothing! Nothing!" [*TTL*, 51]), for she recognizes the impermeable nature of personality, what Pater calls the "thick wall of personality"[50] that makes both union and penetration impossible. Thus, she wonders, "How then . . . did one know one thing or another about people, sealed as they were" (51). Her understanding instead comes from taking up an artistic vision, in which by "subduing all her impressions as a woman to something much more general" (53), she is able to see Mrs. Ramsay sitting with James as part of an aesthetic problem – "how to connect the mass on the right hand with that on the left" (53). Through this androgynous artistic vision, Lily can empathize with Mrs. Ramsay in a way that is blocked both to the men who worship and depend on Mrs. Ramsay and to Lily when she tries to connect with Mrs. Ramsay as a fellow woman.

By reaching toward an androgynous vision, Lily's strategy recalls Lee's emphasis that empathy is not the "*projection of the ego* into the object or shape under observation," because empathy "depends upon a comparative or momentary abeyance of all thought of an ego; if we became aware that it is *we* who are thinking the rising [Lee is discussing looking at a mountain], we who are *feeling* the rising, we should not think or feel that the mountain did the rising."[51] In this formulation the ego of the perceiving subject must be subordinated to the perceived object (in this case a natural object); yet in an earlier book Lee recognizes and argues that this absence of the perceiving ego still involves the attribution, when applied to nonhuman objects, of feelings that the objects cannot possibly have themselves. Lee points out that "What must be grasped by the student of Aesthetic Empathy is that there exists, for one reason or another, an act of attribution of our energies, activities, or feelings to the *non-ego*, an act necessarily preceding all *sympathy*, and that this projection of our inner experience necessitates the revival of subjective states in what we call our memory."[52] To a certain extent there is a contradiction in Lee: empathy involves both the absenting of the ego's experiences and feelings and the projection of the ego's inner experience. The distinction seems to involve the layer of the self that is being projected; while the outer, social "I" – the ego of Freud – must be forgotten, the unconscious self still reaches out and applies itself to the world around.

In the complicated middle section of the novel, "Time Passes," we are both on the level of this unconscious self and in the realm of Mr. Ramsay's own way of viewing the world ("think of a kitchen table . . . when you're not there"). This section functions as a bridge between the first and last parts (and is drawn by Woolf in the manuscript as just such a corridor, with "Time Passes" as the connecting line in an image that resembles a sideways "H").[53] "Time Passes" provides the book's most extended exploration of what it might mean to imagine a world without a human subject. In doing so, however, Woolf challenges the parameters of this very idea of no human subjects; can thought even exist, she asks, if there is no one there? In this world emptied of its inhabitants (though still narrated), nature seems at first to offer a kind of confirmation of its alignment with human experience, its reflection of our own fears and desires. The winds enter the darkened house, and, as they brush the wallpaper and rustle the papers in the waste-paper basket (*TTL*, 126), "one might imagine them" asking the questions about time and longevity that a human would ask. This act of endowing the natural world with human ideas and emotions is undercut, however, in the next vignette; the narrator's questions about the viability of the pathetic fallacy do not lead to a consoling metaphor: "no image with semblance of serving and divine promptitude comes readily to hand bringing the night to order and making the world reflect the compass of the soul" (128). The desire and the attempt to find meaning, reflection, and solace in nature must be put on hold.

This is not, however, Woolf's last attempt in this section to assert the possibility of a comprehending nature or a world in line with humanity. "Time Passes" shows just how terrifying and almost unimaginable a world without a perceiving subject might be. The seeming disaster of this vision emerges after we have read the bracketed news of the deaths of

Mrs. Ramsay (unexpectedly), Prue Ramsay (while pregnant), and Andrew Ramsay (in war). In a moment of narrative reflection on how we are supposed to read this unpeopled, run-down house, she writes:

> Did Nature supplement what man advanced? Did she complete what he began? With equal complacence she saw his misery, his meanness, and his torture. That dream, of sharing, completing, of finding in solitude on the beach an answer, was then but a reflection in a mirror, and the mirror itself was but the surface glassiness which forms in quiescence when the nobler powers sleep beneath … the mirror was broken. (134)

Two levels of disillusionment occur here: not only do we see nothing except a reflection of ourselves in nature, but also this reflection is ephemeral and, upon a moment of insight, destroyed. The greater horror of this vision of nature comes a few paragraphs later, when we see the garden urns filled with a profusion of spring flowers again; what would formerly have seemed a harbinger of coming joy and fecundity is now further evidence of the absence of the human-made meaning, for the flowers are "standing there, looking before them, looking up, yet beholding nothing, eyeless, and so terrible" (135). This image gains its power from its emphasis on the lack of vision – the flowers and nature do *not* see.

This moment may be one of the most uncanny – *unheimlich* – in the section, in the way that the familiar, homey image of the flowers – which we know from "The Window" are the offspring of ones planted by Mrs. Ramsay herself – is rendered so deeply strange. Indeed, this whole section participates in a staging of the uncanny. As we enter into a perspective that is supposed to be devoid of the human, we see the epitome of the familiar now presented as the playground of vagrant airs and breezes; the barrier between inside and outside, nature and the human, disintegrates over time. The lighthouse light takes on the role of observer and participant as "it laid its caress and lingered stealthily and looked" (*TTL*, 132). We are in the realm of illumination without comprehension – the eyeless flowers that look and behold nothing, and the lighthouse light that shines but with the indifference of the inanimate.

And yet, this idea cannot exist for long in an anthropomorphic world, as the novel emphasizes a few lines later. Immediately after the image of the eyeless flowers, the novel gives us Mrs. McNab, the representative of the most base level of humanity presented in this section. She enters the scene and, "Thinking no harm, for the family would not come, never again, some said, and the house would be sold at Michaelmas perhaps, Mrs. McNab stooped and picked a bunch of flowers to take home with her" (135). The primacy of the human over the natural world is made distressingly (and perhaps also reassuringly) clear, when even someone described as "witless" and with a voice "robbed of meaning" (130) can break into this visionless, reasonless world. She plucks the flowers simply because she "was fond of flowers" (135). The *unheimlich* is rendered *heimlich*.

The extended reflection on the world without people ends with the return of the family (though without Mrs. Ramsay, Prue, and Andrew) and of Lily and other guests to the summerhouse. The focus in the final section, "The Lighthouse," is still Mrs. Ramsay, but now we have the question of how to imagine a person, rather than an object, when she is not there – the question of elegy reasserting itself and emerging onto the canvas of Lily's painting. At stake is the *process* of doing this, more than the final product (which we can only visualize in the most general ways). Lily's act of painting participates in this work of elegizing and remembering:

> Certainly she was losing consciousness of outer things. And as she lost consciousness of outer things, and her name and her personality and her appearance, and whether Mr. Carmichael was there or not, her mind kept throwing up from its depths, scenes, and names, and sayings, and memories and ideas, like a fountain spurting over that glaring hideously difficult white space, while she modeled it with greens and blues. (159)

The act of painting begins with a shedding of personality and self-awareness, in addition to a loss of the awareness of others, until the underneath layer of the mind can be receptive to the various deep memories and images that color the present blankness and give it shape and depth. As Laura Marcus has written, *To the Lighthouse* "is all about looking, perspective, distance,"[54] and part of the looking that occurs here is a melding of inward and outward vision. Lily thinks almost deprecatingly about how we tell stories about other people: it is "a whole structure of imagination" (*TTL*, 173) that involves the imagination; "And this, Lily thought, taking the green paint on her brush, this making up scenes about them, is what we call 'knowing' people, 'thinking' of them, 'being fond' of them!" (173). This imaginative play is deeply connected to the kinds of perspective-taking that Lily engages in while painting and, as Lily's painting reveals, making up stories can lead to a kind of truth about the subjects of these stories when the vision is clear, the viewpoint unobstructed.

This aesthetic vision that allows for empathetic understanding – Lily is able to represent, in an abstracted fashion, exactly *how* Mrs. Ramsay feels in her innermost core – thus differs in fundamental ways from Mr. Ramsay's form of imagination; whether Lily is near Mrs. Ramsay or not becomes of central importance, though it is not necessarily better to be near than far. Proximity seems irrelevant for Mr. Ramsay's imaginative act; like the train plowing through the countryside at a pace that blurs the scenery, so does the "scenery" around the viewing subject in Mr. Ramsay's world lose its specific import and become subordinated to abstracted concepts (which are different from abstract images). Yet Lily will remind us in the third section of the novel that questions of proximity and distance reveal things in new and essential ways:

> So much depends then, thought Lily Briscoe, looking at the sea which had scarcely a stain on it, which was so soft that the sails and the clouds seemed set in its blue, so much depends, she thought, upon distance: whether people are near us or far from us; for her feeling for Mr. Ramsay changed as he sailed further and further across the bay. (*TTL*, 191)

What depends upon distance is this question of "feeling," which is far away from the seeming objectivity, and the certain egotism, of Mr. Ramsay's object without a perceiving subject. Feeling and understanding can become more accurate, paradoxically, when their object is far away or even gone. Mrs. Ramsay's actual presence is so overwhelming that Lily, in the first section, can barely resist her pressure to get married. As Lily reflects while watching Mrs. Ramsay reading to James, Mrs. Ramsay was "different too from the perfect shape which one saw there. But why different and how different?" (49). This question of difference is what Lily tries to answer; she reaches at least a partial answer with her purple triangle, which represents Mrs. Ramsay's own sense of herself as a "wedge-shaped core of darkness" (62).

It is only in "The Lighthouse," therefore, after Mrs. Ramsay has died and Lily has returned and begun again to paint the scene, that Lily's most detailed and granular exploration of Mrs. Ramsay can occur; the distance (temporal) has enabled it in a way that presence would not. Though she has been dead a decade, Mrs. Ramsay's absence is felt as resonantly as her presence by those who knew her and loved her. Within Lily's memory she is tangible, so that, while painting, Lily can remember Mrs. Ramsay and reflect:

> That woman sitting there writing under the rock resolved everything into simplicity; made these angers, irritations fall off like old rags; she brought together this and that and then this, and so made out of that miserable silliness and spite ... something ... which survived, after all these years complete, so that she dipped into it to re-fashion her memory of him and there it stayed in the mind affecting one almost like a work of art. (*TTL*, 160)

As a work of art, Mrs. Ramsay has been transformed, occupying the continuous present of one's encounter with art. But like the artwork, she also functions as a transformative agent, operating alchemically to fashion Lily's understanding of other people. The absent figure provides the necessary perspective; Lily cannot think about Charles Tansley with empathy without first occupying Mrs. Ramsay's perspective; the act of thinking empathetically, this moment suggests, depends on finding a perspective that makes the imaginative leap possible: "If she wanted to be serious about him she had to help herself to Mrs. Ramsay's sayings, to look at him through her eyes" (197). Indeed, the issue is even more complex, for in order to understand someone else, you need to have many eyes, many ways of seeing. Lily muses that to understand Mrs. Ramsay, for instance, requires eyes from all around: "One wanted fifty pairs of eyes to see with, she reflected. Fifty pairs of eyes were not enough to get round that one woman with, she thought" (198).

Unlike Mr. Ramsay's fixed and chronological view of reality, Lily has a vision of reality that is more in line with Freud's uncanny and the idea of the shifting and ephemeral dividing lines between subjects and objects and the always fictional nature of reality. The art object of traditional aesthetics enables a transcendence of the estrangement between, in Terry Eagleton's words, a "self-identical subject and a stable object."[55] Here, however, we have a vision of an art object that is also a subject (Mrs. Ramsay), and, what is more, is a subject who identifies with objects (recall the lighthouse light, for example). It is in this complex set of identifications that Mrs. Ramsay becomes both the object of desire and the object of mourning, two experiences that are, Eagleton argues, always linked:

> to be a subject is to be alienated anyway, rendered eccentric to oneself by the movement of desire. And if objects matter at all, they matter precisely in the place where they are absent . . . it is when the object is removed or prohibited that it lays the trace of desire, so that its secure possession will always move under the sign of loss.[56]

Desire only operates in relation to the imagined and foretold loss of the object of desire; this loss is felt physically as well as mentally, as when, in "The Lighthouse," Lily reflects on Mrs. Ramsay's absence: "how could one express in words these emotions of the body? express the emptiness there? . . . It was one's body feeling, not one's mind . . . To want and not to have, sent all up her body a hardness, a hollowness, a strain" (*TTL*, 178). This intrinsic link between desire and loss illuminates not only the final part of the novel where the object of desire and of representation, Mrs. Ramsay, is truly and utterly gone, but also the first part, "The Window," when she is still present and alive. The impending loss is evident in her very being and its inscrutability, her persona that she defines as that wedge of darkness, even as she also identifies herself with the search beam of the lighthouse, with a persona aesthetically mysterious and removed. The key to Mrs. Ramsay's desirability, it appears, is her ultimate mystery. Her "remoteness" (64) pains her husband because he realizes he cannot protect her; people wonder what is behind the beauty of her face, for "she never spoke. She was silent always" (28).

Despite this silence, the book ends with several different moments of completion. Mr. Ramsay, Cam, and James reach the lighthouse; their arrival is noted by both Lily and Mr. Carmichael, those two artist figures who serve as the ultimate observers of the scenes. While the landing occurs in the last lines of the penultimate chapter, the final short chapter is where those on shore note and reflect upon it. That distant landing provides another instance of empathetic communication for Lily; Mr. Carmichael stands and says, "'They will have landed,' and she felt that she has been right. They had not needed to speak. They had been thinking the same things and he had answered her without her asking him anything" (208). This moment of connection allows Lily finally to finish her picture: "With a sudden intensity, as if she saw it clear for a second, she drew a line there, in the centre. It was done; it was finished. Yes, she thought, laying down her brush in extreme fatigue, I have had my vision" (209). It is a triumphant moment in the text, for there has been intersubjective communication mediated by a shared event – an unexpected moment of empathetic thinking based on physical proximity. This triumph leads to Lily's moment of aesthetic insight; her vision emerges at the moment not just of insight, but of physical sight – an ability to share perspectives literally. The painting is far from Freud's uncanny object, for while it is the product of such a shared perspective, it is not a repository of a shared perspective, taking on a life of its own. The line that completes Lily's painting can be seen as dividing or as centering, marking the gap or providing a bridge; it is the dark space, the marker of loss that points to the productive and connecting aesthetic imagination. The gap filled by this line points us back to the underlying problem of silence, absence, and loss so central to modernist writing, and that we first saw in Hardy's elegies with their dipodic rhythms. The aesthetic imagination here provides one method of bridging this gap, as transitory as that bridge may ultimately be.

CONCLUSION

Performing Empathy?

Throughout this book I have argued that we have to recognize how modernist empathy challenges premises about the integrity of the subject and the inviolability of one's own identity. The issue of empathy feels all the more important today as we are asked to limit our imaginative range and to fear, rather than stand in the shoes of, those who seem other. If there is a darkness at the heart of modernist empathy and a threat of loss that defines and delimits every movement outside the self, how can we use our understanding of the writers and places discussed in this book to inform our own representational projects and efforts at empathy today? I am not looking for a prescription – the ten acts of empathy that will help save a refugee or turn the tide against chauvinistic thinking – but rather for how we might see clearly the dangers and benefits of trying to see through someone else's eyes and stand in their shoes.

Debates continue about the ethical necessity of exercising our empathetic imagination; much hinges, I would argue, on our understanding of the preposition that is attached to the act of empathy: feeling *with*. Does this "with" signify an assumption of the perspective, or does it signify a companionship within that perspective? In other words, is this distance between the empathizing subject and the object of empathy maintained or elided? The threat to the subject that we have seen acknowledged and explored by the writers in the preceding chapters suggests that a line will persist between subject and object, self and other, even self and self, but that it can be set differently and is potentially porous. Thus, though the act of empathizing seems ethically good in and of itself, since it necessitates stepping outside the boundaries of the self and acknowledging both those boundaries and the possibility of there being an "outside," it also involves a constant negotiation between the self and the other. Recognizing the gap that exists – indeed, the gap that is a precondition of the empathetic act – is a humbling experience, for it reveals isolation in the very moment of attempting to bridge that isolation and to see beyond the narrow walls of the individual personality.

Turning to an early twentieth-century text that does not perform or manifest this isolation will help to clarify why emphasizing the gap is a useful process. This text, one of the most successful of the "Mass Declamations" of the 1930s, provides a politicized version of literary perspective-taking. The question of unity and of understanding other perspectives seemed increasingly complicated during the tense interwar period of the 1920s and '30s. World War I still loomed large in the imagination and experiences of those in England. The war had created fissures that Evelyn Waugh discussed over a decade after the end of the war in a 1929 article in *The Spectator*, claiming that after the war "a double cleft appeared in the life of Europe dividing it into three perfectly distinct classes between whom none but the most superficial sympathy can ever exist." He categorizes the generations as "a) the wistful generation who grew up and found their opinions before the war and were too old for military service b) the stunted and mutilated generation who fought c) the younger generation."[1] When the Spanish Civil War (1936–1939) broke out, it offered an outlet for that third category in particular.

In the literary world, this "younger generation" of British writers responded to these national and international changes in the form and content of their writing; poets saw the project of poetry as involving an outward turn as much as an inward one; as Michael Roberts writes in his introduction to the 1936 *The Faber Book of Modern Verse*, "Every vital age, perhaps, sees its own time as crucial and full of perils, but the problems and difficulties of our own age necessarily appear more urgent to us than those of any other, and the need for an evaluating, clarifying poetry has never been greater than it appears to be today."[2] Among those things that needed to be evaluated and clarified were the very questions about subjectivity, embodiment, and voice – and where the boundaries between self and other, reader and writer, and subject and object might lie – that we have seen taken up in previous chapters. Even more so, perhaps, the poetry begins to ask what kind of "illocutionary" power poetry might have, to use a term foregrounded first in J. L. Austin's *How to Do Things With Words* (originally presented as a series of talks in 1955) and provocatively reexamined in Judith Butler's *Excitable Speech* (1997).[3] As Butler notes, words that are illocutionary are performative in a literally active way: the word itself is the act; "the pronouncement is the act of speech at the same time as it is the speaking of an act."[4] As such, illocutionary words implicate the speaker in unexpected ways;

questions arise about the relationship of the speaking subject with those illocutionary words. If the words themselves are the action or deed, does the speaker become an actor and/or the creator of those words? When sounds become not simply descriptive, but also prescriptive, what kind of responsibility lies with the sounding voice? As Butler indicates, the questions of moral responsibility for illocutionary speech, and of when the speaking subject becomes the actor herself, are complicated. With her focus on injurious speech, Butler notes that "The question, then, of who is accountable for a given injury precedes and initiates the subject, and the subject itself is formed through being nominated to inhabit that grammatical and juridical site."[5] I want to take up this idea of inhabiting a *grammatical* site – for that is at the heart of the movement enacted by the performative "Mass Declamation" examined here – and to think about what the ethical possibilities are or may be when the project of perspective-taking involves engaging in a public, poetic speech act. A danger emerges, I argue, for an act that seems to inhabit the structure of empathetic thinking turns into one that erases both individual and ideological complexity.

Voicing "Us"

If we speak in unison, we might ask, do we feel more connected? Or, even more specifically when thinking about literature and poetry, if we use the same rhythm, do we feel more empathy? In the last years of the nineteenth century Henri Bergson was making such a claim, describing how central rhythm and music are to the empathetic experience: "The regularity of the rhythm establishes a kind of communication between [the dancer] and us."[6] Recent psychological studies suggest this might be the case: for example, one published in 2011 by the psychologists David DeSteno and Piercarlo Valdesolo showed that participants who engaged in synchronous rhythmic tapping with another person were twice as likely as those who did nonsynchronous tapping with a partner to provide help to someone *after* the experience. They concluded: "synchronous action functionally directs the experience of compassion in response to the plight of those around us, interests us in their well-being, and motivates us to help on their behalf."[7] In this example, which was one of the first to explore the effects on behavior *after* the synchronous experience had occurred, the shared experience simply involved rhythmic movements (tapping) and a uniform sound. It did not address what happens when language enters the mix, however – that change that brings us into the realm of poetry and song.

It also raises more questions about how we might understand lyric, rather than narrative, empathy, if rhythm is an aid to empathetic engagement.

To understand socially embedded questions of how shared rhythmic and linguistic performances might connect to empathetic engagement, specifically in a modern war-torn world, we can examine a curious phenomenon that became popular during the 1930s: Mass Declamations of synchronously performed poetry. The Mass Declamations – which began in 1936 and were choreographed public recitations of poems, usually performed at political meetings[8] – are particularly interesting to examine in terms of how a shared rhythmic experience might connect to the fascination of 1930s' poetry with spatial orientations, geographic location and dislocation, and shifts in perspective. The rhythmic and the spatial have to work in tandem, I believe, because the point of the Mass Declamations is to make the chanters sympathize *not* with each other – those people standing side by side – but with the cause of the Spanish people in a country far from Britain. It requires a form of imaginative empathy with an absent, perhaps never seen other (the Spanish people) and with an abstract concept (the Republican cause).

By moving into this poetry of the 1930s, I am shifting from the high-modernist writers' inward-focused understanding of empathic experience to an urge toward a collective "we." In Hardy's novels, we also saw an effort to position the reader to become a participant, to a certain degree, in the narrative and thereby to empathize (ideally) with the characters (and to increase books sales as well). Yet here the positioning takes another form; while Hardy oriented the readers on the space of the imaginary map of Wessex using narrative description, the Mass Declamations blur the relationship between the audience and the poetry and, using illocutionary language, reformulate the subjects' position in more radical terms: they make the audience into the speakers, indeed almost the creators, of their words as they are being voiced. But a central question is whether or not this experience ultimately is empathy; in other words, is there a moment when the line is crossed between feeling and thinking with another and becoming a part of a shared voice and movement?

With the opening of the Unity Theater in 1936, these group recitations became, in the words of critic Valentine Cunningham, "one of the characteristic (and more successful) attempts by left-wing poets . . . to achieve forms of a 'non-bourgeois' kind."[9] Cunningham quotes the 1943 reminiscences of R. Vernon Beste, who describes how the group, during a recitation of a poem by Jack Lindsay titled "On Guard for Spain!," chanted "Malaga!!" and "Teruel," and these words seemed, according to

Beste, "a deep growl of fury rather than a name, not just a place in Southern Spain, but a word to give vengeance a sharper meaning, a banner rallying the defenceless and shaming the cynical." Beste continues, "I not only knew *intellectually* that the Spanish People's fight was my fight, but for the first time *felt* that it was."[10] Beste's use of italics in this quotation highlights the layered quality – the cognitive as well as emotional assumption of a different perspective – of the empathetic experience he describes, which has been arrived at, it appears, through the recitation of the Spanish place names. And the result is, remarkably, a kind of action: Beste describes how, when a speaker "came on the platform to make her appeal [for contributions] three minutes afterwards there was hardly any need for her to speak – one was ashamed of being able to give no more than money."[11] I say "remarkably" here because one of the most hotly debated issues in empathy studies is whether empathy (and literary empathy in particular) promotes action.[12] In this case it appears to do so; the poem seems to have connected the London audience to the Spanish people's plight through a shared desire for vengeance.

Beste's Mass Declamation experience seems an ideal manifestation of literary empathy – it works not only to engage the participants in the experience, but also to lead to action. Of course, Beste is recounting this several years after the experience and from the perspective of one already convinced of the importance of the battle – hardly a dispassionate narrator. Yet Beste was not the only one affected by this particular poem; Jack Lindsay wrote in his memoir, *Fanfrolico and After*, that "it was continually done all over England by Unity Theatre or groups connected with the Left Book Club. It was performed in Trafalgar Square and at countless rallies," and a friend told Lindsay that "he had never in his life seen an audience so powerfully affected as by the declamation."[13] Moreover, the strategies that Beste describes as so powerful in the Mass Declamation – for one, the use of place names within a shared chant to mobilize identification with those fighting against Franco – emerge in quieter ways in the published poetry from the period. The question is not only whether the solitary "I" of lyric can perform the same work as the collective "growl" of the declamation, but, more importantly, what sort of strategies would be needed to do this. Such a project was desired by some poets; as Kevin Foster states in his essay on intellectuals and the war, poets such as John Cornford "welcomed . . . the subordination of the personal by the collective voice" in their poems.[14]

Yet this idea of subordination raises the question of whether empathy is involved when the personal is suppressed. In other words, poems that, in terms of their effect on the chanters, seem to present a primer on how to create an empathetic audience may in fact be doing something different. We must ask whether the words act in such an illocutionary way that they somehow change the speakers into the "we" that they present. Do they engender, in other words, a set of beliefs and a new identity? And, in doing so, are they shifting away from the project of an empathetic vision that, as Eliot had noted in his discussions of monads, has at its center a recognition of a multiplicity of points of view? As we saw Eliot claiming in a 1914 essay, "The discrimination of these points of view has a certain value inasmuch as we are apt, when we have passed from one point of view to another, let us say, more critical point of view, to forget that the first retains its own rights and is not absorbed" (*Complete Prose I*, 167). Here Eliot emphasizes the difficulty of remembering the possibility and power of each point of view; we forget all perspectives other than the one that we inhabit at the moment. The fundamental complexity and messiness of empathy – the persisting and necessary tension between subject and object – are precisely what Eliot and the other modernist writers have forced us to appreciate.

Work in both lyric studies and social psychology has examined the ambiguous nature of our understanding of the "we": when is "we" a collective of individuals versus a manifestation of a group mind? Does the assumption of a "we" involve the empathetic act of imagining other perspectives, and then aligning oneself with other perspectives into a shared viewpoint and place of action? Do minds merge or remain individual in a "we"? And then what happens when an individual is asked to imagine a group – a "them" – as opposed to another individual or individual object? The behavioral research examined by Mary-Catherine Harrison in relation to Victorian literature has shown that individuals process and respond to groups and individuals in fundamentally different ways: this is due to "our inability to empathize with groups" because when "we cannot imagine the subjective experience of individuals, we perceive instead an undifferentiated whole."[15] This obstacle to empathetic imagination with a group accounts for the problems that emerge when the "I" shifts to a "we" in literature with particularly political aims.

The unique and conflicted nature of the poetic "we" was thoroughly explored for the first time by scholar Bonnie Costello in *The Plural of Us* (2017). Costello argues that "we" can signal not only a "collective subject," but also an "individuated" and indeterminate one; thus, it can perform the seemingly incompatible functions of working as "a powerful communicative tool, perhaps the quintessential pronoun of oratory" as well as "of intimacy."[16] It is this slippage between the intimate and the oratorical that, in some ways, allows poetry to inhabit the interstices between the personal and the social. Yet if I return to my overarching argument about the kinds of gaps and losses that emerge when examining modernist empathy and the move between subject and object, we can also see how "we" functions as a charged term in relation to empathy. Empathy is predicated on the "I" and the "you" – empathizer and empathized – so that "we" may signal a critical change in that act of empathy.

With this reminder and warning, we can see why Lindsay's text might have been so effective when declaimed. Lindsay was an Australian who moved to England in the 1920s and never returned to his home country, publishing vast numbers of poems, memoirs, history, and art criticism throughout his life. He was a strong supporter of Mass Declamations, even writing a piece called "A Plea for Mass Declamations" in the *Left Review* in 1937. "On Guard" is a long poem (346 lines in the published version), and does not include several stanzas that Lindsay added for one of the recitations (the recitation that Beste probably heard, given Beste's description of the moment and the scene). In fact, the poem feels too long when it is read in print, overly and even tiresomely insistent on the theme, repeated at several points, that "the workers, going to battle, / went as to a fiesta."[17] Lindsay seems at pains to instruct the audience about the history of the conflict and the horrors being committed by Franco's troops. He begins:

> What you shall hear is the tale of the Spanish people.
> It is also your own life.
>   On guard, we cry!
> It is the pattern of the world today . . .

> I speak for the Spanish people,
> I speak for the Spanish people to the workers of the world.
> Men and women, come out of the numbered cells
> of harsh privation, mockingly called your homes,
> break through the deadening screen with your clenched fists,
> unrope the bells that jangle in the steeple of the sky,
> make the least gap of silence in the wall of day
> and you will hear the guns in Spain.   (253–4)

Lindsay's rhetorical and perspectival moves become immediately apparent in the first stanzas, for we shift in the first two lines from a recognition of the distance between us ("you," the listeners) and the subject of the poem ("the Spanish people") to an erasure of that distance: "It is also your own life." Of course, saying so does not ensure agreement, and Lindsay goes a step further in that final line of the stanza, moving beyond the elision of personal distance with his statement that "It is the pattern of the world today." The term "pattern" aestheticizes the experience of intersubjective movement that Lindsay proclaims in the first lines, even as it also foreshadows the patterning Lindsay will create through the repetition of lines and phrases and through the movements of stanzas. The second stanza immediately hones in on the issue of authority – "I speak for" – and with the repeated phrase that moves, in its second iteration, into a focus on the indirect object of this speaking (the "workers of the world"), it asks the audience to adopt a new identity, to become the workers of the world. The stanza resolves on what this speech act will do: open the ears of the audience members so that they will "hear" the guns being fired in Spain.

Even as this opening feels somewhat clunky when viewed on the page, the numbers of different perspectival moves that it employs and requires are impressive. We go from individuals listening to a story, to characters within that story, to representatives of a larger pattern, then back to our role as audience members, now abstracted as "workers of the world," and in turn back into an imaginative and a spatial shift that will allow us to escape the prison cells of our isolated existences and become aware of the conflict. Moreover, the poem was written not to be read but to be chanted by a large group of people. The "I" is therefore multiple, and the "you" is both the listeners and the chanters themselves. This is where the power and effectiveness of Lindsay's perspectival shifts emerge; they illustrate the sort of action that is already occurring within the chanters as they voice these lines. The speakers embody – very literally give voice to – the moves that we see on the page.

The perspectival shifts described in Lindsay's Mass Declamation poem bring us back to the aesthetic roots of the word "empathy" and to Lee's discussions of the embodied nature of the empathetic experience. Lee's interest in an empathetic experience of art was sparked by the physical reactions that her lover and collaborator, Kit Anstruther-Thompson, experienced when looking at works of visual art. With Anstruther-Thomson as her model, Lee connected this form of "feeling into" the artwork with theories of empathy, arguing that

> Such projection *of ourselves into* external objects, such interpretation of their modes of existence by our own experience, such *Einfühlung* is not merely manifest throughout all poetry, where it borders on and overlaps moral and dramatic sympathy, but is at the bottom of numberless words and expressions whose daily use has made us overlook this special peculiarity. We say, for instance, that hills *roll* and mountains *rise*, although we know as a geological fact that what they really do is suffer denudation above and thickening below.[18]

Lee's mention of moral sympathy raises the important and essential question of the ethics of this dramatic assumption of another perspective that we see manifested in the Mass Declamation. On the one hand, the perspectival shifts seem to operate for a cause that we can support: the resistance against the spread of fascism in general, and the terrorization of a national population in particular. On the other hand, these shifts raise the question of the ethical implications of claiming the voice of a group that not only is far away, but also is the victim of violence. Lee is talking about occupying and understanding works of art: she writes that "in looking at the Doric column and its entablature, we are attributing to the lines and surfaces, to the spatial forms, those dynamic experiences which we should have were we to put our bodies into similar conditions."[19] The stakes are quite different when the "objects" of this perspective-taking are humans fighting in a war, and perhaps especially when the poem itself is in service of fueling a conflict.

Thus, the performative voicing of the plight of the Spanish people begins to feel more ethically suspect as the poem continues. The poem moves without warning in the different stanzas from a "we" that is the "we" of the Spanish people to a "we" that has a more distanced and authoritative position than of those on the ground in Spain. Lindsay describes how:

> After the February elections
> the people sang in the streets of work.
> . . .
> The sun tied ribbons in all the trees
> when we led the prisoners out of the jails
> . . .
> The locks of the prisons of poverty
> were broken by the hammers of unity,
> and brushing the cobwebs of old night away
> we came out into the factories of day.
>
> (Lindsay, "On Guard," 254)

Voicing memories and making them come to life, the speakers become authors of these memories. In most of the lines the "we" seems to be Spanish, for it has led prisoners out of the jails and emerged from the ignorance of poverty with the help of the clarifying logic of Communism. Yet still, even here, there is a slippage to a more distanced perspective that can view the scene as if from afar: "the people sang in the streets." And these shifts in perspective continue throughout the poem, at times taking on the admonishing voice of the instructor: "Remember, Spanish people, / the humble marchers shot down out of side-streets" and "Remember what

was suffered in 1934. / Cry out, and cry again, / On guard, people of Spain!"
(255). As the poem tracks the rise of Franco and the fascist forces, it shifts
from the distanced description of "the people" and the "Spanish people"
(256) as they dealt with the threats to their freedom to the engaged first-
person plural "We" who "sought the heart of that alarm, / tracking the
spoor of danger. We were freedom's foresters / on that wild morning"
(257). As the poem reaches the climax of the slaughter on July 20, 1936 (the
fourth day after the outbreak of war), the perspective shifts from the
communal to the individual – "we" to the "I" – as it delves into
a personal experience of terror and death:

> We rushed the Montana barracks
> with some old pistols and our bare hands
> through swivelling machine-gun fire.
> I was there.
>   I saw the officers cowering,
> their faces chalked with fear.   (259)

The stark "I was there" locates the speaker – in this case, the many speakers – like a pin placed upon a battle map; it is a linguistic marker, a rooting
of the "I" in space, an embedding of the speaker into the setting and the
events. The poem moves into alternating rhymes at this point, so that the
rhythmic regularity emphasizes the unity of the speaking "I," who
describes how the "fascists shot my children first, / they made me stand
and see" (259). We are in the realm of intense emotional experience, fueled
by the shocking nature of the scene and the acts. Yet even in this movement
inward to the "I," which makes each speaking voice proclaim an individual
set of stakes, we are confronted with the wholly unspecified enemy – the
fascist. The dominant pattern becomes an inward turn followed by an
abstracting outward shift, and from this intense moment of personal
identification and shared suffering the poem moves outward again, to
the forces mustered by the fascists and a view of the destruction wreaked
on Spain.

As the project of fusing the experiences of the British crowd reciting the
poem with those of the Spanish people becomes more explicit, the chanters
are reminded that they not only have a common cause, but should think of
themselves as also having a shared experience: "Have you ever faced your
deepest despair? / Then what you see in the agony of Spain / is your own
body crucified" (262). This equating of sufferings may seem callous –
would most of the reciters have faced despair comparable to seeing their
children killed in front of them or watching their land destroyed? – but it is

remarkably effective, with its conflation of the martyred Spain and the Christ-like martyred body of the listener. And with this appeal for unity, the poem moves into the rhetoric of Communism: "workers of the world, we cry" (262) and "Workers of the world, unite for us" (263). From the individual "I" to the collective Communist "we" – this is the gesture that works to harness the individual subject's experience into a movement; here is where the poem no longer hides its propagandistic agenda.

At this moment, the differences between empathetic imagining and erasure of individuality emerge; the rhetoric of propaganda, even when in support of the most just cause, results in an erasure of the individual experience and therefore a subversion of the possibility of moving from self to other. This is the moment when we can no longer talk about empathy, for two reasons. First, with the shift to a political stance, we no longer are thinking about taking on the perspective of another, but are instead focusing on the immersion of the self within a prescribed and generalized perspective. Second, empathy depends on a distance traversed, a movement between self and other, and when the "other" transforms into an all-encompassing identity that subsumes the self and the other under one mantle (in this case, the British audience member and the Spanish citizen become "workers of the world" fighting fascism), then there is no longer a distance to traverse. Empathy cannot occur, in other words, when a unified identity is assumed.

As an act, therefore, empathy depends on an interest and a belief in the primacy of the individual, since it depends on the acknowledgment of a difference – a distance – between subject and object, even as that distance is bridged (or the attempt to bridge it is made). Thus, a claim like the one made by the editors of a recent collection on *Organizing through Empathy* (2014) only partially rings true. The editors argue that empathy not only leads to prosocial behavior, but also challenges the tenets of global capitalism because "the obvious tension between individualism and self-interest becomes incompatible with the sense of oneness that is experienced through high levels of empathy."[20] First and foremost, what *Modernist Empathy* has shown is that empathy both depends on and engenders an experience of often immolating aloneness – not oneness. When that sense of oneness becomes dominant, as we saw in Lindsay's declamation, we move out of the realm of empathy and into the creation of a political collective – a collective consciousness that needs no empathy, since it is always already shared and unified.[21] Empathy might be a unifying act, but it is the product of an essential disjunction between self and other; should that disjunction disappear, there is no longer the context in which empathy can emerge. A "we" that is a collection of individuals, rather than a group mind, is needed for empathy to work. Recognizing and fostering this self-conscious, yet outward-reaching attitude in the face of the ethical pitfalls that lurk, as well as the near impossibility of maintaining an undamaged individual subject position, is the work that modernist literature presents and encourages. Modernist texts invite us to occupy other perspectives, and simultaneously reveal the perils to our sense of unique subjectivity of such movements; empathy, even if impossible to perform comprehensively, emerges as fundamental to our fractured selves.

Notes

1 Modernizing Empathy, Locating Loss

1. Proust, *Time Regained*, 299.
2. Ibid., 298.
3. Ibid., 301.
4. Wood, "Introduction for Orhan Pamuk," Sept. 22, 2009.
5. See Wispe's "History of the Concept of Empathy" and Hammond's "Introduction" to *Empathy and the Psychology of Modernism*.
6. This speech was given on May 1, 2009. Indeed, from as early as an interview in 2004 by Charlie Rose, Obama identified one of the biggest problems as the "empathy deficit," which he defined as "the inability of people to stand in other folks' shoes." See http://cultureofempathy.com/obama/SpeechIndex.htm.
7. Obama and Robinson, November 19, 2015: www.nybooks.com/articles/2015/11/19/president-obama-marilynne-robinson-conversation-2/.
8. Suzanne Keen takes this up in *Empathy and the Novel*, arguing that literary empathy does not lead to altruistic actions: since "the contract of fictionality offers a no-strings-attached opportunity for emotional transactions of great intensity," expecting altruistic action "puts too great a burden on empathy and the novel" (168; hereafter cited parenthetically). Mary-Catherine Harrison ("The Paradox of Fiction and the Ethics of Empathy") points to the interesting historical example of Dickens's *The Christmas Carol* for an alternative stance. Physicians have been especially interested in the question of whether reading literature can help doctors empathize with patients (see Shapiro and Rucker, "Can Poetry Make Better Doctors?").
9. See Coplan and Goldie's "Introduction" to *Empathy: Philosophical and Psychological Perspectives*.
10. Edward Bradford Titchener's 1909 *Lectures on the Experimental Psychology of Thought-Processes* introduced the term to the world of American psychology. Vernon Lee and C. Ansthruther-Thomson's 1912 book on *Beauty and Ugliness and Other Studies in Psychological Aesthetics* brought to a wider public the essays that Lee had published earlier.

11. See Hulme's "Modern Art and its Philosophy."

12. See Morgan's "Critical Empathy: Vernon Lee's Aesthetics and the Origins of Close Reading."

13. Hulme, "Modern Art and its Philosophy," 273.

14. Hammond, *Empathy and the Psychology of Modernism*, 124, 125. Hereafter cited parenthetically.

15. Blasing, *Lyric Poetry*, 51.

16. Smith, *The Theory of Moral Sentiments*, 12.

17. Ibid., 11.

18. Robert Solomon describes sympathy this way in his *In Defense of Sentimentality*, arguing that empathy "is not as such an emotion. Rather it refers to the *sharing* of emotion (any emotion). Sympathy, by contrast, *is* an emotion, a quite particular though rather suffuse and contextually defined emotion. It is therefore sympathy that does the motivational work which Smith requires [an act of imagination by which one can appreciate the feelings of another (51)], but that in turn requires empathy, the *capacity* to "read" and to some extent share other people's emotions" (69).

19. Greiner, "Thinking of Me Thinking of You," 418. Hereafter cited parenthetically.

20. Culler, *Theory of the Lyric*, 35.

21. James, *Psychology: A Briefer Course*, 209.

22. Blasing, *Lyric Poetry*, 4.

23. Jonathan Cullers and Eva Zettelmann recently debated this at the "Situating Lyric" conference (Boston University, June 7–11, 2017); Zettelmann argued that it is impossible to read most lyrics without a speaking subject and, in fact, that it enriches the experience to be able to imagine an individual.

24. Srikanth, *Constructing the Enemy*, 41.

25. Berlant, "Poor Eliza," 641.

26. Ibid., 648.

27. Sherry, *Ezra Pound, Wyndham Lewis, and Radical Modernism*, 11.

28. See articles in *Narrative* by Mary-Catherine Harrison ("The Paradox of Fiction and the Ethics of Empathy") and D. Rae Greiner ("Sympathy Time"), for example. Amy Coplan and Peter Goldie's *Empathy: Philosophical and Psychological Perspectives* brings together discussions in psychology and philosophy.

29. Mitchell, *Victorian Lessons in Empathy and Difference*, x.

30. Harrison, "The Paradox of Fiction and the Ethics of Empathy," 266.

31. Levine, "Victorian Realism," 98.

32. Jameson, *The Antinomies of Realism*, 5.

33. Quoted in Royle, *The Uncanny*, 258, from Scholes and Kellogg, *The Nature of Narrative*, 272.

34. See Elliott Holt's recent review in the *New York Times*: "Gustave Flaubert believed that the ideal author should be 'present everywhere and visible nowhere,' but in stressing invisibility, Flaubert was ahead of his time. Most 19th-century novelists didn't try to hide their authorial presence. With modernism's emphasis on the self and the rendering of individual consciousness, omniscience became unfashionable. Twentieth-century realists moved closer to their characters and wrote in the first person or limited third" ("The Return of Omniscience," 29). He goes on to make the claim that there is a return to omniscience in some contemporary fiction, but instead of the author as God, we get the author as smartphone.

35. Cristina Griffin argues that we need to read George Eliot as proposing another version of omniscience that emerges from an embodied, sympathetic experience. She writes that, "Eliot's fictions envision omniscience as a consequence of embodiment – and, in particular, a consequence of the embodied experience of sensory sympathy" ("George Eliot's Feuerbach," 489) – the development of what Eliot calls a "fine ear" in *Scenes from A Clerical Life* (ibid., 491). Omniscience therefore emerges from a deeply – and unexpectedly – attuned experience of the world and others.

36. Woolf, "Mr. Bennett and Mrs. Brown," 4. Hereafter cited parenthetically.

37. Hulme, "Romanticism and Classicism," 52.

38. Ibid.

39. Wordsworth, *Selected Poems*, 164.

40. Howarth, *British Poetry in the Age of Modernism*, 25.

41. Woolf, of course, does talk about various moments of ecstasy that can emerge in acts of creation (often in the act that precedes the writing). See my essay, "Masochistic Modernisms," for a discussion of this aspect of Woolf's theory of aesthetic creation.

42. Lee and Ansthruther-Thomson, *Beauty and Ugliness*, 59.

43. See Mitchell's discussion of the distinction between empathy and sympathy, for example; she argues that the realist novel "makes empathy possible by teaching us that the alienation that exists between the self and the other cannot be fully overcome, that the alterity of the human other is infinite and permanent" (*Victorian Lessons in Empathy and Difference*, x).

44. Benjamin, "On the Mimetic Faculty," *Reflections*, 333.

45. Butler, *Excitable Speech*, 16.

46. See Austin's *How to Do Things With Words* (originally presented as a series of talks in 1955); Austin does not focus on the subject ("I") of performative speech acts in his book, but the constitution of the subject through speech acts is implicit, and it is what Butler builds upon.

47. Garber, "Compassion," 24, her italics.

48. Weinstein, *Unknowing: The Work of Modernist Fiction*, 84.

49. Stein, *On the Problem of Empathy*, 63.
50. See her Introduction (and page 7, in particular), for her discussion of the term "fellow feeling."
51. See, for example, Shamay-Tsoory et al. They found that the areas of the brain used for cognitive empathy (which they equate with Theory of Mind – what "someone else thinks about what someone else thinks" ("Two Systems for Empathy," 621)) and for emotional empathy were strikingly different, so that a subject with a lesion on the part used for cognitive empathy, for example, could still prove adept at experiencing emotional empathy. See also Cox et al., "The Balance Between Feeling and Knowing," for further discussion and citations.
52. Jonathan Flatley argues that affect proves more useful as a term in discussions about "the relational more than the expressive" (*Affective Mapping*, 12); affects have come to be defined as irreducible and, to a certain extent, universal, operating separately from cognition in the brain. Emotion, on the other hand, is defined as "the result of the inevitable interaction of affects with thoughts, ideas, beliefs, habits, instincts, and other affects. If affects are not reducible, emotions are, and it is emotions that vary from context to context, person to person" (ibid., 16). Deleuze and Guattari's theory of "nomad thought" similarly works to destabilize the hierarchical nature of subject–object relationships; the nomad is one who stands as the "Deterritorialized par excellance" (*A Thousand Plateaus*, 381). Like the relational nature of affect, these nomad lines of thought traverse paths that redefine the terrain, and such nomad reading practices seem to exist outside of ideological structures of meaning-making
53. Greiner argued that the formal "protocols" of sympathy define the realist novel, while those of empathy "align with poetry, especially modernist and symbolic" (420).
54. Detloff, *The Persistence of Modernism*, 4.
55. Culler, *Theory of the Lyric*, 6.
56. Tiffany, *Infidel Poetics*, 3, 6.
57. Berlant, "Poor Eliza," 648.
58. Freud, "The Uncanny" (1919), 368. Hereafter cited parenthetically.
59. Lee and Ansthruther-Thomson, *Beauty and Ugliness*, 2.
60. Ibid., 18.
61. Woolf, *Diary: Vol. 3*, 104.
62. Woolf, *Mrs. Dalloway*, 186.
63. Eliot, *Collected Poems*, 60.
64. Quoted in Royle, *The Uncanny*, 16.
65. See Crangle's *Prosaic Desires: Modernist Knowledge, Boredom, Laughter, and Anticipation*, and Sumner's *A Route to Modernism: Hardy, Lawrence, Woolf* for such a use of Hardy.

66. Hardy, *Tess of the D'Urbervilles*, 140.
67. Lee, *The Beautiful*, 66 (my emphasis).

2 Disorientation, Elegy, and the Uncanny: Modernist Empathy Through Hardy

1. For critics claiming him as a modernist, see Sara Crangle's *Prosaic Desires: Modernist Knowledge, Boredom, Laughter, and Anticipation*, and Rosemary Sumner's *A Route to Modernism: Hardy, Lawrence, Woolf.*
2. Hardy, *Thomas Hardy's Personal Writings*, 129. Hereafter cited parenthetically.
3. Woolf, "Hours in a Library," 57.
4. See Michael Millgate's *Thomas Hardy* (and the section on revising the novels in his biography of Hardy [chapter 18]); also see Simon Gatrell's *Hardy the Creator: A Textual Biography* for reflections on this whole process, which focuses particularly on the ways that Hardy consolidated and codified his references to Wessex. Millgate and Gatrell hereafter cited parenthetically.
5. See the *Oxford English Dictionary*, online edition (1989) for a comprehensive definition of geography. The first definition deals with the field: "The science which has for its object the description of the earth's surface, treating of its form and physical features, its natural and political divisions, the climate, productions, population, etc., of the various countries"; the third definition focuses on the subject of study: "the geographical features of a place or region; the range or extent of what is known geographically."
6. Hardy anticipates the intersection of the cognitive and the affective theories of empathy that are central to studies of empathy today; as Keen writes, "Empathy studies have from the start challenged the division of emotion and cognition" (Keen, *Empathy and the Novel*, 27).
7. Hardy quotes from a letter by an actress who performed a scene from *Tess* at his house: Hardy "talked of Tess as if she was someone real whom he had known and liked tremendously" (Hardy, *The Life of Thomas Hardy by Florence Hardy: Early Life and Late Life*, 244). Hereafter cited parenthetically as *Life I* or *Life II* to differentiate between the volumes.
8. Quoted in Keen, *Thomas Hardy's Brains*, 181; emphasis in the original. Hereafter cited parenthetically.
9. Scarry, "The Difficulty of Imagining Other People," 103.
10. Cohen, "Faciality and Sensation in Hardy's *The Return of the Native*," 440.
11. Widdowson, "Moments of Vision," 97; his emphasis.
12. Deleuze and Parnet, *Dialogues*, 39–40.
13. Miller, *Topographies*, 40.
14. Hardy met Pater in 1886. Dale Kramer argues that Pater is one of the most pervasive influences on *Tess* in terms of the novel's exploration of perception (Kramer, *Hardy: Tess of the D'Urbervilles*, 31).

15. Hardy's library included a number of books on the field of geography (as well as more than twenty maps, many of which he annotated). A partial list includes: William Hughes, *A Manual of Geography Physical, Industrial and Political* (London: Longman, Green, Longman, Roberts, & Green, 1864), *A Handbook for Residents and Travellers in Wilts and Dorset* (London: John Murray, 1899), and M. J. B. Baddeley, *The English Lake District* (London: Dulau & Co., 1902). Hardy also had one of Patrick Geddes's most famous books, *The Evolution of Sex* (probably an 1890 edition; the volume has no date). This list comes from the wonderful online catalog provided by Michael Millgate at *Thomas Hardy's Library at Max Gate: Catalogue of an Attempted Reconstruction* (http://hardy.library.utoronto.ca/). Hardy also owned an impressive collection of maps of both England and abroad, many of which are housed at the British Library, the Dorset Country Museum, and Colby College.

16. See Irwin ("The Ordnance Survey: Roy's Legacy") or Harris et al. ("British Maps and Charts") for discussions of the Ordnance Survey. Halford Mackinder was the first reader in geography appointed to Oxford (in 1887), and he remained the only one until 1899 (Dickinson, *Regional Concept*, 44).

17. Godlewska, "From Enlightenment Vision to Modern Science?" 237; hereafter cited parenthetically. See also Pite, *Hardy's Geography*, 4–7. Geography was not a recognized field in universities until the last decades of the nineteenth century. The Royal Geographical Society began to push for this recognition in 1871, but it was only in 1886 that Oxford and Cambridge agreed to add geography to their curriculums (Keltie, *The Position of Geography in British Universities*, 1–4).

18. Darby, "Academic Geography in Britain," 15.

19. Geike, *The Teaching of Geography*, 10; hereafter cited parenthetically. See Keltie (*The Position of Geography in British Universities*) and Clark (*Geography in the Schools of Europe*) for the role of geography in the British educational system.

20. Mill, "On Research in the Geographical Science," 416.

21. Quoted in Said, *Orientalism*, 216.

22. Matless, "Regional Surveys and Local Knowledges," 465. Hereafter cited parenthetically.

23. The connections between nineteenth-century geographic practices and contemporary findings in empathy studies emerge in the overlap of spatial and cognitive perspective-taking. Contemporary empirical studies by psychologists have shown that spatially based perspective-taking is central to narrative empathy because, in the words of one group, "perspective-taking in narrative is a form of empathetic identification with the principal protagonist" (Ziegler, Mitchell, and Currie, "How Does Narrative Cue

Children's Perspective Taking?" 16). For example, another experiment found that even very young children would adopt the protagonist's point of view in a narrated scene, engaging in an "imaginative displacement" in which they "imagined themselves at the same location in the same space seeing events from that perspective" (Rall and Harris, "In Cinderella's Slippers," 206). A later study supported this finding by showing how children create mental models of narratives that allow them not simply to remember, but actually to *inhabit* those spaces (Ziegler, Mitchell, and Currie, "How Does Narrative Cue Children's Perspective Taking?" 124). Work on adults has produced similar results – namely, that spatial mental models of narrative actions "allow implicit relations to be computed in working memory" (de Vega, "Characters and their Perspectives in Narratives Describing Spatial Environments," 124). This adoption of narrative-based perspectives implies the ability to see and view things from a protagonist's perspective. The cognitive act of empathy within narrative therefore involves a metaphorical move in space, exactly the kind of move that early geographers worked to literalize when using surveys to move from individual to more distanced perspectives.

24. Hardy, *The Woodlanders*, 5. Unless otherwise cited, references to *The Woodlanders* refer to the 1981 Clarendon Press edition, which follows the Wessex Edition copy. I contrast this version with the Harper book edition, which is based on the text from their first 1887 printing and which was set from proofs from the *Macmillan's Magazine* publication (May 1886–April 1887). See Kramer's list of editions in his introduction to *The Woodlanders* (63–64).

25. Hardy, *The Woodlanders* (HarperCollins, 1905), 3. This edition cited parenthetically as Harper edition.

26. Kramer, Introduction, *The Woodlanders*, 49.

27. Barrell, "Geographies of Hardy's Wessex," 103; his emphasis. Hereafter cited parenthetically.

28. Altick, *The English Common Reader*, 296.

29. Women were counted separately, since they were not categorized by career (Altick, *The English Common Reader*, 236).

30. Rode, *Mapping and Reading Hardy's Roads*, 3.

31. "Thomas Hardy's Wessex," 26. Hereafter cited parenthetically.

32. Laurence Lerner and John Holmstrom, eds. *Thomas Hardy and his Readers*, 60. Hereafter cited parenthetically.

33. Hardy, *Tess of the D'Urbervilles*, 18. Hereafter cited parenthetically. References to *Tess* come from this Oxford edition, which uses the final revised version, except where otherwise noted.

34. See also Pite, *Hardy's Geography*, for a critique of Barrell's position (12–16). Pite hereafter cited parenthetically.

35. Relevant here is Widdowson's argument that Tess's character seems a composite of others' perspectives ("Moments of Vision," 88). Also see Katherine Maynard's discussion of a "Hardyean universe" in which people inevitably "misread their environment" (*Thomas Hardy's Tragic Poetry*, 86).

36. Quoted in Holland, "The Power(?) of Literature," 395. See Holland also for a discussion of why cognitive science seems to support Coleridge's claim.

37. Hardy, *Collected Letters*, 12. Hereafter cited parenthetically.

38. Lea, *Thomas Hardy's Wessex*, xxii. Hereafter cited parenthetically.

39. See Slack, "Hardy's Revisions," for a list of these changes.

40. Levinson, "Object-Loss and Object-Bondage," 571.

41. Rosemary Sumner argues that this picture should be read as part of the Surrealist legacy and as a signal of Hardy's modernist urge to defamiliarize our surroundings (*A Route to Modernism*, 36).

42. Culler, "Why Lyric?" 204.

43. Ibid., 205.

44. Nishimura argues that we should see Hardy's use of the pathetic fallacy as "something more than a stereotypically romantic way of seeing the natural world, a distortion of truth by emotion," because Hardy's poems so fully engage with the way that the pathetic fallacy is linguistically determined due to the "abundance of 'humanizing' terms in the English language" ("Thomas Hardy and the Language of the Inanimate," 898).

45. See Sacks for a list of the conventions (*The English Elegy*, 2) and for a discussion of Hardy's revision of elegiac conventions (ibid., 234–235).

46. Keen, *Hardy's Brains*, 188.

47. Sacks argues that while most of the poems in this sequence emphasize the lack of human impressions on nature, Hardy's use of the pathetic fallacy ultimately works to complete the task of mourning (*The English Elegy*, 254).

48. Shelley, *Poetry and Prose*, 77.

49. Levinson, "Object-Loss and Object-Bondage," 572.

50. Davie, *With the Grain*, 13–14. Hereafter cited parenthetically.

51. See also Pite, *Hardy's Geography*, and Kort, *Place and Space in Modern Fiction*, for further insight into Hardy and place.

52. Ramazani, *Poetry of Mourning*, 4. Hereafter cited parenthetically.

53. The two terms that I use in this sentence – space and place – have been the subject of discussion by both geographers and cultural or literary critics. Space, the more inclusive the two terms, is usually designated as an a priori, abstract arena (see Kort's discussion in *Place and Space in Modern Fiction*). In *The Production of Space*, Henri Lefebvre challenged this Enlightenment model with his version of space as created by social processes. Yet, while space now is seen as constructed and, therefore, ideologically bound, it still functions as an inclusive term that can be applied to both physical and

mental arenas. Place, as we will see later in the chapter, is referred to by scholars such as Timothy Oakes, as the site of agency ("Place and the Paradox of Modernity"). This element of place becomes, I argue, contested in Hardy's elegies.

54. Specifically, *modernist* mourning has been the focus of a number of critical works. Ramazani's *Poetry of Mourning* is, of course, an early example of this. More recent discussions of the connections between modernist aesthetic concerns and the project of mourning occur in Ricardi (*The Ends of Mourning*), Rae's collection of essays (*Modernism and Mourning*), and Moglen (*Mourning Modernity*). All of these works share a commitment to exploring the continuum between mourning and melancholia – a continuum that Rae, for one, asks us to revisit through an examination of the formal strategies of modernist texts that may offer "resistance" to mourning (*Modernism and Mourning*, 16).

55. The *OED* gives as its first definition of "mark": "To trace out boundaries for; to plot out (ground); to set out the ground plan of (a building); (fig.) to plan out, design." It gives in definition 11 the following description and example: "To make perceptible or recognizable, by some sign or indication. 1904 Grove's *Dict. Music* I. 18/1: The famous instrumentalists of the classical school ... were accustomed to mark the natural accent ... by a hardly perceptible prolongation of the first note of the bar" (from the Online *OED* draft revision, March 2005).

56. This view of Hardy's poetry is reinforced by his oft-quoted comment about his method of composition: "Among his papers were quantities of notes on rhythm and metre: with outlines and experiments in innumerable original measures, some of which he adopted from time to time. These verse skeletons were mostly blank, and only designed by the usual marks for long and short syllables, accentuations, etc., but they were occasionally made up of "nonsense verses" – such as, he said, were written when he was a boy by students of Latin prosody with the aid of a 'Gradus'" (*Life II*, 79–80).

57. Taylor, *Hardy's Metres and Victorian Prosody*, 87. Hereafter cited parenthetically.

58. Omond references Patmore's essay and is sympathetic to the idea of a foot containing "action and reaction, systole and diastole," but he dismisses Patmore's claim that dipody necessitates a silent foot at the end of every line (*A Study of Metre*, 80). In his essay, George Stewart tries to make the proof for dipodic meters more scientific with what he calls the "Dipodic Index": an analysis of the stresses accorded different parts of speech in various poems ("A Method Toward the Study of Dipodic Verse," 989). The debate continues today. After hearing my presentation at the 2007 MSA conference, scholar and poet Stephen Burt wrote about it on a Poetry

Foundation blog, www.poetryfoundation.org/harriet/2007/11/the-map-that-hangs-by-me-or-thomas-hardy-or-blogging-the-msa-part-two/, and several people responded to his entry with their own readings regarding whether or not "The Place on the Map" could be considered dipodic.

59. Hardy, *The Literary Notebooks of Thomas Hardy: Volume 2*, 192. Hardy read these lines in 1906 in Patmore's *Ameila, Tamerton, Church-Tower, Etc.* (1878).

60. Campbell, "Tennyson and Hardy's Ghostly Metres," 286. This essay was expanded in *Rhythm and Will in Victorian Poetry*. John Hughes engages in a complementary exploration, though Hughes is less interested in the metrical resonances between the two poets than what he describes as their sharing of a "similar affective scenario" ("Tennyson Revisited: Hardy's 'After a Journey,'" 155).

61. Armstrong, *Haunted Hardy*, 134.

62. My quotation comes from Book XI of the 1805 Prelude (428). See discussions of the "spots of time" by Lucy Newlyn ("The Noble Living and the Noble Dead") and Nicola Trott ("Wordsworth: The Shape of the Poetic Career"). Theresa Kelley enriches her discussion of the "imaginative restoration" of these spots, with insight into how they reveal the various poetic selves that are partially hidden from the reader (*Wordsworth's Revisionary Aesthetics*, 122).

63. The *OED* combines these two seemingly exclusive meanings of pantomime in its first definition: "To express oneself through silent or imitative gestures; (also) to make an absurd spectacle or display of oneself, to go around behaving as though in a pantomime" (Online *OED*, draft revision December 2007).

64. Freud, "The Uncanny," 369–370.

65. Royle, *The Uncanny*, 84.

66. Freud, *Beyond the Pleasure Principle*, 61.

67. To the confusion of his readers, in most of his volumes Hardy arranged his poems in a haphazard order that accounts for neither the chronology of composition nor thematic similarities. In his defensive "Apology" at the beginning of his 1922 book *Late Lyrics and Earlier* (the title of which itself suggests a disrupted chronology and a retrospective process of creation), Hardy provides an inadequate explanation of this seemingly careless practice, claiming that "the difficulties of arranging the themes in a graduated kinship of moods would have been so great that irrelation was almost unavoidable with efforts so diverse" (*Complete Poems*, 559). And while Hardy was known to be careless about certain elements of composition, most notably in the serializations of his novels, I think that a more satisfying reason behind his haphazard ordering is that, in terms of the way that Hardy saw space and time interacting, such juxtapositions are more true to life than would be neat chronologies of cause and effect.

68. Though in Cornwall, Saint-Juliot is an English name and is pronounced phonetically, with the accent on the first syllable and the second two syllables elided (JUL-yot).

69. See *The Complete Poetical Works of Thomas Hardy: Volume II* (58–59), for all of the variations between various editions and the holograph. In the 1915 edition, Hynes notes that the second line is slightly different: "I was but made fancy."

70. "Fancy" is Hardy's chosen term for the project of poetry, as he makes clear with his critique of Wordsworth's choice of the word "imagination" in the Preface to the *Lyrical Ballads*. He boldly rewrites Wordsworth's formulation: "He should have put the matter somewhat like this: In works of *passion and sentiment* (not 'imagination and sentiment') the language of verse is the language of prose. In works of *fancy* (or *imagination*), 'poetic diction' (of the real kind) is proper, and even necessary" (*Life II*, 85).

71. I read the middle two lines, which only have two stresses and are likewise set off by their indentations, as amphibrachs (˘ / ˘), which create a similarly rhythmical movement, though one could also scan them as containing three feet (iamb, pyrrhic, trochee). I find the amphibrach more convincing because of the galloping rhythm of the poem as a whole.

72. Toponymy is the study of place names.

73. Taylor's reading of the first few lines goes as follows, with the circles used to indicate where some might read an accent and others elide (thereby allowing the lines to embody either a tetrameter or a pentameter meter):

> /　　　　•　　/　　　　/　　　　/
> Hereto I come to view a voiceless ghost;
> 　/　　　　/　　　•　　　/　　　　/
> Whither, O whither will its whim now draw me?
> /　　　　/　　　　/　　　　/
> Up the cliff, down, till I'm lonely, lost,
> 　　　/　　　/　　　/　　•　　/
> And the unseen waters' ejaculations awe me. (98)

74. Oakes, "Place and the Paradox of Modernity," 510, 511. Hereafter cited parenthetically. Oakes makes his argument to counteract scholars who have claimed that modernity in general (and modernism, in particular) ignored and suppressed the idea of place (the local and specific) in favor of an abstract, totalizing space. See Harvey, *The Condition of Postmodernity*, especially chapter 15, for a discussion of this Enlightenment model of space.

75. Samuel Hynes points out this choice of order in his explanatory note to the poem (Hardy, *Complete Poetical Works*, 488).

76. In 1896 Hardy was recovering from the uproar around *Jude*. He wrote about his hope to express "more fully in verse ideas and emotions which run counter

to the inert crystallized opinion" (*Life II*, 57). Armstrong describes this as the "crisis poem" (*Haunted Hardy*, 8).

77. Change noted in Hynes, *The Complete Poetical Works*, 25. Hardy uses a number of amphibrachs in this poem, in particular at the end of the first half of the lines ("in **Wes**sex" (1); "no **com**rade" (5), for example (stressed syllables are bold)). The same place in the line is also often held by anapests or dactyls, which create that same feeling of urgency.

78. Taylor, *Hardy's Metres and Victorian Prosody*, 96. We can see the possibility of a dipodic reading in the following stanza, for example (this reading is mine, not Taylor's; he does not actually discuss the poem at any length in his book, though I use the same notation as he does above in "After a Journey"):

/ • / / • /

In the lowlands I have no comrade, not even the lone man's friend—

/ • / / • • /

Her who suffreth long and is kind; accepts what he is too weak to mend:

• / / • / • /

Down there they are dubious and askance; there nobody thinks as I,

/ • / • / • /

But mind-chains do not clank where one's next neighbor is the sky.

79. Weinstein, *Unknowing*, 2.

3 Disorienting Empathy: World War I and the Traumas of Perspective-Taking

1. Sandburg, "Grass," 235.
2. See Sorum, "Thinking about Space: Mapping and Perception in WWI Literature" for a further discussion of Lefebvre.
3. For example, see G. R. Crone's discussion of the effects of war on geographic endeavors. He points out, in particular, that the war inspired interest "in the potentiality of air photography as a method of mapping" ("British Geography in the Twentieth Century," 205).
4. *Parade's End* consists of four volumes: *Some Do Not* (1924), *No More Parades* (1925), *A Man Could Stand Up –* (1926), and *The Last Post* (1928).
5. Hegel, quoted in Culler, *Theory of the Lyric*, 98.
6. Ibid., 226.
7. Freud, "The Uncanny," 397.
8. Leys, *Trauma*, 9.
9. Ibid., 33.
10. Norris, *Writing War in the Twentieth Century*, 21, her italics.
11. Again, a turn to Scarry's work is appropriate here. She writes that "any activity that itself actually occurs in the interior of war will be much more difficult for

the human mind to assess" because there is an epistemological inability to acknowledge that injuring is at the heart of any war act (*Body in Pain*, 68).

12. Norris, *Writing War in the Twentieth Century*, 20.

13. Indeed, Lefebvre's ultimate project is to reveal the connections between these social spaces, but he does not actually follow through with this in his discussion. He hopes to "rediscover the unity of the productive process" (*The Production of Space*, 42) with perceived and imagined space, yet the inquiry primarily concerns itself with defining and explaining the variety of ways in which space can be examined and only gestures to the dialectical relationship between the experienced–perceived–imagined triad. Lefebvre imagines that it is possible for the triad to act as a "coherent whole," but only when society is at a peak of stability and creative innovation (he suggests that the Western town in the Italian Renaissance might offer such an example of a cohesive space; ibid., 40). Yet Lefebvre does not analyze what might happen at a moment of extreme disruption and disintegration – the very sort of moment that the Great War epitomizes.

14. Alan Judd gives an amusing description of Ford's love of "tall tales": "Ford's eye is on the right effect, not the right fact. It is as if he were writing a novel. It is not that he did not see the difference between the truth and what he said but that he chose on the basis of effect, as a novelist would" (*Ford Madox Ford*, 61).

15. Saunders, *Ford I*, 486.

16. Saunders, *Ford II*, 1–2.

17. Judd, *Ford Madox Ford*, 284–285.

18. Ford, *War Prose*, 254. Hereafter essays from *War Prose* cited parenthetically.

19. His impressive list of narratives that involve reflecting on the nature of a particular place also supports this. Those books include *The Soul of London* (1905), *The Heart of the Country* (1906), *The Spirit of the People* (1907), *Between St. Denis and St. George: A Sketch of Three Civilisations* (1915), *A Mirror to France* (1926), *New York is Not America* (1927), and *Provence* (1935).

20. In some ways we can see the metaphorical work of this analogy as connected to Scarry's discussion of Marx's insights into how, with the laborer, the body is projected into the object/artifice ("out of the bodies of women and men, material objects emerge" [*The Body in Pain*, 259]). The other end of this process of objectification emerges in Ford's statement, where we see the body becoming the already created artifact – not the fruits of his own labor, but the representation of someone else's – and of the way that war demands the materialization or "objectification" of the human body, in order to distance the infliction of pain and death from the experienced body and mind of the soldier.

21. Saunders, *Ford II*, 210. One could say the same thing about Saunder's own act in his astoundingly thorough and empathetic biography of Ford.
22. Keen, *Empathy and the Novel*, 87. Keen is quick to point out that the studies show only a very general link between difficulty and empathetic engagement.
23. Ngai, *Ugly Feelings*, 49, 52.
24. McCarthy, "The Foul System," 178.
25. Ford, *A Man Could Stand Up –*, 90. Hereafter cited parenthetically.
26. Ford, *Some Do Not*, 205. Hereafter cited parenthetically.
27. Leys, "Traumatic Cures: Shell Shock, Janet, and the Question of Memory," 104. Hereafter cited parenthetically. Leys discusses one doctor in particular who worked on cases of shell shock: William Brown, who used the "Breuer-Freud formula" on the repressed traumatic memories of hysterics as a template for his work on war neuroses (104). She examines the debate between Brown and other contemporary doctors about the method of treating dissociation and amnesia. At the core of the debate was the role of the patient in effecting his own cure (106).
28. With his repeated references to Tietjens as a lonely representative of the eighteenth-century beliefs in a rational and moral world, Ford presents his protagonist as a symbol of decency that is at odds with the vicious modern antics of his wife and the unthinkable slaughter of the war.
29. Ford, *No More Parades*, 29. Hereafter cited parenthetically.
30. Martin, "Therapeutic Measures," 36. Tietjens's use and then rejection of the sonnet form mirrors the perceived conflict between modernism and more traditional war poetry, epitomized by Yeats's view of Wilfred Owen's poetry as "unworthy of the poets' corner of a country newspaper" (qtd. in Norris, *Writing War in the Twentieth Century*, 38), because of its sentimentality and lack of innovation. Yet, in poems such as "The Show," Owen suggests that an understanding of the war and the modern subject in war must involve unraveling the complex relations among the spaces inhabited, perceived, and imagined by the subject, as well as that central problems in the war will be not about how to empathize with *others*, but how to learn even to see from *one's own* perspective. He thus reshaped traditional forms in a way that clarifies the horror of the war situation.
31. Conrad, *Heart of Darkness*, 9. Comparison with Conrad's work is especially apt in Ford's case, since the two collaborated on several works in the early part of the century.
32. Moretti, *Atlas of the European Novel*, 3.
33. Livesey, *The Viking Atlas of World War I*, 126.
34. Barrell, *The Idea of Landscape and the Sense of Place*, 2.
35. Saunders, *Ford II*, 17–18.
36. Ford, "On Impressionism," 325.

37. Three years later Virginia Woolf would engage in a similar narrative elision of the war in *To The Lighthouse* (1927), though her "Time Passes" section allows the war a haunting, if oblique presence (in contrast to the absolute blankness that Ford gives us between Parts One and Two of his novel).

38. Wordsworth, *The Prelude*, Book 6, 598–599. Thanks to my anonymous reader for noting this connection.

39. Hynes, *The Soldier's Tale*, 100.

40. Vincent Trott explores this gap in his book on the publication history of texts about the Great War, arguing that critics have been too quick to claim the war as accurately represented by the "narrative of disillusionment" (*Publishers, Readers, and the Great War*, 2).

41. Deleuze and Guattari, *A Thousand Plateaus*, 496.

42. Ibid., 477.

43. Ibid., 478.

44. De Certeau, *The Practice of Everyday Life*, 97.

45. Deleuze and Guattari, *A Thousand Plateaus*, 493. Their italics and ellipses.

46. Ibid., 496.

47. Ibid., 499.

48. Quoted in Keen, *Empathy and the Novel*, 87.

49. Quoted in Judd, *Ford Madox Ford*, 254.

50. Eric L. Santner explores a version of this form of denial in World War II; he describes the postwar development of "a set of defense mechanisms that served to burn affective bridges to the past" (*Stranded Objects*, 4). By severing identification with the defeated Nazis and, in many cases, claiming the position of victim, rather than perpetrator, Germans involved in the war bypassed the work of mourning, thus prolonging a cycle of denial for later generations. We can see a similar process in post-World War I England; as Ford's remark to Wyndham Lewis acknowledges, when the war was over, those who had sat it out in England would want to ignore the horrors they helped perpetuate.

51. Quoted in Gregory, *The Silence of Memory*, 59, from the *Liverpool Weekly Post*, London Correspondent, November 12, 1921, 10.

52. Ford, *The Last Post*, 75. Hereafter cited parenthetically.

53. See Froula, "Mrs. Dalloway's Postwar Elegy," 126. Froula argues that, in *Mrs. Dalloway*, Woolf uses a modern elegiac form to explore how England might emerge from the devastation wrought by war. Unlike the ultimately pessimistic view of the future of England that I see in Ford, Froula reads *Mrs. Dalloway* as offering a redemptive vision in her choice of an elegiac insistence on "the necessity of relinquishing the dead and of forming new attachments in order to carry on with life" (129). My reading is more parallel to Tammy Clewell's view of Woolf's desire to "denounce traditional

forms of consolation for loss" ("Consolation Refused,"199) in *Jacob's Room* and *To the Lighthouse*.

54. Ford wrote in a letter to Eric Pinker that "I strongly wish to omit *The Last Post* from the edition. I do not like the book and have never liked it and always intended the series to end with *A Man Could Stand Up –*" (qtd. in Judd, *Ford Madox Ford*, 382).

55. Benjamin, *Illuminations*, 212.

56. Trott, *Publishers, Readers, and the Great War*, 35.

57. Butler, *Precarious Life*, 22.

58. Borden, *The Forbidden Zone*, 15. Hereafter cited parenthetically.

59. See Armantrout, "Poetic Silence," 21.

60. Johnson, "Muteness Envy," 204, 205.

61. Ibid., 205.

62. Ibid.

63. Keats, "Ode on a Grecian Urn," *Poems*, 192.

64. See Zhang, "Naming the Indescribable," 58.

65. Srikanth, "Quiet Prose and Bare Life," 80.

66. Baxter, *Burning Down the House*, 43–44.

67. Ibid., 228.

68. Culler, *Theory of the Lyric*, 98.

69. Baxter, *Burning Down the House*, 222.

4 Elegizing Empathy: Eliot and the Subject–Object Divide

1. Eliot, *The Confidential Clerk*, 49–50.

2. Woolf, *Diary II*, 90.

3. Eliot's comments were recorded by a classmate and are cited in the *Complete Prose I*, note 11, 134. Hereafter cited parenthetically by volume number.

4. Leibniz, *The Monadology and Other Philosophical Writings*, point 19; 230. Hereafter cited parenthetically by point and page number.

5. On the one hand, the monad is an absolutely isolated element – it is a unit of perception and it is a world unto itself in that singular perception. On the other hand, Leibniz notes that monads have relations with other monads, though "such relations consist solely of expressive correspondences, or harmonized perceptual states" (see Tiffany, *Infidel Poetics*, 100). Leibniz says, for example, that "And just as the same town looked at from different sides appears completely different, and as if multiplied in perspective, so through the infinite multitude of simple substances, it is as if there were so many different universes, which nevertheless are only perspectives on a single universe, according to the different point of view of each monad" (point 57; 248). In other words, there are moments of alignment – a moment of orientation – between the perceptions

of different monads that allows them to share, at least for a moment, the same vision of the world. For Leibniz, again, this comes back to God's plan: "For God in regulating the whole has had regard for each part" (point 60; 250). Leibniz returns to the materiality of the monad as definitive: each monad is assigned to a specific body, and the body (some organic being) is its source of self-sustaining energy, what Leibniz calls its "entelechy" (point 63; 253).

6. Chodat, *Wordly Acts and Sentient Things*, 5.

7. As I argue in "Psychology, Psychoanalysis, and New Subjectivities," immediate experiences for Bradley are "the perceptual events in which the boundaries between the self and the surrounding world are no longer visible. These experiences are then resolved, for Bradley, into a unified, unknowable whole called the "Absolute" (164).

8. Eliot, *Collected Poems*, 72. Hereafter cited parenthetically.

9. Quoted in Tiffany, *Infidel Poetics*, 113.

10. "There is no gender identity behind the expressions of gender; that identity is performatively constituted by the very "expressions" that are said to be its results" (Butler, *Gender Trouble*, 25).

11. See Sorum, "Masochistic Modernisms," for a further discussion of the role of masochism in Eliot's aesthetic philosophy.

12. See Sorum, "Psychology, Psychoanalysis, and New Subjectivities," for more discussion of this issue.

13. Eliot clearly likes these "scientific" metaphors; we might think about his comparison in "Tradition and the Individual Talent" of the poet with the "shred of platinum," acted upon by various gases (*Selected Prose*, 41).

14. Eliot, *The Waste Land Facsimile*, 95–97. Hereafter cited parenthetically.

15. As Tim Dean has written, Eliot's theory of impersonality in "Tradition and the Individual Talent," which has been seen as a simple conduit to conservative thinking, can equally lead "toward anti-authoritarian positions because it undermines, first and foremost, the authority of the self" ("T. S. Eliot, Famous Clairvoyante," 50). While Dean focuses on the kind of "self-dispossession" (ibid., 51) that Eliot worked toward in his poetry, his claim is equally useful when thinking about the way that empathetic identification is always figured already as an act that involves recognition of the damage enacted on the self.

16. See Lamos, "The Love Song of T. S. Eliot," 35–36.

17. Bersani, "Is the Rectum a Grave?" 222.

18. Butler, *Precarious Life*, 22.

19. In addition to Gilbert, whom I discuss later in the chapter, another critic interested in the elegiac nature of *The Waste Land* includes James Miller, who wrote an early book that explores the poem as a response to the loss of Eliot's friend, Jean Verdenal.

20. Gilbert, "Rat's Alley," 66.
21. Pater, *The Renaissance*, 234.
22. Fuss, "Corpse Poem," 1. Fuss goes on to probe how an entire body of poetry could be devoted to this seemingly impossible genre of "lyric utterances not from beyond the grave but from inside it" (1–2).
23. Holley, "Words Moving," 160.
24. Boland, "Meter in English: A Response," 46.
25. Rae, "Introduction," *Modernism and Mourning*, 17.
26. Ibid., 16.
27. Freud, "The Ego and the Id," 638.
28. Ibid.
29. Spender, *The Destructive Element*, 134.
30. See Jennifer Sorensen Emery-Peck's argument: "The voice of the speaker-narrator in the pub-sequence – marked by its sex and class and unique in the poem for its deployment of narrative techniques to build heightened readerly desires for story, character, and plot – refuses to be collapsed into an overarching lyric "I" which could potentially connect the lyric sections of the poem" ("Tom and Vivien Eliot do Narrative in Different Voices," 333).
31. Levenson, *A Genealogy of Modernism*, 159.
32. Dickens, *Our Mutual Friend*, 224.
33. Dean, "T. S. Eliot, Famous Clairvoyante," 54.
34. Quoted in Culler, *Theory of the Lyric*, 15.
35. As John Stuart Mill writes, "eloquence is heard; poetry is overheard" ("Thoughts on Poetry and Its Varieties," 95).
36. Brown, "Negative Poetics," 121.
37. Thanks to my anonymous reader for pointing out this connection.
38. Spender, *The Destructive Element*, 146.
39. Moody, *Thomas Stearns Eliot: Poet*, 92.
40. Tiffany, *Infidel Poetics*, 103.
41. Quoted in Tiffany, *Infidel Poetics*, 117.
42. Sorum, "Psychology, Psychoanalysis, and New Subjectivities," 173.
43. He uses the term "sympathise," but the lines that follow the "dayadhvam" suggest that his usage follows our understanding of empathy, which was still not part of common usage.
44. Levenson, *A Genealogy of Modernism*, 201.
45. "transcendence, n." *OED Online*, Oxford University Press, January 2018, www.oed.com/view/Entry/204607.
46. See Whittier-Ferguson, *Mortality and Form in Late Modernist Literature*, ch. 1. He asks for a reading of Eliot's late poetry that sees it as "doctrinally conservative, but … profoundly adventurous and resourceful aesthetically" (78).

47. Ibid., 39.
48. Levinas, quoted in Butler, *Precarious Life*, 134. Hereafter cited parenthetically.
49. Whittier-Ferguson, *Mortality and Form*, 66.
50. Moody, *Thomas Stearns Eliot: Poet*, 205.
51. Ibid.
52. Quoted in Whittier-Ferguson, *Mortality and Form*, 79.
53. Whittier-Ferguson, *Mortality and Form*, 210.
54. According to Gordon, we see here a gesture to Sir Thomas Elyot's 1531 *The Boke Named the Governour* (*T. S. Eliot*, 631, n.348).
55. Gross and McDowell, *Sound and Form in Modern Poetry*, 163.

5 Uncanny Empathy: Woolf's Half-Life of Objects

1. Woolf, "Modern Fiction," 159. Hereafter cited parenthetically.
2. Woolf, *Mr. Bennett and Mrs. Brown*, 13.
3. Benjamin, *Illuminations*, 223.
4. Shohet, "Subjects and Objects in Lycidas," 103.
5. Ibid.
6. Banfield, *The Phantom Table*, 1.
7. Ibid., 3.
8. Ibid., 1.
9. Zhang, "Naming the Indescribable," 52.
10. Quoted in Zhang, "Naming the Indescribable," 57.
11. Zhang, "Naming the Indescribable," 58.
12. Baxter, *Burning Down the House*, 93.
13. Ibid., 92.
14. See the Introduction for the discussion of Worringer and Hulme.
15. Lipps, quoted in Worringer, *Abstraction and Empathy*, 7.
16. Woolf, "An Unwritten Novel," 15. Hereafter cited parenthetically.
17. Lacan, "Death, Desire, and Freud's Radical Turn," 162.
18. Ibid., 163.
19. Ibid.
20. Freud, "The Uncanny," 388.
21. Weinstein, *Unknowing*, 84.
22. Freud, "The Uncanny," 387.
23. Lee and Ansthruther-Thomson, *Beauty and Ugliness*, 48.
24. Ibid.
25. Freud, "The Uncanny," 385.
26. Weinstein, *Unknowing*, 2.
27. Woolf, *Jacob's Room: The Holograph Draft*, 275. Hereafter cited parenthetically.
28. Woolf, *Jacob's Room*, 91–92. Hereafter cited parenthetically.

29. De Man, *The Rhetoric of Romanticism*, 80–81.
30. Ibid., 80.
31. Woolf, *Diary: Vol. 2*, 14.
32. Lee and Ansthruther-Thomson, *Beauty and Ugliness*, 57.
33. Woolf, *Three Guineas*, 106.
34. Woolf, *Diary: Vol. 1*, 186.
35. Woolf, *Diary: Vol. 3*, 104.
36. Worsley, "Ophelia's Loneliness," 524.
37. See Clewell, "Consolation Refused," 199.
38. Woolf, *To the Lighthouse*, 3. Hereafter cited parenthetically as *TTL*.
39. Ruskin, *Modern Painters: Vol. III*, 163.
40. James, *Psychology: A Briefer Course*, 165. While we do not know for sure whether Woolf read William James (his brother, Henry, was both an author she loved and someone she knew personally), writers such as Anne Fernihough ("Consciousness as a Stream") argue that it is likely that Woolf was well aware of James' psychological theories and writings.
41. Ryan, *The Vanishing Subject*, 2.
42. Ibid., 9.
43. Nishimura, "Personification and Narrative," 33.
44. Ibid.
45. Quoted in Hammond, *Empathy and the Psychology of Modernism*, 6.
46. James, *Psychology*, 189.
47. Harker, "Misperceiving Virginia Woolf," 8.
48. Hulme describes the work of the artist with language: "It is only by a concentrated effort of the mind that you can hold it fixed to your own purpose" ("Romanticism and Classicism," 52).
49. Woolf, *Diary: Vol. 4*, 282–283. February 27, 1935.
50. Pater, *The Renaissance*, 151.
51. Lee, *The Beautiful*, 67.
52. Lee and Ansthruther-Thomson, *Beauty and Ugliness*, 47.
53. See Hermione Lee, *Virginia Woolf*, 469.
54. Marcus, *Virginia Woolf*, 99.
55. Eagleton, *Ideology of the Aesthetic*, 267.
56. Ibid.

Conclusion: Performing Empathy?

1. Quoted in Vinem, *A History in Fragments*, 78–79.
2. Roberts, "Introduction," *The Faber Book of Modern Verse*, 515.
3. See Butler's first chapter, "Burning Acts, Injurious Speech," in particular, for a discussion of these terms.

4. Butler, *Excitable Speech*, 44.
5. Ibid., 46. The whole quotation is italicized in the original.
6. Quoted in Sherry, *Ezra Pound, Wyndham Lewis, and Radical Modernism*, 2.
7. Valdesolo and Desteno, "Synchrony and the Social Tuning of Compassion," 265.
8. See, for example, Claire Warden's discussions of Lindsay's Mass Declamation in her book on Avant-Garde theater (*British Avant-Garde Theater*, 105).
9. Cunningham, "Introduction," *The Penguin Book of Spanish Civil War Verse*, 44.
10. Quoted in Cunningham, "Introduction," 46.
11. Ibid.
12. Suzanne Keen argues that it does not; Mary-Catherine Harrison is more optimistic, citing the increased charitable giving after the publication of Dickens's *A Christmas Carol* as a possible example (see Keen, *Empathy and the Novel*, 90–92; Harrison, "The Paradox of Fiction," 271).
13. Lindsay, *Fanfrolico and After*, 264.
14. Foster, "Between the Bullet and the Lie," 22.
15. Harrison, "The Great Sum of Universal Anguish," 137.
16. Costello, *The Plural of Us*, 2, 3.
17. Lindsay, "On Guard for Spain!" 254. Hereafter cited parenthetically.
18. Lee and Anstruther-Thomson, *Beauty and Ugliness*, 18–19.
19. Ibid., 20.
20. Pavlovich and Krahnke, *Organizing through Empathy*, 2.
21. Thanks to one of my anonymous reviewers for pressing this point.

Bibliography

Agamben, Giorgio. "The End of the Poem." *The Lyric Theory Reader: A Critical Anthology*. Eds. Virginia Jackson and Yopie Prins. Baltimore: Johns Hopkins University Press, 2014. 430–434.

Altick, Richard D. *The English Common Reader: A Social History of the Mass Reading Public 1800–1900*. Chicago: The University of Chicago Press, 1957.

Armantrout, Rae. "Poetic Silence." *Writing/Talks*. Ed. Bob Perelman. Carbondale: Southern Illinois University Press, 1985. 31–47. http://epc.buffalo.edu/authors/armantrout/.

Armstrong, Tim. *Haunted Hardy: Poetry, History, Memory*. New York: Palgrave, 2000.

Austin, J. L. *How to Do Things with Words*. 2nd edn. Ed. J. O. Urmson and Marina Sbisà. Cambridge, MA: Harvard University Press, 1975.

Banfield, Ann. *The Phantom Table: Woolf, Fry, Russell and the Epistemology of Modernism*. New York: Cambridge University Press, 2000.

Barrell, John. "Geographies of Hardy's Wessex." *The Regional Novel in Britain and Ireland, 1800–1990*. Ed. K. D. M. Snell. New York: Cambridge University Press, 1998. 99–118.

The Idea of Landscape and the Sense of Place, 1730–1840. London: Cambridge University Press, 1972.

Baxter, Charles. *Burning Down the House*. Saint Paul: Graywolf Press, 1997.

Benjamin, Walter. *Illuminations*. Ed. Hannah Arendt. Trans. Harry Zohn. New York: Schocken Books, 1968.

Reflections. New York: Schocken Books, 1986.

Berlant, Lauren. "Poor Eliza." *American Literature* 70.3 (1999): 635–668.

Bersani, Leo. "Is the Rectum a Grave?" *AIDS: Cultural Analysis/Cultural Activism* October 43 (1987): 197–222.

Blasing, Mutlu Konuk. *Lyric Poetry: The Pain and the Pleasure of Words*. Princeton: Princeton University Press, 2007.

Boland, Eavan. "Meter in English: A Response." *Meter in English: A Critical Engagement*. Ed. David Baker. Fayetteville: The University of Arkansas Press, 1996. 45–57.

Borden, Mary. *The Forbidden Zone*. London: Hesperus Press, [1929] 2009.

Brown, Marshall. "Negative Poetics: On Skepticism and the Lyric Voice." *Representations* 86.1 (2004): 120–140.

Burt, Stephen. "the map that hangs by me (or, thomas hardy, or, blogging the MSA, part two)." www.poetryfoundation.org/harriet/2007/11/the-map-that-hangs-by-me-or-thomas-hardy-or-blogging-the-msa-part-two.

Butler, Judith. *Excitable Speech: A Politics of the Performative.* New York: Routledge, 1997.

   Gender Trouble: Feminism and the Subversion of Identity. New York: Routledge, 1990.

   Precarious Life: The Powers of Mourning and Violence. New York: Verso, 2006.

Campbell, Matthew. "Tennyson and Hardy's Ghostly Metres." *Essays in Criticism* 42.4 (1992): 279–298.

Cannadine, David. "War and Death, Grief and Mourning in Modern Britain." *Mirrors of Mortality: Studies in the Social History of Death.* Ed. Joachim Whaley. New York: St. Martin's Press, 1982. 187–242.

Chodat, Robert. *Worldly Acts and Sentient Things.* Ithaca: Cornell University Press, 2008.

Clark, Rose. *Geography in the Schools of Europe, In Relation to a Program of Geographic Instruction in American Education.* Charles Scribner's Sons, 1934.

Clewell, Tammy. "Consolation Refused: Virginia Woolf, the Great War, and Modernist Mourning." *MFS: Modern Fiction Studies.* 50.1 (2004): 197–223.

Cohen, William A. "Faciality and Sensation in Hardy's *The Return of the Native.*" *PMLA* 121.2 (2006): 437–452.

Conrad, Joseph. *Heart of Darkness.* New York: W. W. Norton & Company, 1988.

Coplan, Amy and Peter Goldie, eds. *Empathy: Philosophical and Psychological Perspectives.* New York: Oxford University Press, 2011.

Costello, Bonnie. *The Plural of Us: Poetry and Community in Auden and Others.* Princeton: Princeton University Press, 2017.

Cox, Christine L., Lucina Q. Uddin, Adriana Di Martino, F. Xavier Castellanos, Michael P. Milham, and Clare Kelly. "The Balance Between Feeling and Knowing: Affective and Cognitive Empathy Are Reflected in the Brain's Intrinsic Functional Dynamics." *Social Cognitive and Affective Neuroscience* 7.6 (August 2012): 727–737. Published online Sept. 5, 2011. DOI: 10.1093/scan/nsr051.

Crangle, Sara. *Prosaic Desires: Modernist Knowledge, Boredom, Laughter, and Anticipation.* Edinburgh: Edinburgh University Press, 2010.

Crone, G. R. "British Geography in the Twentieth Century." *The Geographical Journal* 130.2 (June 1964): 197–220.

Culler, Jonathan. *Theory of the Lyric.* Cambridge, MA: Harvard University Press, 2015.

   "Why Lyric?" *PMLA* 123.1 (January 2008): 201–206.

Cunningham, Valentine. Introduction. *The Penguin Book of Spanish Civil War Verse.* Ed. Cunningham. New York: Penguin, 1996. 25–94.

Daleski, H. M. "Thomas Hardy: A Victorian Modernist?" *The Challenge of Periodization: Old Paradigms and New Perspectives.* Hoboken: Taylor and Francis, 2014. 179–196.

Darby, H. C. "Academic Geography in Britain: 1918–1946." *Transactions of the Institute of British Geographers*, New Series 8.1 (1983): 14–26.

Davie, Donald. *With the Grain: Essays on Thomas Hardy and Modern British Poetry*. Manchester: Carcanet Press, 1998.

Dean, Tim. "T. S. Eliot, Famous Clairvoyante." *Gender, Desire, and Sexuality in T. S. Eliot*. Ed. Cassandra Laity and Nancy K. Gish. New York: Cambridge University Press, 2004. 43–65.

De Certeau, Michel. *The Practice of Everyday Life*. Trans. Steven F. Rendall. Berkeley: University of California Press, 1984.

Deleuze, Gilles and Felix Guattari. *A Thousand Plateaus: Capitalism and Schizophrenia*. Trans. Brian Massumi. Minneapolis: University of Minnesota Press, 1987.

Deleuze, Gilles and Claire Parnet. *Dialogues*. Trans. Hugh Tomlinson and Barbara Habberjam. New York: Columbia University Press, 1987.

De Man, Paul. *The Rhetoric of Romanticism*. New York: Columbia University Press, 1984.

Detloff, Madelyn. *The Persistence of Modernism: Loss and Mourning in the Twentieth Century*. New York: Cambridge University Press, 2009.

De Vega, Manuel. "Characters and Their Perspectives in Narratives Describing Spatial Environments." *Psychological Research* 56 (1994): 116–126.

Dickens, Charles. *Our Mutual Friend*. Portsmouth: Manderin Paperbacks, 1991.

Dickinson, Robert E. *Regional Concept: The Anglo-American Leaders*. Boston: Routledge & Kegan Paul, 1976.

Eagleton, Terry. *The Ideology of the Aesthetic*. Malden: Blackwell, 1990.

Eliot, T. S. *Collected Poems, 1909–1962*. 1st edn. New York: Harcourt Brace Jovanovich, 1991.

The Complete Prose of T. S. Eliot: Volume I: The Critical Edition: Apprentice Years, 1905–1918. Ed. Jewel Spears Brooker and Ronald Schuchard. Baltimore: Johns Hopkins University Press, 2014.

The Confidential Clerk. New York: Harcourt, Brace and Company, 1954.

Knowledge and Experience in the Philosophy of F. H. Bradley. New York: Columbia University Press, 1989.

The Letters of T. S. Eliot: Volume 1: 1898–1922. Rev. edn. Ed. Valerie Eliot and Hugh Haughton. New Haven: Yale University Press, 2011.

Selected Prose of T. S. Eliot. Ed. Frank Kermode. New York: Harcourt Brace Jovanovich, 1988.

The Waste Land: A Facsimile and Transcript of the Original Drafts Including the Annotations of Ezra Pound. Ed. Valerie Eliot. New York: Harcourt, Inc., 1971.

The Waste Land and Other Poems. Peterborough: Broadview Press, 2011.

Fernihough, Anne. "Consciousness as a Stream." *The Cambridge Companion to the Modernist Novel*. Ed. Morag Sciach. New York: Cambridge University Press, 2007. 65–81.

Flatley, Jonathan. *Affective Mapping*. Cambridge, MA: Harvard University Press, 2008.

Ford, Ford Madox. "Antwerp." Reprinted in Alan Judd, *Ford Madox Ford.* Cambridge, MA: Harvard University Press, 1990. 251.

"On Impressionism." *Modernism: An Anthology of Sources of Documents.* Ed. Vassiliki Kolooctroni, Jane Goldman, and Olga Taxidou. Chicago: University of Chicago Press, 1998. 323–331.

Parade's End: Volume I: Some Do Not. Ed. Max Saunders. Manchester: Carcanet Press. [1924] 2011.

Parade's End: Volume II: No More Parades. Ed. Joseph Wiesenfarth. Manchester: Carcanet Press. [1925] 2011.

Parade's End: Volume III: A Man Could Stand Up – . Ed. Sara Haslam. Manchester: Carcanet Press. [1926] 2011.

Parade's End: Volume IV: The Last Post. Ed. Paul Skinner. Manchester: Carcanet Press. [1928] 2011.

War Prose. Ed. Max Saunders. Manchester: Carcanet, 1999.

Foster, Kevin. "'Between the Bullet and the Lie': Intellectuals and the War." *The Spanish Civil War: A Cultural and Historical Reader.* Ed. Alun Kenwood. Oxford: Berg, 1993. 19–25.

Freud, Sigmund. *Beyond the Pleasure Principle.* Ed. Todd Dufresne. Trans. Gregory C. Richter. Buffalo: Broadview, 2011.

"Mourning and Melancholia." *The Standard Edition of the Complete Psychological Works of Sigmund Freud.* Trans. and Ed. James Strachey. London: Hogarth Press, 1957. 14: 237–258.

"The Ego and the Id." *The Freud Reader.* Ed. Peter Gay. New York: W. W. Norton & Co., 1989. 628–660.

"The 'Uncanny.'" *Collected Papers: Volume IV.* Trans. Joan Riviere. New York: Basic Books, 1959. 368–407.

Froula, Christine. "*Mrs. Dalloway's* Postwar Elegy: Women, War, and the Art of Mourning." *Modernism/Modernity* 9.1 (2002): 125–163.

Fuss, Diana. "Corpse Poem." *Critical Inquiry* 30 (Autumn 2003): 1–30.

Garber, Marjorie. "Compassion." *Compassion: The Culture and Politics of an Emotion.* Ed. Lauren Berlant. New York: Routledge, 2004. 15–27.

Gatrell, Simon. *Hardy the Creator: A Textual Biography.* Oxford: Clarendon Press, 1988.

Geddes, Patrick. "The Influence of Geographical Conditions on Social Development." *The Geographical Journal* 12. 6 (1898): 580–586.

Geike, Archibald. *The Teaching of Geography.* 2nd edn. London: Macmillan and Co., 1892.

Gilbert, Sandra. "'Rat's Alley': The Great War, Modernism, and the (Anti) Pastoral Elegy." *New Literary History* 30.1 (1999): 179–201.

Godlewska, Anne Marie Claire. "From Enlightenment Vision to Modern Science? Humboldt's Visual Thinking." *Geography and Enlightenment.* Ed. David N. Livingstone and Charles W. J. Withers. Chicago: University of Chicago Press, 1999. 236–275.

Gordon, Lyndall. *T. S. Eliot: An Imperfect Life.* New York: W. W. Norton & Co., 1998.

Gregory, Adrian. *The Silence of Memory: Armistice Day 1919–1946.* Providence: Berg, 1994.

Greiner, D. Rae. "Thinking of Me Thinking of You: Sympathy Versus Empathy in the Realist Novel." *Victorian Studies* 53.3 (2011): 417–426.

Greiner, Rae. "Sympathy Time: Adam Smith, George Eliot, and the Realist Novel." *Narrative* 17.3 (October 2009): 291–311.

Griffin, Cristina Richieri. "George Eliot's Feuerbach: Senses, Sympathy, Omniscience, and Secularism." *ELH* 84.2 (2017): 475–502. https://doi.org/10.1353/elh.2017.0019.

Gross, Harvey Seymour and Robert McDowell. *Sound and Form in Modern Poetry.* Ann Arbor: University of Michigan Press, 1996.

Hammond, Meghan Marie. *Empathy and the Psychology of Modernism.* New York: Edinburgh University Press, 2014.

Hardy, Thomas. *Collected Letters of Thomas Hardy: Volume Three, 1902–1908.* Ed. R. L. Purdy and M. Millgate. Oxford: Clarendon Press, 1982.

The Complete Poetical Works of Thomas Hardy: Volume II. Ed. Samuel Hynes. Oxford: Clarendon Press, 1984.

The Complete Poems. Ed. James Gibson. New York: Palgrave, 2001

"In a Eweleaze near Weatherbury." *Wessex Poems and Other Verses.* New York: Harper & Brothers, 1899. 181.

The Life of Thomas Hardy by Florence Hardy: Early Life and Late Life. Combined edn. London: Studio Editions, 1994.

The Literary Notebooks of Thomas Hardy: Volume 2. Ed. Lennart A. Björk. New York: New York University Press, 1985.

Tess of the D'Urbervilles. 1891. New York: Oxford University Press, 2005.

Thomas Hardy's Personal Writings: Prefaces, Literary Opinions, Reminiscences. Ed. Harold Orel. Lawrence: University of Kansas Press, 1966.

The Woodlanders. New York: HarperCollins, 1905.

The Woodlanders. Ed. Dale Kramer. Oxford: Clarendon Press, 1981.

Harker, James. "Misperceiving Virginia Woolf." *Journal of Modern Literature* 34.2 (Winter 2011): 1–21.

Harris, L. J., C. A. Biddle, E. H. Thompson, and E. G. Irving. "British Maps and Charts: A Survey of Development." *The Geographical Journal* 130.2 (1964): 226–240.

Harrison, Mary-Catherine. "'The Great Sum of Universal Anguish': Statistical Empathy in Victorian Social-Problem Literature." *Rethinking Empathy Through Literature.* Ed. Megan Marie Hammond and Sue J. Kim. New York: Routledge, 2014. 135–149.

"The Paradox of Fiction and the Ethics of Empathy: Reconceiving Dickens's Realism." *Narrative* 16.3 (October 2008): 256–278.

Harvey, David. *The Condition of Postmodernity.* Cambridge: Blackwell, 1990.

Henchman, Anna. "Hardy's Stargazers and the Astronomy of Other Minds." *Victorian Studies* 51.1 (2008): 37–64.

Holland, Norman N. "The Power(?) of Literature: A Neuropsychological View." *New Literary History* 35 (2004): 395–410.

Holley, Margaret. "Words Moving: Metrical Pleasures of Our Time." *Meter in English: A Critical Engagement.* Ed. David Baker. Fayetteville: The University of Arkansas Press, 1996. 151–168.

Holt, Elliott. "The Return of Omniscience." Sunday Book Review. *The New York Times.* September 11, 2016. 29. www.nytimes.com/2016/09/11/books/review/the-return-of-omniscience.html.

Howarth, Peter. *British Poetry in the Age of Modernism.* New York: Cambridge University Press, 2005.

Hughes, John. "Tennyson Revisited: Hardy's 'After a Journey.'" *The Thomas Hardy Journal* 21 (Autumn 2005): 152–157.

Hulme, T. E. "Modern Art and Its Philosophy." *The Collected Writings of T. E. Hulme.* Ed. Karen Csengari. Oxford: Clarendon Press, 1994. 268–285.

Hulme, T. E. "Romanticism and Classicism." *Poetry in Theory: An Anthology: 1900–2000.* Ed. Jon Cook. Malden: Blackwell, 2009. 47–55.

Hynes, Samuel. *The Soldier's Tale.* New York: Penguin, 1997.

James, William. *Psychology: A Briefer Course. Writings: 1878–1899.* New York: The Library of America, [1892] 1992.

Jameson, Frederic. *The Antinomies of Realism.* New York: Verso, 2015.

Jay, Martin. "Against Consolation: Walter Benjamin and the Refusal to Mourn." *War and Remembrance in the Twentieth Century.* Ed. Jay Winter and Emmanuel Siven. Cambridge: Cambridge University Press, 1999. 221–239.

Joerg, W. L. G. "Recent Geographical Work in Europe." *Geographical Review.* 12.3 (1922): 431–484.

Johnson, Barbara. "Muteness Envy." *The Barbara Johnson Reader: The Surprise of Otherness.* Ed. Melissa Feuerstein, Bill Johnson González, Lili Porten, and Keja Valens. Durham: Duke University Press, 2014. 200–216.

Judd, Alan. *Ford Madox Ford.* Cambridge, MA: Harvard University Press, 1990.

Irwin, B. St. G. "The Ordnance Survey: Roy's Legacy." *The Geographical Journal* 143.1 (1977): 14–26.

Keats, John. *Poems.* London: J. M. Dent & Sons, 1974.

Keen, Suzanne. *Empathy and the Novel.* New York: Oxford University Press, 2007.
Thomas Hardy's Brains. New York: Oxford University Press, 2014.

Kelley, Theresa. *Wordsworth's Revisionary Aesthetics.* New York: Cambridge University Press, 1988.

Keltie, Sir John Scott. *The Position of Geography in British Universities.* New York: Oxford University Press, 1921.

Kort, Wesley. *Place and Space in Modern Fiction.* Gainesville: University Press of Florida, 2004.

Kramer, Dale. *Hardy: Tess of the D'Urbervilles.* New York: Cambridge University Press, 1991.
Introduction. *The Woodlanders. By Thomas Hardy.* Oxford: Clarendon Press, 1981. 1–71.

Lacan, Jacques. "Death, Desire, and Freud's Radical Turn." *Beyond the Pleasure Principle.* Sigmund Freud. Ed. Todd Dufresne. Trans. Gregory C. Richter. Buffalo: Broadview, 2011. 159–175.

Lamos, Colleen. "The Love Song of T. S. Eliot: Elegiac Homoeroticism in the Early Poetry." *Gender, Desire, and Sexuality in T. S. Eliot.* Ed. Cassandra Laity and Nancy K. Gish. New York: Cambridge University Press, 2004. 23–42.

Lea, Hermann. *Thomas Hardy's Wessex.* London: Macmillan, 1913.

Lee, Hermione. *Virginia Woolf.* New York: Vintage, 1996.

Lee, Vernon. *The Beautiful: An Introduction to Psychological Aesthetics.* Cambridge: Cambridge University Press, 1913.

Lee, Vernon and C. Ansthruther-Thomson. *Beauty and Ugliness and Other Studies in Psychological Aesthetics.* New York: John Lane Company, 1912.

Lefebvre, Henri. *The Production of Space.* Trans. Donald Nicholson-Smith. New York: Blackwell, [1974] 1991.

Leibniz, G. W. *The Monadology and Other Philosophical Writings.* Trans. and ed. by Robert Latta. Oxford: Clarendon Press, 1898.

Lerner, Laurence and John Holmstrom, eds. *Thomas Hardy and His Readers: A Selection of Contemporary Reviews.* Toronto: The Bodley Head, 1968.

Levenson, Michael. *A Genealogy of Modernism: A Study of English Literary Doctrine 1908–1922.* New York: Cambridge University Press, 1986.

Levine, Caroline. "Victorian Realism." *The Cambridge Companion to the Victorian Novel.* Ed. Deirdre David. New York: Cambridge University Press, 2015. 84–106. http://dx.doi.org/10.1017/CCO9780511793370.

Levinson, Marjorie. "Object-Loss and Object-Bondage: Economies of Representation in Hardy's Poetry." *ELH* 73 (2006): 549–580.

Leys, Ruth. "Traumatic Cures: Shell Shock, Janet, and the Question of Memory." *Tense Past: Cultural Essays in Trauma and Memory.* Ed. Paul Antze and Michael Lambek. New York: Routledge, 1996. 103–145.

Trauma: A Genealogy. Chicago: University of Chicago Press, 2000.

Lindsay, Jack. *Fanfrolico, and After.* London: Bodley Head, 1962.

"Looking at a Map of Spain on the Devon Coast (August, 1937)." *The Penguin Book of Spanish Civil War Verse.* Ed. Valentine Cunningham. New York: Penguin Books Ltd, 1996. 396–399.

"On Guard for Spain!" *The Penguin Book of Spanish Civil War Verse.* Ed. Valentine Cunningham. New York: Penguin Books Ltd, 1996. 253–263.

Livesey, Anthony. *The Viking Atlas of World War I.* New York: Viking, 1994.

Marcus, Laura. *Virginia Woolf.* 2nd edn. Tavistock: Northcote House, 2004.

Matless, David. "Regional Surveys and Local Knowledges: The Geographical Imagination in Britain, 1918–1939." *Transactions of the Institute of British Geographers* 17.4 (1992): 464–480.

Martin, Meredith. "Thereapuetic Measures: *The Hydra* and Wilfred Owen at Craiglockhart War Hospital." *Modernism/Modernity* 14.1 (2007): 35–54.

Maynard, Katherine Kearney. *Thomas Hardy's Tragic Poetry: The Lyrics and the Dynasts.* Iowa City: University of Iowa Press, 1991.

McCarthy, Jeffrey Mathes. "'The Foul System': The Great War and Instrumental Rationality in *Parade's End.*" *Studies in the Novel* 41.2 (2009): 178–200.

Meller, Helen. *Patrick Geddes: Social Evolutionist and City Planner.* New York: Routledge, 1990.

Mill, Hugh Robert. "On Research in the Geographical Science." *The Geographical Journal* 18.4 (1901): 407–424.

Mill, John Stuart. "Thoughts on Poetry and Its Varieties." *The Crayon* 7.4 (1860): 93–97. www.jstor.org/stable/25528035.

Miller, James. *T. S. Eliot's Personal Waste Land: Exorcism of the Demons.* University Park: Penn State Press, 1977.

Miller, J. Hillis. *Topographies.* Stanford: Stanford University Press, 1995.

Millgate, Michael. *Thomas Hardy.* New York: Random House, 1982.

"Thomas Hardy's Library at Max Gate: Catalogue of an Attempted Reconstruction." Online article: http://hardy.library.utoronto.ca/.

Mitchell, Rebecca. *Victorian Lessons in Empathy and Difference.* Columbus: Ohio State University Press, 2011.

Mitchell, W. J. T. *Landscape and Power.* 2nd edn. Ed. Mitchell. Chicago: University of Chicago Press, 2002.

Moglen, Seth. *Mourning Modernity: Literary Modernism and the Injuries of American Capitalism.* Stanford: Stanford University Press, 2007.

Moody, A. David. *Thomas Stearns Eliot: Poet.* 2nd edn. New York: Cambridge University Press, 1994.

Moretti, Franco. *Atlas of the European Novel.* New York: Verso, 1998.

Morgan, Benjamin. "Critical Empathy: Vernon Lee's Aesthetics and the Origins of Close Reading." *Victorian Studies* 55.1 (2012): 31–56.

Newlyn, Lucy. "'The noble living and the noble dead': Community in *The Prelude.*" *The Cambridge Companion to Wordsworth.* Ed. Stephen Gill. New York: Cambridge University Press, 2003. 59–63.

Ngai, Sianne. *Ugly Feelings.* Cambridge, MA: Harvard University Press, 2005.

Nishimura, Satoshi. "Personification and Narrative: The Blurred Boundaries of the Inanimate in Hardy and Woolf." *Narrative* 23.1 (January 2015): 27–39.

"Thomas Hardy and the Language of the Inanimate." *SEL: Studies in English Literature 1500–1900* 43.4 (2003): 897–912.

Norris, Margot. *Writing War in the Twentieth Century.* Charlottesville: University Press of Virginia, 2000.

Nussbaum, Martha. *Upheavals of Thought: The Intelligence of Emotions.* New York: Cambridge University Press, 2001.

Oakes, Timothy. "Place and the Paradox of Modernity." *Annals of the Association of American Geographers* 87.3 (1997): 509–531.

Obama, Barak and Marilynne Robinson. "A Conversation." *New York Review of Books.* November 19, 2015: www.nybooks.com/articles/2015/11/19/president-obama-marilynne-robinson-conversation-2/.

Omond, Thomas Stuart. *A Study of Metre.* London: Grant Richards, 1903.

Owen, Wilfred. "The Show." *The Penguin Book of First World War Poetry.* 2nd edn. Ed. Jon Silkin. New York: Penguin Books, 1996. 198.

Pater, Walter. *The Renaissance: Studies in Art and Poetry.* London: Macmillan, [1873] 1901.

Pavlovich, Kathryn and Kieko Krahnke. *Organizing Through Empathy.* New York: Routledge, 2014.

Pite, Ralph. *Hardy's Geography: Wessex and the Regional Novel.* New York: Palgrave Macmillan, 2002.

Proust, Marcel. *In Search of Lost Time: Vol. VI: Time Regained.* Trans. Andreas Mayor and Terance Kilmartin. New York: Modern Library, 1999.

Rae, Patricia. "Introduction." *Modernism and Mourning.* Ed. Rae. Lewisberg: Bucknell University Press, 2007.

Rall, Jaime and Paul Harris. "In Cinderella's Slippers? Story Comprehension from the Protagonist's Point of View." *Developmental Psychology* 36.2 (2000): 202–208.

Ramazani, Jahan. *Poetry of Mourning: The Modern Elegy from Hardy to Heaney.* Chicago: University of Chicago Press, 1994.

Ricardi, Alessia. *The Ends of Mourning: Psychoanalysis, Literature, Film.* Stanford: Stanford University Press, 2003.

Roberts, Michael. Introduction. *The Faber Book of Modern Verse.* 1936. Rpt. in *Modernism: An Anthology of Sources and Documents.* Ed. Vassiliki Kolocotroni, Jane Goldman, and Olga Taxidou. Chicago: University of Chicago Press, 1998. 513–518.

Rode, Scott. *Reading and Mapping Hardy's Roads.* New York: Routledge, 2006.

Royle, Nicholas. *The Uncanny.* New York: Manchester University Press, 2003.

Ruskin, John. *Modern Painters: Vol. III.* New York: John Wiley, 1863.

Ryan, Judith. *The Vanishing Subject: Early Psychology and Literary Modernism.* Chicago: University of Chicago Press, 1991.

Sacks, Peter. *The English Elegy: Studies in the Genre from Spenser to Yeats.* Baltimore: Johns Hopkins University Press, 1985.

Said, Edward. *Orientalism.* New York: Vintage Books, [1978] 2003.

Sandburg, Carl. "Grass." *The Penguin Book of First World War Poetry.* 2nd edn. Ed. Jon Silkin. New York: Penguin Books, 1996. 235.

Santner, Erik L. *Stranded Objects: Mourning, Memory, and Film in Postwar Germany.* Ithaca: Cornell University Press, 1990.

Saunders, Max. *Ford Madox Ford: A Dual Life, Volume I: The World Before the War.* New York: Oxford University Press, 1996.

Ford Madox Ford: A Dual Life, Volume II: The After-War World. New York: Oxford University Press, 1996.

Introduction. *War Prose.* By Ford Madox Ford. Ed. Saunders. Manchester: Carcanet, 1999.

Scarry, Elaine. *The Body in Pain: The Making and Unmaking of the World.* New York: Oxford University Press, 1985.

"The Difficulty of Imagining Other People." *For Love of Country: Debating the Limits of Patriotism.* Ed. Martha Nussbaum. Beacon Press: Boston, 1996. 98–110.

Scholes, Robert and Robert Kellogg. *The Nature of Narrative.* New York: Oxford University Press, 1966.

Shamay-Tsoory, Simone G., Judith Aharon-Peretz, and Daniella Perry. "Two Systems for Empathy: A Double Dissociation Between Emotional and Cognitive Empathy in Inferior Frontal Gyrus Versus Ventromedial Prefrontal

Lesions." *Brain* 132 (2009): 617–627. http://brain.oxfordjournals.org/. 10.1093/brain/awn279.

Shapiro, Johanna and Lloyd Rucker. "Can Poetry Make Better Doctors? Teaching the Humanities and Arts to Medical Students and Residents at the University of California, Irvine, College of Medicine." *Academic Medicine* 78.10 (2003): 953–957.

Shelly, Percy Bysshe. *Shelley's Poetry and Prose*. Ed. Donald H. Reiman and Sharon B. Powers. New York: Norton, 1977.

Sherry, Vincent. *Ezra Pound, Wyndham Lewis, and Radical Modernism*. New York: Oxford University Press, 1993.

Shohet, Lauren. "Subjects and Objects in Lycidas." *Texas Studies in Literature and Language* 47.2 (2005): 101–119.

Slack, Robert C. "Hardy's Revisions." *Jude the Obscure*. New York: Norton, 1999. 329–337.

Smith, Adam. *The Theory of Moral Sentiments* [1759]. Ed. Knud Haakonssen. New York: Cambridge University Press, 2002.

Solomon, Robert. *In Defense of Sentimentality*. New York: Oxford University Press, 2004.

Sorensen Emery-Peck, Jennifer. "Tom and Vivien Eliot Do Narrative in Different Voices: Mixing Genres in The Waste Land's Pub." *Narrative* 16.3 (October 2008): 331–358.

Sorum, Eve. "Masochistic Modernisms: A Reading of Eliot and Woolf." *The Journal of Modern Literature* 28.3 (2005): 25–43.

"Psychology, Psychoanalysis, and New Subjectivities." *The Cambridge Companion to* The Waste Land. Ed. Gabrielle McIntire. New York: Cambridge University Press, 2015. 162–177.

"Thinking About Space: Mapping and Perception in WWI Literature." *Teaching Representations of the First World War*. Ed. Debra Rae Cohen and Douglas Higbee. New York: Modern Language Association Press, 2017. 185–192.

Spender, Stephen. *The Destructive Element: A Study of Modern Writers and Beliefs*. London: Jonathan Cape, 1935.

T. S. Eliot. New York: The Viking Press, 1975.

Spenser, Edmund. *The Poetical Works of Edmund Spenser, Volume IV*. Ed. Francis J. Child. Boston: Little, Brown, and Company, 1855.

Srikanth, Rajini. *Constructing the Enemy: Empathy/Antipathy in US Literature and Law*. Philadelphia: Temple University Press, 2011.

"Quiet Prose and Bare Life: Why We Should Eschew the Sensational in Human Rights Language." *Frame* 27.1 (2014): 79–99.

Stein, Edith. *On the Problem of Empathy*. [1917]. Trans. Waltraut Stein. 3rd. Rev. edn. Washington, DC: ICS Publications, 1989.

Stewart, George. "A Method Toward the Study of Dipodic Verse." *PMLA* 39.4 (1924): 979–989.

Sumner, Rosemary. *A Route to Modernism: Hardy, Lawrence, Woolf*. New York: St. Martin's Press, 2000.

Taylor, Dennis. *Hardy's Metres and Victorian Prosody*. Oxford: Clarendon Press, 1988.

Tennyson, Alfred. *The Poetical Works of Tennyson*, ed. G. Robert Stange. Boston: Houghton Mifflen, 1974.

"Thomas Hardy's Wessex." *The Bookman* (1891): 26–28. https://babel.hathitrust.org/cgi/pt?id=uc1.31210017702182;view=1up;seq=9.

Titchener, Edward Bradford. *Lectures on the Experimental Psychology of Thought-Processes*. New York: Macmillan, 1909.

Tiffany, Daniel. *Infidel Poetics: Riddles, Nightlife, Substance*. Chicago: University of Chicago Press, 2009.

Todd, Ruthven, Peter Hewett, Herbert B. Mallalieu, Ruthven Todd, and Robert Waller. *Poets of Tomorrow: First Selection*. London: Hogarth Press, 1939.

Trott, Nicola. "Wordsworth: The Shape of the Poetic Career." *The Cambridge Companion to Wordsworth*. Ed. Stephen Gill. New York: Cambridge University Press, 2003. 16–19.

Trott, Vincent. *Publishers, Readers, and the Great War: Literature and Memory Since 1918*. New York: Bloomsbury, 2017.

Valdesolo, Piercarlo, and David Desteno. "Synchrony and the Social Tuning of Compassion." *Emotion* 11.2 (2011): 262–266.

Vickery, John B. *The Prose Elegy: An Exploration of Modern American and British Fiction*. Baton Rouge: Louisiana State University Press, 2009.

Vinem, Richard. *A History in Fragments: Europe in the Twentieth Century*. Cambridge, MA: DeCapo Press, 2001.

Visher, Robert. "On the Optical Sense of Form: A Contribution to Aesthetics" [1873]. Trans. H. F. Mallgrave. *Empathy, Form, and Space: Problems in German Aesthetics, 1873–1893*. Ed. Harry Francis Mallgrave and Eleftherios Ikonomou. Santa Monica: The Getty Center for the History of Art and the Humanities, 1994. 89–122.

Warden, Claire. *British Avant-Garde Theater*. London: Palgrave Macmillan, 2012.

Weinstein, Philip. *Unknowing: The Work of Modernist Fiction*. Ithaca: Cornell University Press, 2006.

Whittier-Ferguson, John. *Mortality and Form in Late Modernist Literature*. New York: Cambridge University Press, 2014.

Widdowson, Peter. "'Moments of Vision': Postmodernizing *Tess of the d'Urbervilles*; or, *Tess of the d'Urbervilles* Faithfully Presented by Peter Widdowson." *New Perspectives on Thomas Hardy*. Ed. Charles P. C. Pettit. New York: St. Martin's Press, 1994. 80–100.

Wispe, Lauren. "History of the Concept of Empathy." *Empathy and Its Development*. Ed. Nancy Eisenberg and Janet Strayer. New York: Cambridge University Press, 1987: 17–37.

Wood, James. "Introduction for Orhan Pamuk." Harvard University. Sanders Theater, Cambridge, MA. Sept. 22, 2009.

Woolf, Virginia. "An Unwritten Novel." *A Haunted House and Other Short Stories*. New York: Harcourt, Inc. 1972.

The Diary of Virginia Woolf: Volume One 1915–1919. Ed. Anne Olivier Bell. New York: Harcourt Brace & Co. 1977.

The Diary of Virginia Woolf: Volume Two 1920–1924. Ed. Anne Olivier Bell and Andrew McNeillie. New York: Harcourt Brace & Co., 1978.

The Diary of Virginia Woolf: Volume Three 1925–1930. Ed. Anne Olivier Bell. New York: Harcourt Brace & Co., 1980.

The Diary of Virginia Woolf: Volume Four 1931–1935. Ed. Anne Olivier Bell. New York: Harcourt Brace & Co., 1983.

"Hours in a Library." *The Essays of Virginia Woolf. Vol. 2: 1912–1918*. Ed. Andrew McNeillie. New York: Harcourt Brace Jovanovich, 1990. 55–61.

Jacob's Room. New York: Harcourt Brace & Company, 1978.

Jacob's Room: The Holograph Draft. Ed. Edward L. Bishop. New York: Pace University Press, 1998.

"Modern Fiction." *The Essays of Virginia Woolf: Volume 4: 1925 to 1928*. Ed. Andrew McNeillie. London: The Hogarth Press, 1984. 157–165.

Mr. Bennett and Mrs. Brown. London: The Hogarth Press, 1924.

Mrs. Dalloway. New York: Harcourt, 1990.

Three Guineas. New York: Harcourt Brace & Company, 1966.

To the Lighthouse. New York: Harcourt Brace Jovanovich, 1981.

Wordsworth, William. *The Prelude 1799, 1805, 1850: A Norton Critical Edition*. Ed. Jonathan Wordsworth, M. H. Abrams, and Stephen Gill. New York: Norton, 1979.

Selected Poems. Ed. Stephen Gill. New York: Penguin, 2004.

Worringer, Wilhelm. *Abstraction and Empathy: A Contribution to the Psychology of Style*. Trans. Michael Bullock. Chicago: Elephant Paperbacks, [1908] 1997.

Worsley, Amelia. "Ophelia's Loneliness." *ELH* 82.2 (2015): 221–251.

Zhang, Dora. "Naming the Indescribable: Woolf, Russell, James, and the Limits of Description." *New Literary History* 45.1 (2014): 51–70.

Ziegler, Fenja, Peter Mitchell, and Gregory Currie. "How Does Narrative Cue Children's Perspective Taking?" *Developmental Psychology* 41.1 (2005): 115–123. www.psychology.nottingham.ac.uk/staff/Peter.Mitchell/narrative2005.pdf

Index